# Student Activities Manual

# IMÁGENES

## AN INTRODUCTION TO SPANISH LANGUAGE AND CULTURES

### THIRD EDITION

**Debbie Rusch**

Boston College

———

**Marcela Domínguez**

———

**Lucía Caycedo Garner**

University of Wisconsin–Madison, Emerita

HEINLE
CENGAGE Learning

Australia • Brazil • Japan • Korea • Mexico • Singapore • Spain • United Kingdom • United States

## HEINLE
### CENGAGE Learning·

ISBN-13: 978-1-133-95233-6

ISBN-10: 1-133-95233-X

**Heinle**
20 Channel Center Street
Boston, MA 02210
USA

Cengage Learning is a leading provider of customized learning solutions with office locations around the globe, including Singapore, the United Kingdom, Australia, Mexico, Brazil, and Japan. Locate your local office at: **www.cengage.com/global**

Cengage Learning products are represented in Canada by Nelson Education, Ltd.

To learn more about Heinle, visit **www.cengage.com/heinle**

Purchase any of our products at your local college store or at our preferred online store **www.cengagebrain.com**

Printed in the United States of America
1 2 3 4 5 6 7 16 15 14 13 12

# Contents

# To the Student

The *Student Activities Manual* to accompany *Imágenes*, *Third Edition* is divided in two parts: Workbook Activities and Lab Manual Activities.

## Workbook

The Workbook activities are designed to reinforce the chapter material and to help develop your writing skills. Each chapter in the Workbook parallels the organization of your textbook so that you can begin doing the activities after studying each **Vocabulario esencial** and **Gramática para la comunicación** section in the text.

The **Un poco de todo** sections in the middle and end of each chapter include activities that focus on more than one concept. This helps you apply your learning to more real-life like situations in which multiple topics come into play at once. At the end of the chapter, reading activities reinforce the strategies introduced in the textbook as you read about the Hispanic world. Becoming a better reader can also help you in other aspects of the language such as increasing your vocabulary.

The **Repaso** sections, after odd-numbered chapters, will help you review some key concepts and are especially useful for review prior to midterm or final exams.

Answers to the Workbook activities may be made available to you by your instructor.

Here are some tips for using the Workbook:

- Before doing the exercises, study the corresponding vocabulary or grammar sections in the textbook.
- Do the activities with the textbook closed and without looking at the answer key.
- Write what you have learned. Be creative, but not overly so. Try not to overstep your linguistic boundaries.
- Try to use dictionaries sparingly and NEVER use an online translator.
- Check your answers against the answer key, if provided by your instructor, marking all incorrect answers in a different color ink.
- Check any wrong answers against the grammar explanations and vocabulary lists in your textbook. Make notes to yourself in the margins to use as study aids.
- Use your notes to help prepare for exams and quizzes.
- If you feel you need additional work with particular portions of the chapter, do the corresponding activities on the Student Website at **CengageBrain.com.** The online activities can be done prior to doing or after completing any section of the Workbook or as review to prepare for quizzes and exams.

## Lab Manual

The activities in the Lab Manual are designed to help improve your pronunciation and listening skills. Each chapter contains two main parts.

- **Mejora tu pronunciación:** Contains an explanation of the sounds and rhythm of Spanish, followed by pronunciation exercises. This section can be done at the beginning of a chapter.
- **Mejora tu comprensión:** Contains numerous listening comprehension activities. As you listen to these recordings, you will be given a task to perform (for example, writing down the order in a restaurant as you hear a conversation between a waiter and diners). This section should be done after studying the last grammar explanation. It will help prepare you for the listening comprehension sections of the quizzes and exams.
- To listen to the audio program go to the *Imágenes Student Website* at **CengageBrain.com.**

Tips for improving pronunciation and listening skills:

- While doing the pronunciation exercises, listen carefully, repeat accurately, and speak up.
- Read all directions and items before doing the listening comprehension activities. This will help to focus you.
- Pay specific attention to the setting and type of spoken language (for example, an announcement in a store, a radio newscast, a conversation between two students about exams, and so forth).
- Do not be concerned with understanding every word; your goal should be to do the task that is asked of you in the activity.
- Replay the activities as many times as needed.
- Listen to the recordings again after correction to hear what you missed.

Conscientious use of the Workbook and Lab Manual will help you make good progress in your study of the Spanish Language. Should you need or want additional practice, the *Imágenes Student Website* at **CengageBrain.com** has activities that provide excellent review for exams and quizzes.

# WORKBOOK

# Bienvenidos al mundo hispano

Capítulo

**P**

## Las presentaciones

**ACTIVIDAD 1** **¿Cómo te llamas?** Complete the following sentences with the correct word or words (**me, te, se, llamo, llamas, llama**).

1. Ud. se _____ Pedro Lerma, ¿no?

2. Me _____ Francisco.

3. ¿Cómo te _____?

4. ¿Cómo se _____ Ud.?

5. Ud. _____ _____ Julia Muñoz, ¿no?

6. _____ llamo Ramón.

7. ¿Cómo _____ _____ tú?

8. Hola, tú _____ _____ Patricia, ¿no?

**ACTIVIDAD 2** **El origen** Complete the following sentences with the correct word (**soy, eres, es**).

1. Yo _____ de Cali, Colombia.

2. ¿De dónde _____ Ud.?

3. Tú _____ de California, ¿no?

4. Tomás, ¿ _____ de México?

5. Ud. _____ de Valencia, ¿no?

6. ¿De dónde _____ tú?

7. Yo _____ de San José.

**ACTIVIDAD 3** **¿Cómo se llama Ud.?** Two business people are sitting next to each other on a plane, and they strike up a conversation. You can hear the woman, Mrs. Beltrán, but not the man, Mr. García. Write what you think Mr. García is saying.

SRA. BELTRÁN    Buenas tardes.

SR. GARCÍA      _____.

SRA. BELTRÁN    Me llamo Susana Beltrán, y ¿cómo se llama Ud.?

| | |
|---|---|
| SR. GARCÍA | _____ . |
| | ¿ _____ ? |
| SRA. BELTRÁN | Soy de Guatemala, ¿y Ud.? |
| SR. GARCÍA | _____ . |
| SRA. BELTRÁN | Encantada. |
| SR. GARCÍA | _____ . |

**ACTIVIDAD  4  Buenos días** Today is Pepe's first day at a new school. He is meeting his teacher, Mr. Torres, for the first time. Complete the following conversation. Remember, when Pepe speaks to his teacher he will use **usted**.

| | |
|---|---|
| SR. TORRES | Buenos días. |
| PEPE | _____ . |
| SR. TORRES | ¿ _____ ? |
| PEPE | _____ Pepe. |
| SR. TORRES | ¿De dónde _____ ? |
| PEPE | _____ Buenos Aires. |
| SR. TORRES | Ahhh... Buenos Aires. |
| PEPE | Señor, ¿ _____ ? |
| SR. TORRES | Soy el Señor Torres. |

© Cengage Learning 2013

# Los saludos y las despedidas

**ACTIVIDAD  5  ¿Cómo estás?** Complete the following sentences with the correct word (**estás, está**).

1. ¿Cómo _____ Ud.?

2. Pepe, ¿cómo _____ ?

3. Sr. Guzmán, ¿cómo _____ ?

4. Srta. Ramírez, ¿cómo _____ ?

**ACTIVIDAD  6  En la universidad** Finish the following conversation between two college students who are meeting for the first time.

| | |
|---|---|
| ÁLVARO | ¿Cómo te _____ ? |
| TERESA | Me _____ . ¿Y _____ ? |
| ÁLVARO | _____ . |
| TERESA | ¿De _____ eres? |
| ÁLVARO | _____ Córdoba, España. ¿Y _____ ? |
| TERESA | _____ Ponce, Puerto Rico. |
| ÁLVARO | _____ . |
| TERESA | Igualmente. |

**ACTIVIDAD** **7** **¡Hola!** **Parte A.** Two friends see each other on the street. Complete their brief conversation with what you think they said.

MARIEL   Hola, Carlos.

CARLOS   _____, _____.

   ¿_____?

MARIEL   Bien, ¿_____?

CARLOS   Muy bien.

MARIEL   Hasta luego.

CARLOS   _____.

**Parte B.** Rewrite the preceding conversation from **Parte A** so it takes place between two business acquaintances who meet at a conference at 10:00 in the morning.

SR. MARTÍN   _____, _____.

SR. CAMACHO   _____, _____.

   ¿_____?

SR. MARTÍN   _____ · ¿_____?

SR. CAMACHO   _____.

SR. MARTÍN   _____.

SR. CAMACHO   _____.

# Países de habla española y sus capitales

**ACTIVIDAD** **8** **La capital es...** Mr. Torres is teaching Latin American capitals and asks students the following questions. Write the students' answers using complete sentences.

1.  ¿Cuál es la capital de Panamá? _____

2.  ¿Cuál es la capital de Honduras? _____

3.  ¿Cuál es la capital de Colombia? _____

4.  ¿Cuál es la capital de Puerto Rico? _____

5.  ¿Cuál es la capital de Chile? _____

**ACTIVIDAD 9** **Países** As a student, Luis Domínguez has many opportunities to travel. Look at the button collection on his backpack and list the countries he has visited.

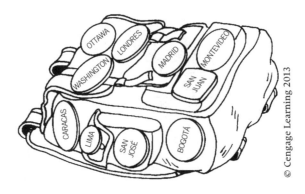

© Cengage Learning 2013

_____

_____

_____

**ACTIVIDAD 10** **Población** Look at the following data provided by the U.S. Census Bureau. Then answer the questions that follow.

| POBLACIÓN DE LOS ESTADOS UNIDOS | | |
|---|---|---|
| **Proyección para el año 2020** | | |
| Número total de habitantes | 341.387.000 | 100% |
| Blancos (no hispanos) | 205.255.000 | 60,1% |
| Negros (no hispanos) | 44.389.000 | 13,0% |
| Hispanos (todas las razas) | 66.365.000 | 19,4% |
| **Proyección para el año 2030** | | |
| Número total de habitantes | 373.504.000 | 100% |
| Blancos (no hispanos) | 207.217.000 | 55,5% |
| Negros (no hispanos) | 48.728.000 | 13,0% |
| Hispanos (todas las razas) | 85.931.000 | 23,0% |
| **Proyección para el año 2050** | | |
| Número total de habitantes | 439.010.000 | 100% |
| Blancos (no hispanos) | 203.347.000 | 46,3% |
| Negros (no hispanos) | 56.944.000 | 13,0% |
| Hispanos (todas las razas) | 132.792.000 | 30,2% |

1. Do all groups mentioned increase in number of inhabitants from 2020 to 2050? _____ yes _____ no

2. In terms of percentage of the overall population, which group is increasing quickly?

   a. Whites (non-Hispanic)        b. Blacks (non-Hispanic)        c. Hispanics (all races)

3. In terms of percentage of the overall population, which group is declining?

   a. Whites (non-Hispanic)        b. Blacks (non-Hispanic)        c. Hispanics (all races)

**ACTIVIDAD** **11** **Opinión** In English, briefly discuss what you think may be some of the implications for the United States of the population trends seen in **Actividad 10**. When considering what the implications may be, think about them at the national, state, local, and even personal levels.

_____

_____

_____

_____

_____

# Deletreo y pronunciación de palabras: el alfabeto

**ACTIVIDAD** **12** **¿Cómo se escribe?** Write out the spellings for the following capitals.

▶ Asunción   *A-ese-u-ene-ce-i-o con acento-ene*

1. Caracas _____

2. Tegucigalpa _____

3. San Juan _____

4. Quito _____

5. Santiago _____

6. La Habana _____

7. Managua _____

8. Montevideo _____

# Acentuación

**ACTIVIDAD** **13** **Los acentos** Write accents on the following words, if needed. The stressed syllables are in boldface.

1. televi**sor**
2. **fa**cil
3. impor**tan**te
4. den**tis**ta

5. Ra**mon**
6. **Me**xico
7. ri**di**culo
8. conti**nen**te

9. fi**nal**
10. fan**tas**tico
11. ciu**dad**
12. invita**cion**

**ACTIVIDAD** **14** **Puntuación** Punctuate the following conversation.

MANOLO    Cómo te llamas

RICARDO    Me llamo Ricardo Y tú

MANOLO    Me llamo Manolo

RICARDO    De dónde eres

MANOLO    Soy de La Paz

# ¿Quién es?

## Vocabulario esencial I

### Los números del cero al cien

**ACTIVIDAD 1** **¿Qué número es?** Write out the following numbers.

a. 25 _____

b. 15 _____

c. 73 _____

d. 14 _____

e. 68 _____

f. 46 _____

g. 17 _____

h. 82 _____

i. 54 _____

j. 39 _____

k. 91 _____

**ACTIVIDAD 2** **¿Cuál es tu número de teléfono?**
You are talking to a friend on the phone, and she asks you for a few phone numbers. Write how you would say the numbers.

▶ Juana
*dos, cincuenta y ocho, setenta y seis, quince*

| Nombre | Teléfono |
|--------|----------|
| Juana | 258 76 15 |
| Paco | 473 47 98 |
| Marisa | 365 03 52 |
| Pedro | 825 32 14 |

© Cengage Learning 2013

1. Paco _____

2. Marisa _____

3. Pedro _____

# Las nacionalidades

**ACTIVIDAD 3** **¿De qué nacionalidad es?** Indicate the nationality of the following people in complete sentences.

▶ Juan es de Madrid.  *Juan es español.*

1. María es de La Paz. _____

2. Hans es de Bonn. _____

3. Peter es de Londres. _____

4. Gonzalo es de Buenos Aires. _____

5. Jesús es de México. _____

6. Ana es de Guatemala. _____

7. Irene es de París. _____

8. Marta es de Quito. _____

9. Frank es de Ottawa. _____

10. Soy de los Estados Unidos. _____

**ACTIVIDAD 4** **¿De dónde son?** Look at the accompanying map and state each person's nationality using adjectives of nationality and complete sentences.

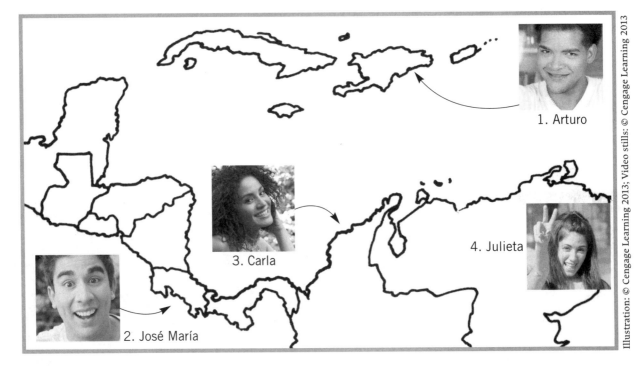

1. Arturo
2. José María
3. Carla
4. Julieta

1. _____

2. _____

3. _____

4. _____

# Gramática para la comunicación I

## Talking about Yourself and Others (Part I): Subject Pronouns, *llamarse*, and *ser*

**ACTIVIDAD  5**  *Llamarse y ser*  Complete the following sentences with the appropriate form of the indicated verbs.

1. ¿Cómo _____ _____ él? (llamarse)

2. ¿De dónde _____ ella? (ser)

3. David _____ de Lisboa, ¿no? (ser)

4. ¿Cómo _____ _____ Ud.? (llamarse)

5. Yo _____ _____ Ramón y _____ de España. (llamarse, ser)

6. Felipe _____ boliviano, ¿no? (ser)

7. ¿Cómo _____ _____ tú? (llamarse)

8. Sra. Gómez, ¿de dónde _____ Ud.? (ser)

**ACTIVIDAD  6**  **En orden lógico**  Put the following conversation in a logical order by numbering the lines from 1 to 10.

_____ ¿De dónde es?

_____ ¿España?

_____ ¿Quién, ella?

_____ ¡Ah! Hola, ¿cómo estás?

_____ Antonio.

_____ Bien... ¿Cómo se llama?

_____ Es de Córdoba.

___1___ Hola, Carlos.

_____ No, Argentina.

_____ No, él.

## Indicating One's Age: *Tener*

**ACTIVIDAD  7**  **¿Cuántos años tienes?**  Complete the following sentences with the appropriate form of **tener**.

1. ¿Cuántos años _____ tú?

2. Ud. _____ treinta y siete años, ¿no?

3. Ella _____ veinticinco años.

4. Yo _____ dieciocho años.

5. Laura, ¿cuántos años _____?

6. ¿Cuántos años _____ la señora Madariaga?

7. Ana _____ diecinueve años y Pepe _____ veinte.

# Un poco de todo

**ACTIVIDAD 8** **¿Quién es?** Write a brief paragraph saying all that you can about the two people shown in the accompanying student IDs.

| Universidad de California – Los Ángeles |
|---|
| **Nombre:** Sonia |
| **Apellidos:** Lerma-Jiménez |
| **Ciudad:** Chicago    **País:** Estados Unidos |
| **Edad:** 20 |

| Universidad de Puerto Rico – Río Piedras |
|---|
| **Nombre:** Arturo |
| **Apellidos:** López Cano |
| **Ciudad:** Santo Domingo  **País:** República Dominicana |
| **Edad:** 23 |

Video stills: © Cengage Learning 2013

_____

_____

_____

_____

_____

_____

# Vocabulario esencial II

## Las ocupaciones

**ACTIVIDAD 9** **¿Masculino o femenino?** Change the following words from masculine to feminine or from feminine to masculine. Note that some words may not change.

1. ingeniero _____
2. doctora _____
3. actriz _____
4. abogada _____
5. secretaria _____
6. artista _____
7. profesora _____
8. director _____
9. camarero _____
10. vendedora _____
11. comerciante _____
12. economista _____

**ACTIVIDAD  10** **¿Qué hacen?** Associate each of the following words or groups of words with an occupation; then write your answer. Include both masculine and feminine forms if applicable and use the articles **el** or **la.**

1. Steven Spielberg, Kathryn Bigelow, Pedro Almodóvar _____

2. Colgate, Crest _____

3. hospital, clínica _____

4. Alex Rodríguez, Lebron James, Serena Williams _____

5. Swiffer, Dyson, Lysol, Betty Crocker _____

6. Dell, Mac _____

7. Hollywood, los Oscars _____

8. Wall Street _____

9. micrófono, música _____

10. J.C. Penney, Bloomingdale's, comisión _____

11. British Airways, hoteles, *tour* _____

12. examen, universidad, quince créditos _____

# Gramática para la comunicación II

## Talking about Yourself and Others (Part II)

**ACTIVIDAD  11** **Verbos** Complete the following sentences with the appropriate form of the indicated verbs.

1. Ellos _____ paraguayos. (ser)

2. ¿Cuántos años _____ Uds.? (tener)

3. Nosotros _____ abogados. (ser)

4. Él _____ veinticinco años y _____ ingeniero.
   (tener, ser)

5. Juan y yo _____ veintiún años. (tener)

6. ¿De dónde _____ Clara y Miguel? (ser)

7. Ella _____ _____ Pilar, _____
   veinticuatro años y _____ artista.
   (llamarse, tener, ser)

8. El Sr. Escobar y la Sra. Beltrán _____ ecuatorianos. (ser)

**ACTIVIDAD 12** **¿De qué nacionalidad son?** Rewrite the following sentences using subject pronouns (**yo, tú, Ud., él, ella, nosotros/as, vosotros/as, Uds., ellos, ellas**) and adjectives of nationality. Remember that an adjective of nationality agrees with the noun or pronoun it modifies (**él/mexicano; ella/mexicana; ellos/mexicanos; ellas/mexicanas**).

▶ Los dentistas son de México. ***Ellos son mexicanos.***

1. Tus padres son de Ecuador. _____

2. El economista es de Venezuela. _____

3. Las señoras son de Francia. _____

4. Alberto y yo somos de Paraguay. _____

5. Las ingenieras son de Chile. _____

6. Laura es de Portugal. _____

7. Los deportistas son de la República Dominicana. _____

8. Mi padre es de Honduras. _____

9. Los vendedores son de Cuba. _____

10. Las profesoras son de España. _____

11. Las periodistas son de Costa Rica. _____

12. El cantante es de Irlanda. _____

13. El Sr. Moreno y yo somos de Inglaterra. _____

14. Mis padres son de los Estados Unidos. _____

**ACTIVIDAD 13** **Un párrafo** Write a paragraph about yourself and your parents. Tell your names, nationalities, how old you are, and what each of you does.

_____

_____

_____

_____

_____

_____

## Asking Information and Negating

**ACTIVIDAD 14** **Preguntas y respuestas** Answer the following questions both affirmatively and negatively in complete sentences.

1. ¿Eres de Chile? Sí, _____

   No, _____

2. Ud. es colombiano, ¿no? Sí, _____

   No, _____

3. Ella se llama Piedad, ¿no? Sí, _____

   No, _____

4. ¿Son españoles Pedro y David? Sí, _____

No, _____

5. Uds. tienen veintiún años, ¿no? Sí, _____

No, _____

**ACTIVIDAD 15 Las preguntas** Write questions for the following answers.

1. —¿_____?

—Sí, es Ramón.

2. —¿_____?

—Ellos son de Panamá.

3. —¿_____?

—Tenemos treinta años.

4. —_____, ¿no?

—No, me llamo Felipe.

5. —¿_____?

—Se llaman Pepe y Ana.

6. —¿_____?

—Es abogado.

7. —_____, ¿no?

—No, es abogada.

8. —_____, ¿no?

—No, no es abogado.

9. —¿_____?

—Soy guatemalteca.

**ACTIVIDAD 16 ¿Recuerdas?** What do you remember about Sonia's family and friends? Answer the following questions in complete sentences. You might have to scan the end of the Preliminary Chapter and Chapter 1 of your textbook for information.

1. ¿Cuántos años tiene Pablo? _____

2. ¿Qué hace Sonia? _____

3. ¿Cómo se llaman los padres de Sonia? _____

4. ¿Qué hace Julieta y de dónde es ella? _____

5. Andrés es centroamericano, ¿no? _____

6. ¿Es de origen mexicano la familia de Sonia? _____

7. ¿Es vendedor Pablo? _____

8. ¿Qué hace el padre de Sonia? ¿Y su madre? _____

# Un poco de todo

**ACTIVIDAD 17** **La respuesta correcta** Select the correct responses to complete the following conversation.

| PERSONA A | ¿Quiénes son ellas? | | |
|---|---|---|---|
| PERSONA B | a. Felipe y Juan. | b. Felipe y Rosa. | c. Rosa y Marta. |
| PERSONA A | ¿De dónde son? | | |
| PERSONA B | a. Soy de Ecuador. | b. Son de Ecuador. | c. Eres de Ecuador. |
| PERSONA A | Son estudiantes, ¿no? | | |
| PERSONA B | a. No, son abogadas. | b. No, no son abogadas. | c. No, son estudiantes. |
| PERSONA A | Y tú, ¿qué haces? | | |
| PERSONA B | a. Soy economista. | b. Soy doctor. | c. Somos ingenieros. |
| PERSONA A | ¡Yo también soy economista! | | |

**ACTIVIDAD 18** **En el aeropuerto** You are in the airport, and you overhear bits and pieces of five different conversations. Fill in the missing words.

1. —¿De dónde eres?

   —_____ de Monterrey, México.

2. —¿De dónde _____ Uds.?

   —_____.

   —Yo también _____ de Panamá.

3. —¿Cómo se _____ ellos?

   —Felipe y Gonzalo.

4. —¿_____?

   —¿Cómo?

   —¿_____?

   —¡Ah! Yo tengo veinte años y ella veintidós.

5. —¿_____ hacen Uds.?

   —_____ cantantes.

Nombre _____ Sección _____ Fecha _____

**ACTIVIDAD 19 La tarjeta** Look at the business card and answer the questions that follow in complete sentences.

Sociedad Industrial de Productos Siderúrgicos S.A.

HUMBERTO HINCAPIÉ VILLEGAS
INGENIERO INDUSTRIAL

CARRERA 13 No. 26-45. OF. 1313          TELS. 828-10-76 - 828-14-75
TELEX 044-1435                          BOGOTÁ. D. E.
hicapivill@correo.com

Courtesy of Humberto Hincapié Villegas

1. ¿Es el Sr. Hincapié o el Sr. Villegas? _____
2. ¿Qué hace Humberto? _____
3. ¿De qué país es? _____
4. ¿Cuáles son sus números de teléfono? _____

**ACTIVIDAD 20 ¿Quién es quién?** Read the clues and complete the following chart. You may need to find some answers by process of elimination.

| Nombre | Primer apellido | Segundo apellido | Edad | País de origen |
|---|---|---|---|---|
| Ricardo | López | Navarro | 25 | Venezuela |
| Alejandro | | | | |
| | | Martínez | | |
| | | | 24 | |
| | | | | Argentina |

La persona de Bolivia no es el Sr. Rodríguez.

La persona que tiene veinticuatro años es de Chile.

Su madre, Carmen Sánchez, es de Suramérica pero su padre es de Alemania.

Miguel es de Colombia.

La madre de Ramón se llama Norma Martini.

La persona de Chile se llama Ana.

La persona que es de Argentina tiene veintiún años.

El primer apellido de Ramón es Pascual.

El Sr. Rodríguez tiene veintidós años.

El segundo apellido del Sr. Fernández es González.

El primer apellido de Ana es Kraus.

La persona que tiene veintiún años no se llama Miguel.

El señor de Bolivia tiene diecinueve años.

**ACTIVIDAD 21** **Jorge Fernández Ramiro** Jorge is a contestant on a TV show and is being interviewed by the host. Read the following description of Jorge and his family. Then complete the conversation between Jorge and the host.

Se llama Jorge Fernández Ramiro. Tiene veinticuatro años y es ingeniero civil. Su padre también es ingeniero civil. Él también se llama Jorge. Su madre Victoria es ama de casa. Ellos tienen cincuenta años. Jorge tiene una novia que se llama Elisa. Ella es estudiante y tiene veinte años. Ellos son de Managua, la capital de Nicaragua.

CONDUCTOR   Buenas tardes. ¿_____?

JORGE   Buenas tardes. Me llamo _____.

CONDUCTOR   ¿_____?

JORGE   Jorge, también.

CONDUCTOR   ¿_____?

JORGE   Victoria.

CONDUCTOR   ¿_____?

JORGE   Tienen cincuenta años.

CONDUCTOR   ¿_____?

JORGE   Veinticuatro.

CONDUCTOR   ¿_____?

JORGE   Sí, tengo novia. Se llama Elisa. (¡Hola, Elisa!)

CONDUCTOR   ¿_____?

JORGE   Soy ingeniero civil y ella es estudiante.

CONDUCTOR   ¿_____?

JORGE   Él es ingeniero también y ella es ama de casa.

CONDUCTOR   ¿_____?

JORGE   Somos de Managua.

CONDUCTOR   Muchas gracias, Jorge.

**ACTIVIDAD 22** **Biografías** Read the following information about famous Hispanics and fill in the blanks with a logical word.

1. Alex Rodríguez (1975– ) _____ deportista de béisbol para los Yankees de Nueva York. Es de Washington Heights, un barrio de la Ciudad de Nueva York, pero su familia es _____ origen dominicano.

2. Wilmer Valderrama (1930– ) es _____, famoso por el papel de Fez en el programa de televisión *That '70s Show*. Valderrama _____ de Miami, pero _____ familia es de origen colombiano y venezolano.

3. Ellen Ochoa (1958– ) es astronauta _____ ingeniera. Es de Los Ángeles, California, pero su _____ es de origen mexicano.

4. Marco Rubio (1971– ) es senador federal del estado de Florida en Washington, DC. Es _____ Miami, pero sus padres _____ exiliados cubanos.

5. Zoe Saldana (1978– ) es una actriz famosa por papeles como Uhura en *Star Trek* y Neytiri en *Avatar*. Su nombre real _____ Zoe Yadira Saldaña Nazario. Es de Nueva Jersey, pero su padre es dominicano y su _____ es de Puerto Rico.

6. Bill Richardson (1947– ) es exgobernador del estado de Nuevo México, exembajador de los Estados Unidos en la ONU y exministro de Energía a nivel federal. Es _____ California, pero su familia es de _____ mexicano.

7. Christina Aguilera (1980– ) es cantante, actriz y *exmouseketeer* del *Mickey Mouse Club*. Es _____ Staten Island en Nueva York. _____ padre es de Ecuador.

**ACTIVIDAD 23** **Personas de origen hispano** Here are some famous people of Hispanic origin. See if you can match the person with the nationality of their family. It is okay to guess answers; you will not be graded on this.

**Famosos**

1. Raquel Welch (actriz) _____
2. Soledad O'Brien (periodista) _____
3. Carlos Santana (músico) _____
4. Cameron Díaz (actriz) _____
5. Hulk Hogan (deportista) _____
6. Tony Romo (deportista) _____
7. Cheech Marin (comediante) _____
8. Martin Sheen (actor) _____
9. Jimmy Smits (actor) _____
10. Rebecca Lobo (deportista) _____

**Origen**

a. boliviano
b. cubano
c. mexicano
d. panameño
e. puertorriqueño
f. español

**ACTIVIDAD 24** **El censo** Mark the following sentences true (T) or false (F) based on the data from the last U.S. census. It is okay to guess answers; you will not be graded on this.

1. _____ More than half of the total growth of the population of the United States between 2000 and 2010 was due to an increase in the number of Hispanics.

2. _____ Hispanic origin can be viewed as the heritage, nationality group, lineage, or country of birth of the person or the person's parents or ancestors before their arrival in the United States.

3. _____ People who identify their origin as Hispanic, Latino, or Spanish may be of any race.

4. _____ 23.1% of children under the age of 17 are Hispanic.

5. _____ The states experiencing the largest percentage growth of Hispanics between 2000 and 2010 were South Carolina and Alabama.

# Repaso

## Geografía

**ACTIVIDAD 1** **Zonas geográficas** Match the following countries with their geographic area.

1. _____ Venezuela
2. _____ Honduras
3. _____ España
4. _____ México
5. _____ Cuba
6. _____ Chile
7. _____ Panamá
8. _____ República Dominicana
9. _____ Ecuador
10. _____ El Salvador

a. Norteamérica
b. Centroamérica
c. el Caribe
d. Suramérica
e. Europa

**ACTIVIDAD 2** **Países y capitales** Label the Spanish-speaking countries (one is actually a Commonwealth of the United States) and their capitals.

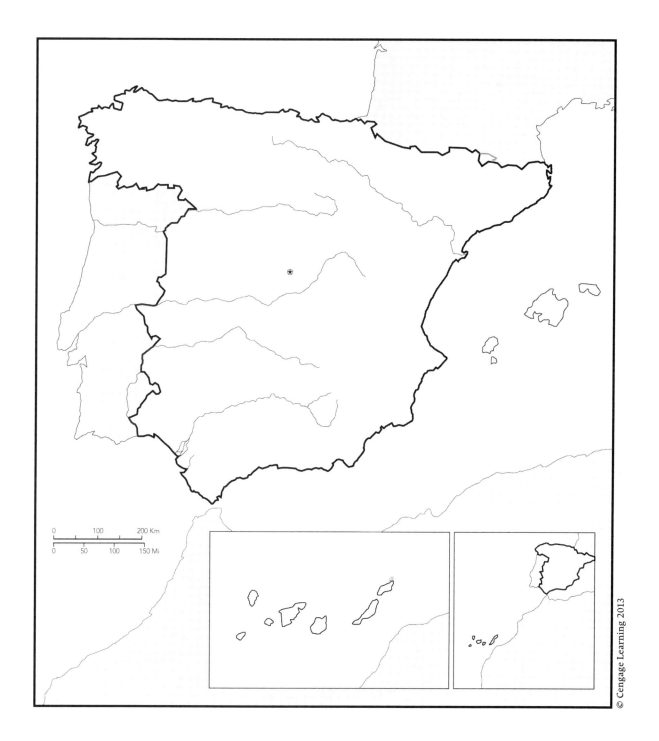

© Cengage Learning 2013

Ecuador

Trópico de Capricornio

| 0 | 250 | 500 Kilómetros |
| 0 | 250 | 500 Millas |

© Cengage Learning 2013

# ¿Te gusta?

## Vocabulario esencial I

### La habitación de un estudiante universitario

**ACTIVIDAD 1** **La palabra no relacionada** In each of the following word groups, select the word that doesn't belong.

1. champú, pasta de dientes, crema de afeitar, silla

2. cama, mesa, móvil, sofá

3. periódico, lápiz, revista, papel

4. reloj, jabón, radio, televisor

5. cepillo, lámpara, escritorio, libro

6. novela, diccionario, peine, periódico

7. foto, cafetera, cámara, álbum

8. toalla, mochila, jabón, perfume

**ACTIVIDAD 2** **¿Qué es?** Write the word that you would associate with each of the following names or products. Include the definite article **el** or **la.**

1. Crest _____

2. *New York Times, Washington Post* _____

3. *Time, Rolling Stone, Newsweek* _____

4. (3452 × 897) – 798 _____

5. Webster's, Oxford _____

6. Ivory, Dove, Dial antibacteriano _____

7. 800-555-1212, Nokia, Samsung, iPhone _____

8. Dell, Compaq, Mac _____

9. Finesse, Pantene, Paul Mitchell _____

10. Sealy, King Koil, Serta, Tempur-Pedic _____

11. Rolex, Timex, Casio, Tag Heuer _____

12. Sandra Cisneros, Stephen King, Agatha Christie, Gabriel García Márquez _____

13. NPR, 1430AM, 980FM _____

14. NBC, CNN, HBO, Sony, alta definición _____

15. Sony, Nikon, Canon, zoom óptico, 14 megapíxeles _____

# Gramática para la comunicación I

## Using Gender and Number

**ACTIVIDAD 3** *El, la, los o las* Add the proper definite article for each of the following words.

1. _____ calculadora

2. _____ plantas

3. _____ papel

4. _____ fotos

5. _____ lámparas

6. _____ escritorios

7. _____ impresora

8. _____ días

9. _____ cama

10. _____ champú

11. _____ desodorante

12. _____ guitarras

13. _____ jabón

14. _____ clase

15. _____ mochilas

16. _____ peines

**ACTIVIDAD 4** **¿Cuál es el plural?** Change the following words, including the articles, from singular to plural.

1. la ciudad _____

2. la nación _____

3. un estudiante _____

4. una revista _____

5. un reloj _____

6. el papel _____

7. el artista _____

8. el lápiz _____

9. el televisor _____

10. un problema _____

## Expressing Likes and Dislikes (Part I): *Gustar*

**ACTIVIDAD 5** **Los gustos** Complete each sentence by writing the appropriate word or words (**a, al, a la, a mí, a ti, a ella, a él, a Ud., me, te, le**) and a form of the verb **gustar.**

1. A mí _____ _____ las novelas.

2. Sr. García, _____ _____ le _____ la computadora, ¿no?

3. _____ Juan _____ _____ los perfumes de Armani.

4. _____ _____ me _____ las plantas.

5. ¿A _____ te _____ el programa de Conan O'Brien?

6. A Elena _____ _____ la universidad.

7. _____ _____ Srta. Martínez _____ _____ la música clásica.

8. _____ mí _____ gusta tu móvil.

9. Marta, ¿ _____ _____ te _____ el café de Guatemala?

10. _____ Sr. Navarro _____ _____ las cámaras digitales simples.

**ACTIVIDAD 6** **Las asignaturas** Parte A. Write the letter of the item in Column B that you associate with each subject in Column A.

| A | B |
|---|---|
| 1. _____ matemáticas | a. animales y plantas |
| 2. _____ sociología | b. fórmulas y números |
| 3. _____ historia | c. Wall Street |
| 4. _____ economía | d. Picasso, Miró, Velázquez, Kahlo |
| 5. _____ literatura | e. adjetivos, verbos, gramática |
| 6. _____ arte | f. 1492, 1776 |
| 7. _____ inglés | g. $H_2O$ |
| 8. _____ biología | h. Freud |
| 9. _____ psicología | i. la sociedad |
| 10. _____ química | j. Isabel Allende y Gabriel García Márquez |

**Parte B.** Now answer these questions based on the subjects listed in Column A of **Parte A.**

1. ¿Qué asignaturas tienes? _____

   _____

2. ¿Qué asignatura te gusta? _____

   _____

3. ¿Qué asignatura no te gusta? _____

   _____

4. ¿Te gusta más el arte o la biología?

   _____

**ACTIVIDAD** **7** **¿A quién le gusta?** Form sentences by selecting one item from each column.

| | | | | |
|---|---|---|---|---|
| A mí | | | | el café de Colombia |
| A ti | | | | el jazz |
| A él | | me | | la música clásica |
| A ella | | te | | las novelas de Julia Álvarez |
| A Ud. | (no) | le | gusta | las computadoras |
| A nosotros | | nos | gustan | las matemáticas |
| A vosotros | | os | | el actor Benicio del Toro |
| A Uds. | | les | | los exámenes |
| A ellos | | | | la televisión |
| A ellas | | | | los relojes Rolex |

1. _____

2. _____

3. _____

4. _____

5. _____

6. _____

7. _____

8. _____

## Expressing Possession

**ACTIVIDAD** **8** **La posesión** Create sentences from the following words. You may need to add words or change forms.

▶ mesa / Carlos **La mesa es de Carlos.**

1. lápiz / Manuel _____

2. papeles / el director _____

3. planta / mi madre _____

4. libros / la profesora _____

5. computadora / el ingeniero _____

**ACTIVIDAD 9** **Es mi móvil.** In Spanish, one can express possession using **de** or by using **mi/s, tu/s, su/s,** etc. Follow the models to create sentences that state who owns what.

▶ Yo tengo móvil.  *Es mi móvil.*
Tú tienes libros de historia.  *Son tus libros de historia.*

1. Ella tiene guitarra. _____

2. Ellos tienen televisor. _____

3. Nosotros tenemos plantas. _____

4. Tú tienes cepillo de dientes. _____

5. Uds. tienen sofá. _____

6. Él tiene novelas. _____

7. Nosotros tenemos impresora. _____

8. Yo tengo reloj. _____

9. Ud. tiene fotografías. _____

**ACTIVIDAD 10** **¿De quién es?** Look at the drawing of these four people moving into their apartment. Tell who owns which items. Follow the example.

▶ Pablo y Mario:  *El televisor es de Pablo y Mario.*

1. Pablo y Mario: _____

2. Ricardo: _____

3. Manuel: _____

**ACTIVIDAD** **11** **¿Es tu televisor?** As a college student, you probably live with a roommate or roommates. Look at the following list of items and state who owns what. (If you live alone, make it up.) Follow the model.

▶ las plantas  *Son mis plantas.*
*Las plantas son de Jazmine.*
*Son nuestras plantas.*
*No tenemos plantas.*

1. el televisor _____

2. las toallas _____

3. los carteles _____

4. la cafetera _____

5. el sofá _____

# Un poco de todo

**ACTIVIDAD** **12** **Una conversación** Complete the following conversation between Beto and Bárbara by writing a logical word in each blank. Only one word per blank.

BETO        Hola. ¿Cómo _____?

BÁRBARA     Bien. Oye, ¿qué tienes?

BETO        Un libro.

BÁRBARA     Ahhhhh. ¿Y cómo _____ llama el libro?

BETO        *El reino de este mundo*, de Alejo Carpentier.

BÁRBARA     ¡Huy! Me _____ mucho sus libros. Alejo Carpentier es _____ autor favorito. ¿Es _____ libro?

BETO        No, es _____ mi profesor de literatura.

BÁRBARA     El profesor Menéndez, ¿no?

BETO        Sí, Menéndez es muy inteligente, pero no me gustan _____ clases.

# Vocabulario esencial II

## Acciones

**ACTIVIDAD** **13** **Asociaciones** Associate the words in the following list with one or more of these actions: **escribir, leer, escuchar, hablar, mirar.**

1. canción _____

2. novela _____

3. televisión _____

4. computadora _____

5. revista _____

6. periódico _____

7. radio _____

8. guitarra _____

9. álbum de fotos _____

10. teléfono _____

**ACTIVIDAD 14** **Verbos** Write the verb that you associate with the following word or group of words.

1. Michael Phelps, agua, Malibu, Dara Torres _____

2. ballet, tango, rumba _____

3. sándwich, papas fritas, pizza _____

4. Coca-Cola, Pepsi, vino, café _____

5. examen, universidad, libros _____

6. Blockbuster, Netflix, Hulu _____

7. el maratón de Boston, Florence Griffith Joyner _____

8. Vail, Steamboat, Aspen _____

9. examen de historia A+, examen de biología A, examen de química A _____

10. Plácido Domingo, ópera _____

11. composiciones _____

12. periódicos, novelas, revistas _____

13. de 9:00 a 5:00 _____

14. número de teléfono, amigo _____

## Los días de la semana

**ACTIVIDAD 15** **El calendario** Complete this calendar by writing the missing days of the week. Note: A Spanish calendar does not start with the same day as one in English.

| AGOSTO | | | | | | |
|---|---|---|---|---|---|---|
| | | | jueves | | | domingo |
| | | 1 | 2 | 3 | 4 | 5 |
| 6 | 7 | 8 | 9 | 10 | 11 | 12 |
| 13 | 14 | 15 | 16 | 17 | 18 | 19 |
| 20 | 21 | 22 | 23 | 24 | 25 | 26 |
| 27 | 28 | 29 | 30 | 31 | | |

**ACTIVIDAD 16** **¿Qué día es?** Complete the following sentences in a logical manner.

1. Si hoy es martes, mañana es _____.

2. Si hoy es viernes, mañana es _____.

3. No tenemos clases los _____ y los _____.

4. Si hoy es lunes, mañana es _____.

5. Tengo clase de español los _____.

# Gramática para la comunicación II

## Expressing Likes and Dislikes (Part II): *Gustar*

**ACTIVIDAD 17** **Le gusta...** Complete each sentence by writing the appropriate word or words (**a, al, a la, a los, me, te, le, nos, os, les**) and a form of the verb **gustar.**

1. _____ Juan _____ _____ las cámaras Nikon.

2. _____ _____ Sres. Ramírez les _____ vivir en la ciudad.

3. ¿_____ Ud. le _____ estudiar inglés?

4. _____ _____ profesora Vázquez _____ _____ la revista *Hola*.

5. Nos _____ cantar y visitar museos.

6. ¿A Ud. _____ _____ los apartamentos o las residencias estudiantiles?

7. _____ Pepe y _____ mí _____ _____ bailar salsa.

8. A mí no _____ _____ los exámenes de química.

9. _____ Diana y a Carlos _____ _____ escuchar música clásica.

10. _____ Sr. Cabrera _____ _____ mirar películas románticas.

11. _____ ellos _____ _____ leer novelas de detectives.

**ACTIVIDAD 18** **Tus gustos Parte A.** On the first line of each item, state whether you like or dislike what is listed. On the second line, state whether your parents like it or not. Remember to include an article if necessary (**el, la, los, las**) and to use **gusta** before one or more infinitives.

► comer pizza  *A mí (no) me gusta comer pizza.*
  *A mis padres (no) les gusta comer pizza.*

1. los programas de MTV

_____

_____

2. escuchar música rock

_____

_____

3. correr

_____

_____

4. sacar fotos con cámaras pequeñas

_____

_____

5. las canciones de los Black Eyed Peas

_____

_____

6. usar computadoras y navegar por Internet

_____

_____

7. las películas de ciencia ficción

_____

_____

**Parte B.** Look at the preceding list and indicate the things that both you and your parents like or dislike. Remember to use **gusta** before an infinitive or infinitives.

▶ *(No) nos gusta comer pizza.*

1. _____
2. _____
3. _____
4. _____
5. _____
6. _____
7. _____

## Expressing Obligation and Making Plans: *Tener que* and *ir a*

**ACTIVIDAD 19** **Preguntas y respuestas** Answer the following questions in complete sentences according to the cues given.

1. ¿Qué vas a hacer mañana? (leer / novela) _____

_____

2. ¿Qué tiene que hacer tu amigo esta noche? (trabajar) _____

_____

3. ¿Tienes que escribir una composición? (sí) _____

_____

4. ¿Tienen que estudiar mucho o poco los estudiantes? (mucho) _____

_____

5. ¿Van a hacer una fiesta tus amigos el sábado? (no) _____

_____

6. ¿Vas a visitar a tus padres la semana que viene? (sí) _____

_____

**ACTIVIDAD 20** **Hoy y mañana** **Parte A.** List three things that you are going to do tonight. Use **ir a** + *infinitive.*

1. _____

2. _____

3. _____

**Parte B.** List three things that you have to do tomorrow. Use **tener que** + *infinitive.*

1. _____

2. _____

3. _____

**ACTIVIDAD 21** **¿Obligaciones o planes?** Write an **O** if the following phrases refer to future obligations or a **P** if they simply refer to future plans. Then write a sentence saying what you are going to do or have to do.

▶ ___*P*___ comer en un restaurante con tus amigos
*Voy a comer en un restaurante con mis amigos.*

1. _____ estudiar para el examen de historia

_____

2. _____ nadar

_____

3. _____ hacer la tarea de filosofía

_____

4. _____ salir a comer con Margarita

_____

5. _____ ir al cine

_____

6. _____ comprar el libro de álgebra

_____

**ACTIVIDAD** **22** **La agenda de Arturo** Look at Arturo's date book and answer the following questions.

| OCTUBRE | ACTIVIDADES |
|---------|-------------|
| lunes 15 | *estudiar para el examen; llamar a mis padres* |
| martes 16 | *examen de tecnologías de la información; ir a bailar* |
| miércoles 17 | *salir con Diana y Marisel a comer; nadar* |
| jueves 18 | *leer y hacer la tarea* |
| viernes 19 | *mirar una película con Jorge* |
| sábado 20 | *nadar e ir a la fiesta - llevar cámara y música de Proyecto Uno y Aventura* |
| domingo 21 | *comer con Sonia* |

1. ¿Adónde va a ir Arturo el sábado? _____

2. ¿Qué tiene que hacer el lunes? _____

3. ¿Cuándo va a salir con Diana y Marisel y qué van a hacer? _____

   _____

4. ¿Qué tiene que llevar a la fiesta? _____

   _____

5. ¿Cuándo va a nadar? _____

6. ¿Qué va a hacer el domingo? _____

**ACTIVIDAD** **23** **Tus planes** **Parte A.** Use the accompanying date book to list the things that you have to do or are going to do next week, and indicate with whom you are going to do them. Follow the sample entry.

| OCTUBRE | ACTIVIDADES |
|---------|-------------|
| lunes | |
| martes | *Pablo y yo tenemos que estudiar - examen mañana* |
| miércoles | |
| jueves | |
| viernes | |
| sábado | |
| domingo | |

**Parte B.** Based on your date book notations, write a description in paragraph form of what you are going to do and what you have to do next week. Be specific.

El lunes _____

_____

_____

_____

_____

## Un poco de todo

**ACTIVIDAD 24 La vida de Julio** Complete this paragraph about what Julio does in a typical day. Fill in each blank with a logical verb.

Por la mañana, a Julio le gusta _____ (1) café, _____ (2) el periódico y

_____ (3) música. Va a sus clases y por la tarde, no le gusta _____ (4)

sándwiches, pero le gusta mucho la pizza. Tiene que _____ (5) mucho para sus clases

para _____ (6) buenas notas. Tiene que _____ (7) novelas para la clase

de literatura y _____ (8) composiciones. Tiene que _____ (9) de 5 a 7 en

la cafetería (recibe $10 la hora). Por la noche le gusta _____ (10) 2 o 3 kilómetros en un

parque, _____ (11) películas de Netflix o _____ (12) merengue y salsa en un

club con sus amigos.

**ACTIVIDAD 25 Gustos y obligaciones** Answer the following questions.

1. ¿Qué tienes que hacer mañana por la mañana? _____

_____

2. ¿Qué van a hacer tus amigos mañana? _____

_____

3. ¿Qué les gusta hacer a tus amigos y a ti los sábados? _____

_____

4. ¿Qué van a hacer Uds. el sábado? _____

_____

**ACTIVIDAD 26 Planes y gustos** Complete the following paragraph to describe yourself and your friends.

A mí me gusta _____ ; por eso, tengo _____.

A mis amigos les gusta _____. Este fin de semana yo tengo que

_____ , pero mis amigos y yo también vamos a _____

_____.

# Lectura

## Estrategia de lectura: Scanning

When scanning a written text, you look for specific information and your eyes search like radar beams for their target.

**ACTIVIDAD 27 La televisión** Scan these TV listings to answer the following question: ¿Cuáles son los programas de los Estados Unidos?

_____

_____

**PROGRAMAS DE TV**

**MIÉRCOLES**
5 de abril

**18:00 hs**

7  **BOB ESPONJA PANTALONES CUADRADOS**
Bob tiene problemas en el restaurante el Krustáceo Krujiente. Calamardo Tentáculos no está contento. Pero, Patricio Estrella tiene una solución. ¿Va a funcionar?

13  **CASI ÁNGELES**
Programa infantil.

**19:00 hs**

7  **BÉISBOL: CAMPEONATO CUBANO**
Final. Pinar del Río vs. Ciego de Ávila.

9  **MENTES CRIMINALES: EPISODIO 21**
Agentes de la FBI viajan a San Antonio donde el Dr. Reid analiza la mente del asesino. Todo cambia cuando Penélope encuentra una pista en su computadora.

13  **LABERINTOS DE PASIÓN**
Telenovela.

**19:30 hs**

11  **CONCIERTOS EN VIVO**
Segmentos de los últimos conciertos de Olga Tañón, Marc Anthony y Calle 13.

**20:00 hs**

9  **LOS SIMPSON: UN TRANVÍA LLAMADO MARGE**
¡Marge es actriz! Marge hace el papel de Blanche DeBois en un teatro. A Homer no le gusta la idea.

13  **TELE SIETE NOTICIAS**
Noticiero.

© Cengage Learning 2013

**ACTIVIDAD 28** ¿Qué sabes? Read the following sentences and match each one with the country it describes.

1. El país forma parte con Haití de la isla de La Española. _____
2. Es una isla del Caribe que es un Estado Libre Asociado de los Estados Unidos. _____
3. Su música incluye el merengue y la bachata. _____
4. Es la isla más grande del Caribe. _____
5. Su moneda (currency) oficial es el dólar estadounidense. _____
6. Al pasar por su canal del Atlántico al Pacífico, vas del norte al sur y no del este al oeste. _____
7. Muchos refugiados políticos de este país están en los Estados Unidos. _____
8. Normalmente no tiene huracanes. _____

a. Cuba
b. República Dominicana
c. Panamá
d. Puerto Rico

**ACTIVIDAD 29** Personas célebres Read the following sentences and pick the correct answer. If you don't know, guess and see if you are correct. You will not be graded on this activity.

1. Pablo Casals (1876–1973), a famous _____, fled Spain after the Spanish Civil War and moved to Puerto Rico where today there is an annual **Festival Pablo Casals (www.festcasalspr.gov.pr).**

   a. artist               b. author               c. cellist

2. Óscar de la Renta (1932– ), a renowned _____ from the Dominican Republic, trained in New York with leaders in the industry prior to starting his own business.

   a. fashion designer     b. chef                 c. architect

3. _____ (1853–1895), known as the *apostle of Cuban independence,* was not only a patriotic political activist, but also a poet, who gave his life in battle before seeing Cuba free from Spanish rule. A stanza from the first poem in the collection *Versos sencillos (Simple Verses)* was the inspiration for the lyrics of the song *Guantanamera.*

   a. José Martí           b. Bernardo O'Higgins    c. Simón Bolívar

4. _____ (1945– ), from Panama, played major league baseball for the Twins and the Angels from 1967–1985. He played in the All-Star Game every year except his last. He was the 1967 Rookie of the Year and in 1977 the American League MVP. He was inducted into the Baseball Hall of Fame in 1991.

   a. Roberto Clemente     b. Rod Carew            c. Moisés Alou

# ¿Qué haces hoy?

**Capítulo 3**

## Vocabulario esencial I

### Lugares

**ACTIVIDAD 1 Asociaciones** What places do you associate with the following names, items, and actions? Follow the model and be sure to give an indefinite article with each noun.

▶ Whole Foods, Albertson's, Shaw's **un supermercado**

1. Gap, TJ Maxx _____
2. Walgreens, CVS _____
3. libros, estudiar _____
4. libros, comprar, Barnes & Noble _____
5. arte, Picasso _____
6. nadar _____
7. médicos, operaciones _____
8. $$$$, Chase, Citibank _____
9. kleenex, aspirinas _____
10. Broadway, Shakespeare _____
11. mirar películas _____
12. Harvard, Wellesley, Duke, UCLA _____
13. comer, TGI Fridays, Applebee's, Olive Garden _____
14. AAA, vacaciones, agente _____

**ACTIVIDAD 2 ¿Al o a la?** Complete the following sentences with **al** or **a la.**

1. Tengo que ir _____ banco.
2. Los domingos Juana va _____ iglesia.
3. Mañana vamos a ir _____ cine.
4. Tengo que comprar champú. Voy _____ farmacia.
5. Tenemos que trabajar. Vamos _____ oficina.

**ACTIVIDAD 3** **Los lugares** Fill in the following crossword puzzle with the appropriate names of places. In crossword puzzles accent marks are not used.

```
          1
          [ ]
 2 [ ][ ][ ][ ]  3 [ ][ ][ ][ ]
          [ ]
          [ ]     4 [ ][ ][ ]  5 [ ][ ]
          [ ]     [ ]           [ ]
          [ ]  7 [ ][ ][ ][ ][ ][ ]     6 [ ]
          [ ]     [ ]           [ ]       [ ]
          [ ]     [ ]    8 [ ][ ][ ][ ][ ][ ]
                  [ ]  9 [ ]            [ ]
               10 [ ][ ][ ][ ]         [ ]
                        [ ]            [ ]
                   11 [ ][ ][ ][ ][ ][ ]
```

**Horizontales**

2. un lugar donde estudias

4. _____ de viajes

7. El _____ Central está en Nueva York.

8. El hotel tiene una _____ para las personas que les gusta nadar.

10. Para comprar cosas vas a una _____.

11. A la Sra. Ramírez le gustaría trabajar con niños en una _____ primaria.

**Verticales**

1. una tienda que vende libros

3. Vas allí para ver un ballet o un concierto de música clásica.

5. Mis amigos católicos van a la _____ los domingos.

6. Voy al _____ para depositar dinero.

7. Para nadar, vamos a la _____ de Jacó en Costa Rica.

9. Vas allí para ver *Casablanca*, *Titanic*, *Avatar*, etc.

**ACTIVIDAD 4** **¿Adónde vas?** Imagine that this is your schedule for the week. State what you have to do (**tengo que** + *infinitive*) or are going to do (**voy a** + *infinitive*) and where you are going to go.

▶ domingo   correr cinco kilómetros
   *El domingo voy a correr cinco kilómetros; por eso voy al parque.*

1. lunes   estudiar para un examen

_____

2. martes   comprar desodorante y champú

_____

3. miércoles   nadar

_____

4. jueves   comprar libros para la clase de literatura

_____

5. viernes   mirar una película

_____

6. sábado   comprar papas fritas, hamburguesas, café y Coca-Cola

_____

7. domingo   ver la exhibición de Francisco Amighetti

_____

# Gramática para la comunicación I

## Indicating Location: *Estar* + *en* + place

**ACTIVIDAD 5** **Siempre está en...** Some people love doing certain things, so you can always find them in one place. Write complete sentences describing where the following people are, based on their likes. Follow the model.

▶  A Marta y a mí nos gusta la ópera.   *Estamos en un teatro.*

1. A Felipe le gusta nadar, pero no le gusta la piscina. _____

2. Me gusta mucho el arte. _____

3. Nos gusta comer bien. _____

4. Te gusta estudiar en silencio. _____

5. A Uds. les gusta bailar. _____

6. A Ana y a Sofía les gusta Angelina Jolie. _____

7. A nosotros nos gusta leer y comprar libros. _____

**ACTIVIDAD 6** **¿Dónde están?** While Salvador is at home alone, he receives a phone call from his wife, Paquita, asking where their children are. Read the entire conversation; then go back and fill in the missing words.

SALVADOR   ¿Aló?

PAQUITA   Hola, Salvador. ¿Está Fernando?

SALVADOR   No, no _____.

PAQUITA   ¿Dónde _____?

SALVADOR   Fernando y su novia _____ _____ el cine.

PAQUITA   ¿Y Susana?

| | |
|---|---|
| SALVADOR | Susana _____ _____ la librería. Tiene que trabajar esta tarde. |
| PAQUITA | ¿ _____ _____ Pedro y Roberto? |
| SALVADOR | _____ _____ la piscina. Yo _____ solo en casa. ¿Dónde _____ tú? |
| PAQUITA | _____ _____ la oficina. Voy a ir al supermercado y después voy a casa. |
| SALVADOR | Bueno, hasta luego. |
| PAQUITA | Chau. |

## Talking about the Present (Part I): The Present Indicative of Regular Verbs

**ACTIVIDAD 7** **Verbos** Complete the following sentences with the appropriate form of the logical verb.

1. Pablo _____ francés muy bien. (hablar, caminar)

2. Ellos _____ en la discoteca. (nadar, bailar)

3. Tú _____ en la cafetería. (comer, llevar)

4. Nosotros _____ novelas. (leer, visitar)

5. Me gusta _____ música. (mirar, escuchar)

6. ¿ _____ Uds. impresoras? (vender, aprender)

7. Yo _____ Coca-Cola. (beber, comer)

8. Carlota y yo _____ a las ocho. (regresar, necesitar)

9. Uds. tienen que _____ champú. (estudiar, comprar)

10. Nosotros _____ mucho en clase. (vender, escribir)

11. Mi padre _____ el piano. (leer, tocar)

12. Tú _____ cinco kilómetros todos los días. (recibir, correr)

13. Ellos _____ en Miami. (vivir, hacer)

14. Margarita _____ en una biblioteca. (esquiar, trabajar)

15. Yo _____ por Internet todos los días. (navegar, usar)

16. Mis padres _____ en Managua, Nicaragua. (desear, estar)

17. Guillermo, Ramiro y yo _____ la televisión. (mirar, hacer)

18. Mis amigos siempre _____ en Vail, Colorado. (esquiar, regresar)

19. Tú _____ buenas notas en la clase de historia. (tocar, sacar)

20. Paula _____ álgebra en la escuela. (recibir, aprender)

21. Uds. _____ películas de Netflix, ¿no? (alquilar, leer)

## Talking about the Present (Part II): The Present Indicative of Verbs with Irregular *yo* Forms

**ACTIVIDAD  8  Más verbos** Change the following sentences from **nosotros** to **yo.** Follow the model.

▶ ¿Salimos mañana?  *¿Salgo mañana?*

1. Traducimos cartas al francés. _____

2. Nosotros salimos temprano. _____

3. Traemos la Coca-Cola. _____

4. Vemos bien. _____

5. Producimos música rap. _____

6. ¿Qué hacemos? _____

7. Ponemos los papeles en el escritorio. _____

**ACTIVIDAD  9  Una conversación** Ana and Germán are at an art gallery organizing a party for an art exhibition. Complete their conversation with the present tense of the indicated verbs.

ANA        ¿Qué _____ yo? (traer)

GERMÁN    Tú _____ los álbumes de música clásica, ¿no? (traer)

ANA        Bien. ¿Quién va a _____ el café? (hacer)

GERMÁN    Yo _____ un café muy bueno. _____ un café de

Costa Rica que es delicioso. (hacer, tener)

ANA        Perfecto.

GERMÁN    ¿Dónde _____ la cafetera? (poner)

ANA        En la mesa.

GERMÁN    Oye, ¿quién está con el director? Yo no _____ bien. (ver)

ANA        Es Patricia, y ella _____ traer Coca-Cola y vino. (ofrecer)

GERMÁN    O.K. Ahora yo _____ que hablar con el director porque nosotros

_____ los programas. ¿Adónde _____ tú ahora?

(tener, necesitar, ir)

ANA        _____ para la universidad. Chau. (salir)

# Un poco de todo

**ACTIVIDAD 10 Una nota** Eugenia has promised her uncle **(tío),** who owns a travel agency in San José, to baby-sit his children while he and his wife lead a tour this weekend. This note from him gives Eugenia some instructions. Complete the sentences with the appropriate form of the verbs indicated.

Eugenia:

Nosotros _____ (1. tener) que ir a Monteverde el viernes con un grupo

de turistas y _____ (2. regresar) el domingo por la mañana. Rosaura

_____ (3. ir) a visitar a unos amigos y yo voy a _____

(4. trabajar). Pero me gusta el trabajo: yo _____ (5. traducir) para los turistas,

_____ (6. ofrecer) un *tour* opcional de la ciudad, _____

(7. hacer) reservas en restaurantes y por las noches _____ (8. salir) con ellos a

las discotecas. ¡Me gusta ser agente de viajes!

Vas a estar con los niños, ¿no? En general, los niños _____ (9. mirar) la

televisión después del colegio y luego _____ (10. ir) al parque. Por la noche,

ellos _____ (11. comer) poco y solo _____ (12. beber) agua.

Mientras *(While)* los niños _____ (13. estudiar) el sábado por la mañana, tú

debes *(should)* comprar unos sándwiches para comer después en la piscina. En la piscina no vas

a _____ (14. tener) problemas porque Carlitos siempre _____

(15. estar) con sus amigos y Cristina _____ (16. nadar). Generalmente

los niños van al cine el sábado por la tarde. Y tú, _____ (17. salir),

_____ (18. estudiar) o _____ (19. usar) mi computadora.

Gracias por todo. Tu tío,

*Alejandro*

**ACTIVIDAD 11** **La rutina diaria** Answer the following questions about yourself.

1. Cuando vas al cine, ¿con quién vas? _____

_____

2. ¿Nadas? Si contestas que sí, ¿con quién nadas? ¿Dónde nadan Uds.?

_____

_____

3. ¿Corres con tus amigos? ¿Corren Uds. en un parque? _____

_____

4. En las fiestas, ¿qué beben Uds.? _____

5. ¿Lees mucho o poco? ¿Qué lees? _____

_____

6. ¿Sales con tus amigos los sábados? ¿Adónde van Uds.? _____

_____

7. Cuando estás en la universidad, ¿escribes muchos emails o hablas mucho por teléfono?

_____

_____

8. ¿Ves a tu familia mucho? Si contestas que no, ¿te gustaría ver más a tu familia? _____

_____

# Vocabulario esencial II

## El físico y la personalidad: *Ser* + adjective

**ACTIVIDAD 12** **Opuestos** Write the opposites of the following adjectives.

1. guapo _____
2. alto _____
3. bueno _____
4. tonto _____
5. nuevo _____
6. moreno _____
7. simpático _____
8. joven _____
9. delgado _____
10. corto _____

**ACTIVIDAD 13** **Una descripción**

Describe your aunt and uncle to a friend who is going to pick them up at the bus station. Base your descriptions on the accompanying drawing. Use the verb **ser**.

_____

_____

_____

_____

_____

## Las emociones y los estados: *Estar* + adjective

**ACTIVIDAD 14** **¿Cómo están?** Look at the accompanying drawings and describe how each person or persons feel. Use the verb **estar** and an appropriate adjective in your responses. Remember to use accents with **estar** when needed.

1. _____

2. _____

3. _____

4. _____

5. _____

**ACTIVIDAD 15** **Hoy estoy...** Finish the following sentences in an original manner.

1. Me gustaría _____ porque hoy estoy _____.

2. Hoy voy a ir _____ porque estoy muy _____.

3. Hoy tengo que _____ porque necesito _____.

4. Deseo _____ porque estoy _____.

# Gramática para la comunicación II

## Describing Yourself and Others: Adjective Agreement, Position of Adjectives, and *ser/estar* + Adjective

**ACTIVIDAD 16** **El plural** Change the following sentences from singular to plural.

1. Pablo es guapo. Pablo y Ramón _____.

2. Yo soy inteligente. Miguel y yo _____.

3. Ana es simpática. Ana y Elena _____.

4. Maricarmen es delgada. Maricarmen y David _____.

**ACTIVIDAD 17** **Descripción** Complete the following sentences with the correct form of the indicated descriptive or possessive adjectives.

1. Lorenzo y Nacho son _____. (simpático)

2. La chica _____ está en la cafetería. (guapo)

3. _____ amigas están _____. (mi, aburrido)

4. _____ padres son _____. (su, alto)

5. _____ clases son muy _____. (nuestro, interesante)

6. Ellos están _____. (borracho)

7. Voy a descargar un álbum de música _____. (clásico)

8. Daniel y Rodrigo están _____. Vamos al cine. (listo)

9. Marcos y Ana tienen un Mini Cooper. _____ carro es muy _____. (su, bueno)

10. Elena está muy _____. (preocupado)

**ACTIVIDAD 18** **En orden lógico** Form complete sentences by putting the following groups of words in logical order.

1. altos / Pablo / son / y / Pedro

   _____

2. profesores / los / inteligentes / son

   _____

3. álbumes / unos / tengo / de / Norah Jones

   _____

4. amigos / muchos / simpáticos / tenemos

   _____

5. madre / tres / tiene / farmacias / su

   _____

**ACTIVIDAD 19** *¿Ser o estar?* Complete the following sentences with the correct form of **ser** or **estar.**

1. Mis amigos Sara y Hernán _____ enamorados.
2. Ellos _____ peruanos.
3. Yo _____ aburrida porque el profesor _____ terrible.
4. Carmen, tenemos que salir. ¿ _____ lista?
5. Nosotros _____ nerviosos porque tenemos un examen de biología.
6. Mi novio _____ muy alto.
7. Mi profesor de historia _____ joven.
8. Tú _____ muy simpático.
9. Es muy tarde y Felipe no _____ listo.
10. Julián y yo _____ enojados.

**ACTIVIDAD 20** **Mi familia** Finish the following sentences with adjectives to describe yourself and your parents.

1. Mi padre es _____, _____ y _____,

   y siempre está _____.

2. Mi madre es _____, _____ y _____,

   y siempre está _____.

3. Yo soy _____, _____ y _____,

   y siempre estoy _____.

Nombre _____ Sección _____ Fecha _____

**ACTIVIDAD** **21** **¿La familia típica?** Look at the accompanying drawing and describe the mother, the father, and their son, Alfonso. Tell what they look like **(ser)** and how they feel **(estar).**

© Cengage Learning 2013

_____

_____

_____

_____

_____

_____

## Discussing Actions in Progress: Present Indicative and Present Progressive

**ACTIVIDAD** **22** **En este momento** Say what the following people are doing right now, using the indicated verbs.

1. Chino Espinoza _____ _____ salsa. (cantar)

2. Felipe y Silvia _____ _____. (comer)

3. Usher _____ _____. (bailar)

4. Yo _____ _____ una respuesta. (escribir)

5. Lindsey Vonn, Picabo Street y Shaun White _____ _____. (esquiar)

**ACTIVIDAD 23** ¿Qué están haciendo? Say what the following people are doing right now. Fill in the blanks with the name of your friends when prompted. Use the following phrases: **mirar la televisión, leer una novela, escuchar música, ver una película, escribir un examen, comer en un restaurante, correr en el parque, estudiar en la biblioteca, hablar con amigos, subir fotos a Internet.**

1. Mi profesor/a de español _____

2. Mi madre _____

3. Mi amiga _____ (nombre) _____

4. Mi amigo _____ (nombre) _____

5. Mis amigos _____ y _____ (nombres) _____

# Un poco de todo

**ACTIVIDAD 24** **Los problemas** Ignacio wrote an email to his friend Jorge, who replied. Read both notes first; then go back and fill in the missing words with the appropriate forms of the following verbs: **bailar, cantar, escuchar, estar, estudiar, gustar, leer, ser, tener, tocar.** You can use a verb more than once.

---

Hola, Jorge:

Por supuesto, yo _____ una persona muy simpática y _____ una novia que

también es simpática. Nos gusta hacer muchas cosas: nosotros _____ muchos tipos de

música, _____ en las discos, yo _____ la guitarra y ella _____. Ella

y yo _____ Literatura en la universidad; nos _____ mucho _____

poemas. Nosotros _____ enamorados, pero yo _____ un problema: ella

_____ muy alta. Yo no _____ contento porque _____ muy bajo.

*Ignacio*

---

Ignacio:

Tu novia es fantástica. Tú _____ un problema: ¡tu ego!

*Jorge*

---

**ACTIVIDAD 25** **Eres profesor/a.** You are the teacher. Correct the grammar in the following sentences. The bolded words contain no errors and will help you find the mistakes. (There are ten mistakes.)

**Mi familia y yo** regreso mañana de nuestros **viaje** a San José. Mi hermano Ramón no regresa porque

**él** viven en San José. Su novia es **en San José,** también. **Ella** es guapo, inteligente y simpático. Ellos

van a una fiesta esta noche y van a llevar su **cámaras.** A **ellos** le gusta mucho la fotografía. Siempre saca

muchos **fotos** en las fiestas.

**ACTIVIDAD 26** **El cantante famoso** Freddy Fernández, a famous Nicaraguan rock singer, was interviewed by a reporter. Write an article based on the following notes that the reporter took. Remember to add words such as **en, el, la, al, a la,** etc. where needed; use **ser** and **estar** correctly with adjectives; use present tense to say what he does every day; use **ir a** + *infinitive* to discuss the future; and use **le gustaría** + *infinitive* to state what he would like to do.

## Descripción
alto, guapo, simpático

## Estado
contento, enamorado

## Un día normal
cantar por la mañana / guitarra

leer / periódico

correr / 10 kilómetros / parque

él / novia / comer / restaurante

él / novia / mirar / películas

## Planes futuros
él / novia / ir / hotel / la playa de Tamarindo / sábado

él / ir / cantar / San José / programa de televisión

## Le gustaría
cantar / Carnegie Hall en Nueva York

ir / novia / teatro en Broadway

_____

_____

_____

_____

_____

_____

_____

_____

_____

_____

_____

_____

_____

_____

_____

_____

_____

# Lectura

## Estrategia de lectura: Dealing with Unfamiliar Words

When reading, we frequently come across unfamiliar words. Sometimes we consult a dictionary to find the exact meaning, but more often than not, we simply guess the meaning from context. You will practice guessing meaning from context in **Actividad 29**.

### Email de Nicaragua

Carolina and Mario are from Chile and have just begun internships. She is in San José, Costa Rica, and he is in Managua, Nicaragua. Read the email he sent her, and answer the questions that follow.

**ACTIVIDAD 27** **Ideas principales** Each paragraph in the following email expresses one of the main ideas in the list. Scan the email and put the correct paragraph number next to its corresponding idea.

a. _____ las actividades de Mario

c. _____ las preguntas para Carolina

b. _____ los amigos de Mario

d. _____ la composición étnica

---

Querida Carolina:

Por fin tengo tiempo para escribir. ¿Cómo estás? Espero que bien. Tengo muchas preguntas porque deseo saber cómo es tu vida en San José y cuáles son tus planes y actividades. ¿Te gusta San José? ¿Tienes muchos amigos? ¿De
5   dónde son y qué **estudian**? ¿Qué haces los sábados y los domingos? Escribe pronto y contesta todas mis preguntas.

Yo estoy muy bien. Voy a la universidad todas las noches y trabajo por las mañanas en American Express. Soy agente de viajes y me gusta mucho el trabajo. Por las tardes voy a la biblioteca y estudio con Luis Sosa, es
10  chileno también. **Tengo** que estudiar dos años más y termino mi carrera; voy a ser hombre de negocios. ¿Te gusta la idea? A mí me gusta mucho.

Por cierto, uno de mis cursos es geografía social de Hispanoamérica y es muy interesante, pero tengo que memorizar muchos datos. Por ejemplo, en la República Dominicana el 16% de las personas son blancas de origen europeo,
15  un 11% de la población es negra y el grupo étnico más grande, un 73%, **es** mulato y casi no hay indígenas; pero en Nicaragua el 17% es de origen europeo, el 9% son negros, mientras que el 5% es indígena, pero el grupo más grande son los mestizos que forman el 69% de la población. Necesito tener buena memoria porque hay mucha variedad en todos los países, ¿verdad?

20  Por aquí, todos bien. Un compañero de trabajo y yo vivimos ahora en el centro de Managua. Nos gusta mucho el apartamento. Mis amigos son interesantes. Marta estudia y trabaja todo el día. Tomás es deportista profesional, practica fútbol ocho horas diarias y Maite, que trabaja en American Express también, va a comprar una computadora Mac. Ahora **escribe**
25  en mi computadora y quiere aprender todo en tres días. Bueno, no tengo más noticias. Ah sí, el fin de semana mis amigos y yo vamos a ir a la playa y voy a aprender a hacer surf.

Carolina, **espero** recibir un email muy pronto. Contesta todas mis preguntas, ¿O.K.? Adiós.
30  Cariños,
Mario
P.D. Tengo celular nuevo; el número es +505 8555 2121.

---

**ACTIVIDAD 28** **¿Quién es el sujeto?** To whom do the following verbs refer? Reread the email; note the verb endings and the context given before choosing an answer.

1. "¿De dónde son y qué **estudian**?" (línea 5)

   a. Carolina y Mario      b. los amigos de Carolina      c. los amigos de Carolina y Mario

2. "**Tengo** que estudiar dos años más... " (línea 10)

   a. Mario             b. Carolina             c. Luis

3. "Por ejemplo, en la República Dominicana... **es** mulato... " (líneas 15–16)

   a. los amigos de Mario    b. el grupo étnico más grande    c. los hispanoamericanos

4. "Ahora **escribe** en mi computadora... " (línea 24)

   a. Alejandra          b. Tomás             c. Maite

5. "Carolina, **espero** recibir un email muy pronto." (línea 28)

   a. Mario             b. Carolina             c. Maite

**ACTIVIDAD 29** **Contexto** Refer to the reading to determine which translation best fits each word in bold.

1. "Tengo que estudiar dos años más y termino mi **carrera**; voy a ser hombre de negocios." (línea 10)

   a. career            b. internship           c. university studies

2. "...el grupo étnico más grande, un 73%, es **mulato**..." (líneas 15–16)

   a. white + indigenous    b. white + black        c. indigenous + black

3. "...pero el grupo más grande son los **mestizos**..." (líneas 17–18)

   a. white + indigenous    b. white + black        c. indigenous + black

**ACTIVIDAD 30** **Preguntas** Answer the following questions based on the email you read.

1. ¿Dónde trabaja Mario y qué hace? _____

   _____

2. ¿Cuál es el grupo étnico más grande de la República Dominicana? _____

   _____

3. En Nicaragua, ¿qué porcentaje de las personas son mestizas? _____

   _____

4. ¿Qué practica Tomás todos los días? _____

   _____

5. ¿Qué va a comprar Maite? _____

   _____

6. ¿Adónde va a ir Mario el fin de semana? ¿Con quiénes va? ¿Qué va a hacer? ____

   _____

**ACTIVIDAD 31 Respuesta de Carolina Parte A.** Read the following reply from Carolina to Mario. Fill in the blanks with a logical word. Only one word per blank.

Querido Mario:

Me gusta mucho Costa Rica y mi trabajo _____ fabuloso. Tengo muchos amigos, pero tengo uno que a _____ te gustaría mucho. Se llama Vicente y estudia música. Canta muy bien. Su cantante favorita _____ la costarricense Xiomar. ¡Pura vida! Para Vicente, ella es una persona que cuando _____ una canción también vive la canción. Es una cantante dinámica. Tengo _____ salir de casa en este momento. Voy a llegar tarde al trabajo.

Besos,

*Carolina*

**Parte B.** Now read Mario's response and fill in the blanks of his email with a logical word. Only one word per blank.

¡Hola!

Xiomar, cantante costarricense... interesante. Normalmente yo _____ por la mañana en American Express, _____ en la biblioteca por la tarde y por la _____ voy a clase. Pero mañana no voy a ir a clase. Pues mañana voy _____ hacer algo muy interesante. Voy a escuchar hablar a Bianca Jagger que _____ nicaragüense. Es la exesposa de Mick Jagger de los Rolling Stones. Ella es activista política y va a hablar de los cambios climáticos y los efectos que producen en _____ poblaciones indígenas de Nicaragua.

Chau,

*Mario*

**Parte C.** Answer the following questions based on the contents of the two emails.

1. ¿De dónde es Xiomar? ¿Qué hace ella? _____

_____

2. ¿De dónde es Bianca Jagger? ¿Qué hace ella? _____

_____

# Repaso

## Ser, estar, tener

In Chapter 3, you learned how to describe someone using **ser** or **estar** with adjectives. In previous chapters, you already learned other uses of **ser** and **estar.**

| | | |
|---|---|---|
| **Ser:** | ¿De dónde **eres**? | **Soy** de Wisconsin. Soy norteamericana. |
| | ¿Qué haces? | **Soy** economista. |
| | ¿Cuál **es** tu número de teléfono? | Mi número de teléfono **es** 448 22 69. |
| | ¿**Es** tu padre? | Sí, él **es** mi padre. |
| | ¿Quién **es** ella? | **Es** mi madre. |
| | ¿De quién **es** el carro? | **Es** de mi madre. |
| | ¿Cuándo **es** tu examen de historia? | **Es** el lunes. |
| | ¿Cómo **es** tu profesor de historia? | **Es** muy simpático, pero la clase **es** difícil. |
| **Estar:** | ¿Cómo **estás**? | **Estoy** bien. |
| | ¿Dónde **está** tu madre? | **Está** en casa, está enferma. |
| | ¿Dónde **está** tu casa? | **Está** en la parte vieja de Managua. |
| | ¿Qué **estás** haciendo? | **Estoy** escribiendo la tarea. |

You also learned that to express age in Spanish, you use the verb **tener.**

¿Cuántos años **tienes**?                    **Tengo** veinte años.

**ACTIVIDAD  1  En el aeropuerto** Paula and Hernán are sitting next to each other in the airport when they find out their flight will be delayed for a few hours. Fill in the blanks in their conversation with the appropriate forms of **ser, estar,** or **tener.**

COMPUTADORA   Bip... Bip... Bip...

HERNÁN      ¿Qué haces?

PAULA      _____ (1) trabajando con la computadora, pero ya no tiene batería.

HERNÁN      ¿Cómo te llamas?

PAULA      _____ (2) Paula, Paula Barrero. ¿Y tú?

HERNÁN      Hernán Gálvez. Encantado. ¿De dónde _____ (3)?

PAULA      _____ (4) de León.

HERNÁN      ¿En qué país _____ (5) León?

PAULA      Ay, perdón, _____ (6) en Nicaragua.

HERNÁN   Pues, yo también _____ (7) de León, pero León en España. Y ¿qué haces?

PAULA    _____ (8) programadora de computadoras.

HERNÁN   ¿Para qué compañía trabajas?

PAULA    Para IBM.

HERNÁN   ¿Tu oficina _____ (9) en León?

PAULA    No, _____ (10) en Managua. Y tú, ¿qué haces?

HERNÁN   _____ (11) director de cine.

PAULA    Entonces, _____ (12) muy creativo, ¿no?

HERNÁN   No exactamente; _____ (13) un poco creativo e idealista, pero también

         _____ (14) muy responsable... Si _____ (15) programadora

         de computadoras, te gustan los números, ¿no?

PAULA    No sé... _____ (16) posible, pero ahora _____ (17)

         aburrida en el trabajo. Todos los días _____ (18) iguales.

HERNÁN   Todos los días _____ (19) diferentes y activos para mí. Y tus padres, ¿viven

         en León?

PAULA    No, _____ (20) en Managua.

HERNÁN   ¿Trabajan?

PAULA    No. Mi padre _____ (21) enfermo. _____ (22) un poco

         gordo y tiene diabetes; por eso mi madre _____ (23) en casa con él.

         _____ (24) mayores.

HERNÁN   _____ (25) preocupada, ¿no?

PAULA    Sí, un poco. Mi padre siempre _____ (26) en el sofá con el televisor todo el

         día y el pobre _____ (27) aburrido y mi madre _____ (28)

         un poco triste últimamente.

HERNÁN   ¿Cuántos años _____ (29) ellos?

PAULA    Mi madre _____ (30) sesenta y cinco años y mi padre

         _____ (31) setenta y cinco.

HERNÁN   Bueno, _____ (32) un poco mayores... ¿Te gustaría tomar una

         Coca-Cola o algo?

PAULA    Bueno. Gracias.

HERNÁN   La cafetería Los Galgos _____ (33) en este aeropuerto y

         _____ (34) muy bonita. Vamos.

# Un día típico

## Vocabulario esencial I

### Las partes del cuerpo

**ACTIVIDAD 1** **¿Qué parte es?** Look at the following drawing and label the parts of the body. Be sure to include the definite article.

1. _____
2. _____
3. _____
4. _____
5. _____
6. _____
7. _____
8. _____
9. _____
10. _____
11. _____
12. _____
13. _____
14. _____
15. _____
16. _____
17. _____
18. _____
19. _____
20. _____

© Cengage Learning 2013

**ACTIVIDAD 2** **La parte más interesante** Stars are constantly scrutinized for their appearance, either in a positive or a negative manner. Associate these people with their most distinctive body part; then write if you like it or not. If you don't, indicate what that person should do to improve. Here are a few suggestions for what they should do: **consultar con un cirujano plástico, ir al dentista, hacer ejercicio, ir a un peluquero** (hair stylist / barber) **bueno, comprar una peluca** (wig).

▶ nariz / Adrien Brody *Me gusta la nariz de Adrien Brody. ¡Qué bonita/atractiva!*
*No me gusta la nariz de Adrien Brody. ¡Qué fea/horrible!*
*Adrien debe consultar con un cirujano plástico.*

1. pelo / Donald Trump _____

_____

2. dientes / Madonna _____

_____

3. piernas / Heidi Klum _____

_____

4. estómago / Homer Simpson _____

_____

5. labios / Steven Tyler _____

_____

6. bigote / el Dr. Phil _____

_____

7. boca / Julia Roberts _____

_____

8. orejas / el príncipe Carlos de Inglaterra _____

_____

9. ojos / Amanda Seyfried _____

_____

10. brazos / Michelle Obama _____

_____

## Acciones reflexivas

**ACTIVIDAD 3** **Los verbos reflexivos** Select the word that does not belong in each of the following groups.

1. bañarse, lavarse, levantarse, ducharse
2. la barba, el bigote, afeitarse, quitarse la ropa
3. cepillarse, la pasta de dientes, el pelo, peinarse
4. el jabón, lavarse la espalda, afeitarse, ducharse
5. ducharse, el pelo, cepillarse, los dientes
6. quitarse, ponerse, la ropa, lavarse

**ACTIVIDAD 4** **Asociaciones** Write a reflexive action that you associate with each of the following items. Try not to repeat items.

▶ los dientes *cepillarse*

1. la cara _____

2. la barba _____

3. la ropa _____

4. las manos _____

5. el cuerpo _____

6. los ojos _____

7. las piernas _____

# Gramática para la comunicación I

## Describing Daily Routines: Reflexive Verbs

**ACTIVIDAD 5** **Las rutinas** Complete the following sentences with the appropriate form of the indicated reflexive verbs.

1. Los domingos yo _____ _____ tarde. (levantarse)

2. Mi novio no _____ _____ porque a mí me gusta la barba. (afeitarse)

3. Todos los niños _____ _____ el pelo con champú Johnson para no llorar. (lavarse)

4. Nosotros siempre _____ _____ tarde. (levantarse)

5. ¿Tú _____ _____ o _____ _____ por la mañana? (ducharse, bañarse)

6. Yo _____ _____ los dientes después de comer. (cepillarse)

7. El niño tiene cuatro años, pero _____ _____ la ropa solo. (ponerse)

8. Las actrices de Hollywood _____ _____ mucho. (maquillarse)

**ACTIVIDAD 6** **Posición de los reflexivos** Write the following sentences a different way by changing the position of the reflexive pronoun, but without changing their meaning. Remember to use accents if needed.

1. Voy a lavarme el pelo. _____

2. Ella tiene que maquillarse. _____

3. Juan se va a afeitar. _____

4. Tenemos que levantarnos temprano. _____

5. Me estoy poniendo la ropa. _____

**ACTIVIDAD 7** **¡Qué tonto!** Rewrite the following nonsense sentences in a logical manner, changing whatever elements are necessary.

1. El señor se afeita los brazos.

   _____

2. La señora se maquilla el pelo.

   _____

3. Me levanto, me pongo la ropa y me ducho.

   _____

4. Antes de comer, los chicos se quitan las manos.

   _____

5. Antes de salir de la casa, me cepillo la nariz y me maquillo las orejas.

   _____

**ACTIVIDAD 8** **Una familia extraña** Pedro's family seems to be caught in a routine. First read the entire paragraph; then go back and fill in the missing words with the appropriate forms of the verbs in the list. You can use verbs more than once. When finished, reread the paragraph and check to see that each verb agrees with its subject. Note: Some verbs are reflexive and some aren't.

| | | | | |
|---|---|---|---|---|
| **afeitarse** | **ducharse** | **levantarse** | **mirar** | **salir** |
| **cepillarse** | **leer** | **maquillarse** | **peinarse** | **tomar** |

En mi casa todos los días son iguales (the same). Mis padres _____ temprano. Mi

madre va al baño y _____. Mi padre prepara el café. Después, él _____

el periódico. Al terminar de ducharse, mi madre _____ los dientes con Crest (mi

padre usa Colgate) y _____ la cara con productos de Revlon. Luego, mi padre

_____ , _____ con su Gillette, _____ los dientes y

_____ (¡tiene poco pelo, pero tiene peine!). Después, ellos _____ café.

Finalmente, ellos _____ los dientes otra vez y _____ para el trabajo.

Luego, yo _____ y _____ café. Después, _____ los

dientes y _____ la televisión. Voy a la universidad, pero por la tarde, no por la mañana.

## The Personal *a*

**ACTIVIDAD 9** *A, al, a la, a los, a las* Complete the following sentences with **a, al, a la, a los,** or **a las** only if necessary; otherwise, leave the space blank.

1. Voy a ir _____ ciudad.

2. No veo bien _____ actor.

3. ¿ _____ ti te gusta esquiar?

4. Escucho _____ música muy interesante.

5. Tengo _____ un profesor muy interesante.

6. Siempre visitamos _____ padres de mi novio.

7. Vamos a ver _____ la película mañana.

8. Me gustar caminar _____ parque.

**ACTIVIDAD 10** **El día de Noemí** Finish the following paragraph about what Noemí is doing today. Use **a, al, a la, a los,** or **a las** only if necessary; otherwise, leave the space blank.

Hoy Noemí va _____ (1) levantarse temprano. Normalmente escucha _____ (2) álbumes de salsa y merengue cuando se ducha y se pone la ropa. Después va _____ (3) universidad. Hoy tiene que ver _____ (4) profesor Aguirre para hablar sobre un examen. Por la tarde va _____ (5) llamar _____ (6) Enrique y _____ (7) Diana para tomar un café con ellos. _____ (8) Enrique le gusta el bar Jazz Zone porque siempre ponen _____ (9) música vieja de John Coltrane, Charlie Parker y Ella Fitzgerald. Pero _____ (10) Noemí no le gusta mucho escuchar _____ (11) jazz. Por eso, van _____ (12) ir _____ (13) Café de la Paz porque es más tranquilo. Después Noemí tiene que ir _____ (14) Biblioteca Nacional para hacer _____ (15) investigación para una clase. Más tarde tiene que ir _____ (16) oficina para hablar un poco del trabajo. Por la noche, _____ (17) Noemí le gustaría ir _____ (18) bailar. _____ (19) amigos de Noemí les gusta mucho la música criolla afroperuana y tienen _____ (20) música de Susana Baca y Eva Ayllón, pero el grupo Novalima es su favorito.

# Un poco de todo

**ACTIVIDAD 11** **Una carta** Finish the following letter to your Spanish-speaking grandmother, who has asked you to describe a typical day at the university.

Universidad de _____, 12 de septiembre de 20 _____

Querida Abuela:

¿Cómo estás? Yo _____. Me gusta mucho _____

_____. Estudio mucho pero

también _____. Tengo muchos amigos que son

_____. A ellos les

gusta _____.

Todos los días son iguales; normalmente me levanto y _____

_____.

Después de clase, llamo por teléfono a _____. Y por la noche

_____

_____.

Un abrazo *(hug),*

_____

(tu nombre)

# Vocabulario esencial II

## El tiempo, las estaciones y las fechas

**ACTIVIDAD 12** **Las fechas y las estaciones** Write out the following dates and state what season it is in the Northern and Southern Hemispheres. Remember that the day is written first in Spanish. The first one has been done for you.

| | | Fecha | Hemisferio norte | Hemisferio sur |
|---|---|---|---|---|
| a. | 15/2 | el quince de febrero | invierno | verano |
| b. | 3/4 | _____ | _____ | _____ |
| c. | 15/12 | _____ | _____ | _____ |
| d. | 30/8 | _____ | _____ | _____ |
| e. | 25/10 | _____ | _____ | _____ |
| f. | 1/2 | _____ | _____ | _____ |

**ACTIVIDAD 13** **El tiempo** Look at the accompanying drawings. Using complete sentences, state what the weather is like in each case. The first one has been done for you.

Illustrations: © Cengage Learning 2013

1. _____ *Hace sol.* _____   5. _____
2. _____   6. _____
3. _____   7. _____
4. _____   8. _____

**ACTIVIDAD 14** **Fechas importantes** Complete the following lists with names, events, and dates (e.g., **el doce de marzo**) that are important to you.

| | | Fecha |
|---|---|---|
| **Cumpleaños:** | madre<br>padre<br>_____<br>_____<br>_____ | _____<br>_____<br>_____<br>_____<br>_____ |
| **Aniversario:** | padres | _____ |
| **Último (last) día de clases:** | | _____ |
| **Exámenes finales:** | español<br>_____<br>_____<br>_____<br>_____ | _____<br>_____<br>_____<br>_____<br>_____ |

**ACTIVIDAD 15** **Asociaciones** Associate the following words with actions, weather expressions, months, and other nouns.

▶ otoño *clases, noviembre, hace fresco, estudiamos*

1. julio _____

2. primavera _____

3. Acapulco _____

4. diciembre _____

5. invierno _____

6. hacer viento _____

7. octubre _____

**ACTIVIDAD 16** **¿Qué tiempo hace?** You are on vacation in Atacames, Ecuador, and you call a friend in Cleveland. As always, you begin your conversation by talking about the weather. Complete the following conversation based on the accompanying drawings.

**Atacames, Ecuador**          **Cleveland, Ohio**

TU AMIGO    ¿Aló?

TÚ          Hola. ¿Cómo estás?

TU AMIGO    Bien, pero _____

_____.

TÚ          ¿También llueve?

TU AMIGO    _____.

¿_____?

TÚ          ¡Fantástico! _____

_____.

TU AMIGO    ¿Cuál es la temperatura?

TÚ          _____.

TU AMIGO    Creo que voy a visitar Ecuador.

# Gramática para la comunicación II

## Talking about Who and What You Know: *Saber* and *conocer*

**ACTIVIDAD 17** **¿Saber o conocer?** Complete the following sentences with the appropriate form of the verbs **saber** or **conocer**.

1. ¿_____ tú a mi padre?

2. Yo no _____ tu número de teléfono.

3. ¿_____ Uds. dónde está la casa de Fernanda?

4. Ellos _____ Caracas muy bien porque trabajan allí.

5. ¿_____ nadar Teresa?

6. ¿_____ Uds. cómo se llama el profesor nuevo?

7. Yo no _____ la nueva película de Almodóvar.

8. Jorge _____ bailar muy bien porque es bailarín profesional.

**ACTIVIDAD 18** **Ana Sofía y sus amigos** Finish the following story about Ana Sofía, Carlos, Aarón, and Eva. Fill in the blanks with the correct form of **saber** or **conocer**.

Ana Sofía desea _____ más de Carlos; por eso llama a Eva porque ella

_____ a Carlos. Eva _____ que Carlos va a llamar a Ana Sofía

para salir con ella. Eva también _____ que a Carlos le gusta ir a discotecas y que

_____ bailar salsa muy bien. Él _____ una discoteca que se llama Son

Latino, pero Eva no _____ exactamente dónde está.

Aarón también _____ a Carlos. Ana Sofía _____ que a Eva le gusta

mucho Aarón. Eva no _____ su número de teléfono, pero ella ve a Aarón todos los días

en la cafetería. Entonces, mañana Eva va a hablar con Aarón para ir al cine con Ana Sofía y Carlos el

domingo.

Así que Eva va a salir con Aarón y Ana Sofía con Carlos. ¿Va a pasar algo interesante? Quién

_____, pero es posible...

**ACTIVIDAD 19** **Muchas preguntas pero poco dinero** You work for a low-budget advertising agency that makes ads for TV and radio. Complete your boss's questions, using **saber** or **conocer,** and then answer them in complete sentences.

1. ¿_____ el número de teléfono de la compañía de champú?

_____

2. ¿Tú _____ personalmente a un actor famoso?

_____

3. Necesito un pianista para un anuncio comercial (ad). ¿ _____ tocar el piano?

_____

4. Necesito un fotógrafo. ¿ _____ a un fotógrafo bueno?

_____

5. ¿_____ tus amigos nuestros productos?

_____

## Pointing Out and Referencing: Demonstrative Adjectives and Pronouns

**ACTIVIDAD 20** **¿Cuál es?** Complete these mini-conversations with the appropriate demonstrative adjective or pronoun (**esta, esos, aquellas, ese, aquellos,** etc...)

1. —Me gustan las plantas que están cerca de la puerta.

   —¿ _____ plantas que están allí?

2. —¿Te gustan _____ jabones que tengo en la mano?

   —Sí, me gustan mucho.

3. —¿Dónde está el restaurante?

   —Tenemos que caminar mucho. Es _____ restaurante que está allá.

4. —¿Vas a comprar una revista?

   —Sí, pero ¿cuál quieres? ¿ _____ que tengo aquí o

   _____ que está allí?

   —Me gusta más *People en español.*

# Un poco de todo

**ACTIVIDAD 21** **Lógica** Finish the following series of words in a logical manner.

1. junio, julio, _____

2. hacer frío, hacer fresco, _____

3. afeitarse, crema de afeitar; lavarse el pelo, champú; cepillarse los dientes,

   _____

4. este libro, ese libro, _____

5. verano, _____, _____, primavera

6. noviembre, _____, enero

7. el brazo, el codo, _____, los dedos

**ACTIVIDAD 22** **Una conversación** Luis calls Marcos on his cell phone. Complete the conversation by selecting the correct responses.

LUIS      ¿Qué estás haciendo?

MARCOS    a. Te estás duchando.

          b. Voy a ir a Cochabamba mañana.

          c. Estoy lavando el carro.

LUIS      a. Yo estoy estudiando y tengo una pregunta.

          b. No tengo carro.

          c. También estoy duchándome.

MARCOS    a.   Ud. es el profesor.

           b.   Bueno, pero no sé mucho.

           c.   Eres experto.

LUIS    a.   ¡Hombre! Por lo menos sabes más que yo.

           b.   Claro que soy inteligente.

           c.   Siempre saca buenas notas.

MARCOS    a.   O.K. ¿Conoces al profesor?

           b.   ¿Por qué no hablas con el médico? Sabe mucho.

           c.   O.K., pero estoy lavando el carro. Más tarde, ¿eh?

**ACTIVIDAD 23** **El fin de semana**   Look at the accompanying map and plan your weekend. You can only go to **one** place. Say where you are going to go and why. Use phrases such as **voy a ir a...**, **porque hace...**, and **me gusta....**

_____

_____

_____

_____

**ACTIVIDAD** **24** **La fiesta** You and your friend are at a party. You are standing close to the people on the right of the illustration and you begin discussing the physical variety that exists among people. Study the drawing and complete the conversation that follows by supplying the word that is missing for each blank.

TÚ          No hay dos personas iguales. _____ (1) señor es gordo, bajo y tiene poco

            pelo. Y _____ (2) hombres son guapos, altos y delgados. Uno tiene barba y

            el otro, _____ (3).

TU AMIGA    Sí, y _____ (4), que _____ (5) bailando,

            _____ (6) muy alto.

TÚ          Y _____ (7) mujer, que _____ (8) bailando con él, es

            _____ (9) también.

TU AMIGA    ¿Y esta señora?

TÚ          ¡Huy! _____ (10) señora, que está _____ (11), es un poco

            fea, ¿no?

TU AMIGA    No, no es fea, pero tampoco _____ (12) muy guapa.

TÚ          Es verdad, todos somos diferentes.

# Lectura

## Estrategia de lectura: Using Background Knowledge and Identifying Cognates

The following is about the Inti Raymi festival in Perú. By using your general knowledge and your ability to recognize cognates (words in Spanish that are similar to English), you should be able to obtain a great deal of information about this intriguing place.

When doing the following activities, assume that you are a tourist in Peru and do not have a bilingual dictionary. Simply try to get as much information as you can from the reading.

**ACTIVIDAD 25** **Cognados** In the excerpt that follows, underline all the cognates (words that are similar in Spanish and English) you can identify. Also underline all the words you may have already learned in Spanish. Then read the entire description of **Inti Raymi** to extract as much information as you can.

### INTI RAYMI

Francisco Pizarro conquista a los incas y poco después, en 1572, el festival Inti Raymi deja de existir por orden de la Iglesia católica. Esta institución considera el festival una celebración pagana. En el año 1944, los habitantes de Cuzco, muchos de ellos descendientes de los incas, celebran Inti Raymi por primera vez en 372 años. Inti Raymi es el festival del sol porque marca el solsticio de invierno. La fiesta dura una semana y marca el final de un año y el principio de otro en el calendario inca.

El 24 de junio todos los años hay una procesión de dos kilómetros de largo en la ciudad de Cuzco.

**Festival de Inti Raymi en las ruinas de Sacsayhuaman**

Nevada Wier/Corbis

Esta procesión va hasta las ruinas de Sacsayhuaman donde las personas representan una antigua ceremonia incaica en la que el jefe de los incas honra a su dios, el Sol. Participan cientos de personas que llevan ropa tradicional mientras peruanos de todo el país y unos 100.000 turistas extranjeros van a mirar la ceremonia. Como en el siglo XVI, habla el líder de los incas, que se llama Sapa Inca, y también hablan tres personas vestidas de serpiente, puma y cóndor. Los animales representan el mundo que existe debajo de la tierra, la Tierra y el mundo de los dioses, respectivamente. Todo es igual que antes, excepto que hoy día no sacrifican una llama, solo representan esta antigua tradición.

**ACTIVIDAD 26** **¿Qué sabes ahora?** Make a list of all the information you have been able to obtain from the above reading. You can make this list in English.

_____

_____

_____

_____

_____

_____

_____

_____

_____

# Los planes y las compras

## Vocabulario esencial I

### La hora, los minutos y los segundos

**ACTIVIDAD 1** **¿Qué hora es?** Write out the following times in complete sentences.

▶ 2:00 *Son las dos.*

a. 9:15 _____

b. 12:05 _____

c. 1:25 _____

d. 5:40 _____

e. 12:45 _____

f. 7:30 _____

**ACTIVIDAD 2** **La hora** Answer each of the following questions according to the cue in parentheses. Use complete sentences.

▶ A qué hora vamos a comer? (2:00) *Vamos a comer a las dos.*

1. ¿A qué hora es la película? (8:30) _____

2. ¿Qué hora es? (4:50) _____

3. ¿A qué hora es el examen? (10:04) _____

4. ¿Cuándo va a llegar el médico? (1:15) _____

5. ¿Qué hora es? (12:35) _____

6. ¿A qué hora es el programa? (2:45) _____

## Las sensaciones

**ACTIVIDAD 3** **¿Tiene calor, frío o qué?** Read the following situations and indicate how each person or group of people feels: hot, cold, hungry, etc. Use complete sentences. Remember to use the verb **tener** in your responses.

1. Una persona con una pistola entra en la casa de Esteban. Esteban llama al 911.

   Esteban _____

2. Es el mes de julio y estoy en los Andes chilenos.

   _____

3. Son las tres y media de la mañana y estamos estudiando en la biblioteca.

   _____

4. Estoy en clase y veo mis medias (socks). ¡Por Dios! Las dos son de colores diferentes.

   _____

5. Después de jugar al fútbol, Sebastián compra una Coca-Cola.

   Sebastián _____

6. Volvemos de estudiar, vemos una pizzería, entramos y compramos una pizza grande con todo.

   _____

7. Mis amigos están en Cabo San Lucas, México, en el invierno porque no les gusta el frío de Minnesota.

   Mis amigos _____

# Gramática para la comunicación I

## Expressing Habitual and Future Actions and Actions in Progress: Stem-changing Verbs

**ACTIVIDAD 4** **En singular** Change the subjects of the following sentences from **nosotros** to **yo** and make all other necessary changes.

1. Podemos ir a la fiesta. _____

2. Dormimos ocho horas todas las noches. _____

3. No servimos vino. _____

4. Nos divertimos mucho. _____

5. Nos acostamos temprano. _____

6. Jugamos al fútbol. _____

**ACTIVIDAD 5** **Verbos** Complete the following sentences by selecting a logical verb and writing the appropriate form.

1. María no _____ venir hoy. (poder, entender)

2. Los profesores siempre _____ las ventanas. (jugar, cerrar)

3. Carmen y yo _____ estudiar esta noche. (volver, preferir)

4. Josefina siempre _____ temprano. (dormirse, encontrar)

5. Yo no _____ francés. (entender, pedir)

6. ¿A qué hora _____ el concierto? (despertarse, empezar)

7. Juan _____ ir a bailar esta noche. (decir, pensar)

8. Pablo es camarero; ahora está _____ cerveza. (servir, comenzar)

9. Nosotros _____ a casa esta tarde. (volver, poder)

10. ¿Qué _____ hacer Uds.? (querer, dormir)

11. ¿_____ Ricardo y Germán mañana? (despertar, venir)

12. Los niños están jugando al fútbol y están _____ mucho. (querer, divertirse)

13. Yo siempre _____ la verdad. (sentarse, decir)

14. ¿Cuándo _____ Ud. las clases? (comenzar, servir)

15. Ellos dicen que _____ ir. (decir, querer)

**ACTIVIDAD 6** **Preguntas** Answer the following questions about your life in complete sentences.

1. ¿A qué hora empiezan tus clases los lunes? _____

_____

2. ¿A qué hora te acuestas los domingos por la noche? _____

_____

3. ¿Con quién almuerzas durante la semana? _____

_____

4. ¿Dónde almuerzan Uds.? _____

_____

5. ¿Puedes estudiar por la tarde o tienes que trabajar? _____

_____

6. ¿Prefieres estudiar por la tarde o por la noche? _____

_____

7. Generalmente, ¿cuántas horas duermes cada noche? _____

_____

**ACTIVIDAD 7** **Un email a Chile** Leticia, a college student in Mexico City, is writing an email to a friend in Chile. First read the entire message; then reread it and complete it with the appropriate forms of the verbs found to the left of each paragraph. Note: You may use verbs more than once.

divertirse
entender
estar
querer
salir
ser

...¿y cómo están tus clases? ¿Tienes mucho trabajo? Tengo unos amigos fantásticos. Una se llama Sara; _____ (1) de los Estados Unidos, pero _____ (2) en México estudiando literatura. Habla y _____ (3) español como tú y yo porque su familia _____ (4) de origen mexicano. Yo _____ (5) mucho cuando _____ (6) con ella porque siempre pasa algo interesante. Nosotras _____ (7) ir a Guadalajara el fin de semana que viene y después ir a Puerto Vallarta para _____ (8) en la playa.

encontrar
poder
ponerse
saber
ser

Tengo otra amiga que a ti te gustaría. Se llama Mónica; _____ (9) de Venezuela. Tiene ropa, ropa y más ropa. Ella _____ (10) ropa muy moderna. Yo siempre tengo problemas con la ropa; voy a muchas tiendas, pero no _____ (11) cosas bonitas. _____ (12) que no soy fea, pero no hay ropa para mí. En cambio, Mónica siempre _____ (13) encontrar algo que es perfecto para ella.

conocer
pensar
poder
querer
vivir

Si vienes al D. F., vas a _____ (14) a dos chicos muy simpáticos. _____ (15) en un apartamento y si tú _____ (16), _____ (17) vivir con ellos. Debes _____ (18) en venir porque te gustaría y tienes que...

**ACTIVIDAD 8** **Dos conversaciones** Complete the following conversations with verbs from the lists provided. Follow this procedure: first, read one conversation; then go back, select the verbs, and fill in the blanks with the appropriate forms; when finished, reread the conversations and check to see that all the verbs agree with their subjects. Note: You may use verbs more than once.

1. Una conversación por teléfono (**divertirse, empezar, mirar, preferir, querer, saber, volver**)

—¡Aló!

—¿Jesús?

—Sí.

—Habla Rafael. Carmen y yo _____ (1) ver la película de Gael García Bernal. ¿Quieres ir?

—¿A qué hora _____ (2) la película?

—No _____ (3).

—¿Por qué no _____ (4) en el periódico?

—Buena idea... Es a las siete y cuarto en el Cine Rex.

—¿_____ (5) Uds. comer un sándwich antes?

—Claro. Siempre tengo hambre. Hoy Carmen _____ (6) a casa a las cinco. ¿Dónde _____ (7) comer tú?

—_____ (8) la comida del restaurante Casa Oaxaca porque es barata y es un lugar bonito.

—Buena idea; yo siempre _____ (9) en esa cafetería porque los camareros son muy cómicos.

2. Una conversación con el médico (**acostarse, despertarse, dormir, dormirse, entender**)

—Normalmente, ¿a qué hora _____ (1) Ud. por la noche?

—A la una y media.

—¡Qué tarde! ¿Y a qué hora _____ (2)?

—_____ (3) a las siete.

—¡Cinco horas y media! ¿No _____ (4) Ud. en la oficina?

—No, pero yo _____ (5) la siesta todos los días.

—Ah, ahora _____ (6). En mi casa, nosotros también _____ (7) la siesta.

**ACTIVIDAD 9 El detective** A detective is watching the woman. Today is very boring because the woman isn't leaving her apartment and the detective has to watch everything through the windows. Write what the detective says into his digital voice recorder, including the time and the activity in progress. Use the verb **estar** + *present participle* (**-ando, -iendo**) to describe the activity in progress.

1.

2.

3.

4.

5.

6.

1. estar / mirar _____

_____

2. estar / preparar / el almuerzo *(lunch)* _____

_____

3. hombre / estar / entrar _____

_____

4. estar / servir / el almuerzo _____

_____

5. hombre / estar / salir _____

_____

6. estar / dormir _____

_____

# Un poco de todo

**ACTIVIDAD** **10** **El horario de Lupe** Lupe is a first-year student of philosophy. Look at her schedule (**horario**) and then answer the questions that follow.

|  | lunes | martes | miércoles | jueves | viernes |
|---|---|---|---|---|---|
| 9:00–9:50 | Antropología I | La herencia socrática | Antropología I | La herencia socrática | |
| 10:05–11:05 | Filosofía de la naturaleza | Teorías científicas de la cultura | Filosofía de la naturaleza | Teorías científicas de la cultura | Filosofía de la naturaleza |
| 11:20–12:10 | Metafísica I | | Metafísica I | | |
| 12:25–1:25 | | Filosofía de la religión | | Filosofía de la religión | |
| 1:40–2:30 | Fenomenología de la religión | Nihilismo y metafísica | Fenomenología de la religión | Nihilismo y metafísica | Fenomenología de la religión |

1. ¿A qué hora empieza la clase de Antropología I los lunes y los miércoles?

   _____

2. ¿A qué hora puede tomar un café en la cafetería los martes?

   _____

3. ¿A qué hora termina la clase de Filosofía de la religión?

   _____

4. Normalmente las clases empiezan a las nueve. ¿A qué hora empiezan sus clases los viernes?

   _____

5. ¿Prefieren estudiar Antropología I o Nihilismo y metafísica tú y tus amigos?

   _____

6. ¿Te gustaría tener este horario o prefieres tu horario de este semestre?

   _____

# Vocabulario esencial II

## Los colores

**ACTIVIDAD 11** **Asociaciones** Write the color or colors that you associate with each of the following things.

▶ las plantas *verde*

1. el sol _____

2. los dientes _____

3. el océano Atlántico _____

4. el elefante Dumbo _____

5. el chocolate _____

6. la ecología _____

7. la bandera (*flag*) de Canadá _____

8. Tropicana, el pelo de Donald Trump y Sunkist _____

9. las bananas _____

10. la bandera de los Estados Unidos _____

11. el jugo Welch's _____

## La ropa y los materiales

**ACTIVIDAD 12** **La ropa** Identify the clothing items in this drawing. Include the definite article in your response.

1. _____

2. _____

3. _____

4. _____

5. _____

6. _____

7. _____

8. _____

9. _____

10. _____

© Cengage Learning 2013

**ACTIVIDAD 13** **En orden lógico** Put the following words in logical order to form sentences. Make all necessary changes.

1. tener / suéter / ella / de / azul / lana / mi _____

_____

2. camisas / el / para / comprar / yo / verano / ir a / algodón / de _____

_____

3. gustar / rojo / me / pantalones / tus _____

_____

4. yo / los / probarse / zapatos / alto / de / tacón / querer / negro _____

_____

**ACTIVIDAD 14** **La importación** Answer the following questions in complete sentences based on the clothes you are wearing.

1. ¿De dónde es tu camisa? _____

2. ¿De qué material es? _____

3. ¿Son de los Estados Unidos tus pantalones favoritos? _____

4. ¿De dónde son tus zapatos? _____

5. ¿Son de cuero? _____

**ACTIVIDAD 15** **Descripción** Look at the accompanying drawing and describe what the people in it are wearing. Use complete sentences and be specific. Include information about colors and fabrics.

© Cengage Learning 2013

_____

_____

_____

_____

_____

_____

**ACTIVIDAD** **16** **Tu ropa** Using complete sentences, describe what you normally wear to class.

_____

_____

_____

_____

_____

# Gramática para la comunicación II

## Indicating Purpose, Destination, and Duration: *Para* and *por*

**ACTIVIDAD** **17** *Por o para* Complete the following sentences with **por** or **para**.

1. La blusa es _____ mi madre porque mañana es su cumpleaños.

2. Salimos el sábado _____ Lima.

3. Voy a vivir en la universidad _____ dos años más.

4. Benjamín estudia _____ ser abogado.

5. Ahora Carlos trabaja los sábados _____ la noche.

6. Vamos a Costa Rica _____ dos semanas.

7. No me gusta ser camarero pero trabajo _____ poder vestirme bien.

8. Tenemos que leer la novela _____ mañana.

9. Mi amigo estudia _____ ser médico.

10. Esta noche tengo que estudiar _____ un mínimo de seis horas.

11. ¿Vas _____ tu casa ahora?

12. Durante los veranos yo trabajo _____ un banco en mi pueblo.

## Indicating the Location of a Person, Thing, or Event: *Estar en* and *ser en*

**ACTIVIDAD** **18** **¿Dónde es o dónde está?** Complete each sentence with the appropriate form of **ser** or **estar**.

1. Mi padre _____ en Acapulco este fin de semana.

2. La fiesta _____ en casa de Paco.

3. ¿Dónde _____ los niños?

4. El concierto de Julieta Venegas _____ en el estadio.

5. Los libros _____ en la biblioteca.

6. ¿Dónde _____ la exhibición de Frida Kahlo?

7.  Muchos murales de Diego Rivera _____ en el Palacio Nacional de la Ciudad de México.

8.  El presidente _____ en la Casa Blanca.

9.  La bufanda que quieres _____ en Bloomingdale's.

**ACTIVIDAD 19** **Los viajes** All of the following people are currently traveling. Say where they are from and imagine where they are right now. Use complete sentences.

1.  Salma Hayek _____

_____

2.  George Clooney _____

_____

3.  Tus padres _____

_____

4.  Shakira _____

_____

# Un poco de todo

**ACTIVIDAD 20** **Ser o estar** Complete the following sentences with the appropriate form of **ser** or **estar**. Don't forget the other uses of **ser** and **estar** you've studied. See **Capítulo 3** if needed.

1.  Tu camisa _____ de algodón, ¿no?

2.  Mis padres _____ en Paraguay.

3.  ¿De dónde _____ tus zapatos?

4.  ¿Dónde _____ tus zapatos?

5.  El concierto _____ en el Teatro Colón.

6.  Tus libros _____ en la biblioteca.

7.  ¿Dónde _____ la fiesta?

8.  ¿Dónde _____ Daniel?

9.  Daniel _____ de Cuba, ¿no?

10. ¿ _____ de plástico tus gafas de sol?

**ACTIVIDAD 21** **¿Dónde están?** Read the following mini-conversations and complete the sentences with an appropriate verb form. Afterward, tell where each conversation is taking place.

1. —¿A qué hora _____ la película, por favor?

   —A las nueve y cuarto.

   ¿Dónde están estas personas? _____

2. —¿Cuánto _____ la habitación?

   —52 euros.

   —¿Tiene dos camas o una cama?

   —Dos.

   ¿Dónde están? _____

3. —¿Qué hora es?

   —_____ las dos y media.

   —¿Siempre _____ Ud. aquí?

   —Sí, es un lugar excelente para pedir hamburguesas vegetarianas.

   ¿Dónde están? _____

4. —¿Aló?

   —Hola, Roberto. _____ hablar con tu padre.

   —Está _____ en el sofá.

   —Bueno. Voy a llamar más tarde.

   ¿Dónde están Roberto y su padre? _____

**ACTIVIDAD 22** **¡A comprar!** Complete the following conversation between a store clerk and a customer who is looking for a gift for his girlfriend.

| CLIENTE | Buenos días. |
|---|---|
| VENDEDORA | ¿En qué _____ servirle? |
| CLIENTE | Me gustaría ver una blusa. |
| VENDEDORA | ¿_____ quién? |
| CLIENTE | _____ mi novia porque es su cumpleaños. Es que ella |

_____ Ecuador y yo salgo _____ Quito

mañana.

| VENDEDORA | Muy _____. ¿De qué color? |
| CLIENTE | _____, _____ o |

_____.

| VENDEDORA | Aquí tiene tres blusas. |

CLIENTE      ¿Son de _____?

VENDEDORA    Esta es de algodón, _____ las otras

             _____ seda.

CLIENTE      No, no quiero una de algodón; _____ una blusa de seda.

VENDEDORA    ¿ _____?

CLIENTE      Creo que es 36.

VENDEDORA    Bien, 36. Aquí están. Son muy _____.

CLIENTE      ¡Ay! Estas sí. Me gustan mucho.

VENDEDORA    Y _____ solamente 60 euros. ¿Cuál quiere?

CLIENTE      Quiero la blusa _____.

VENDEDORA    Es un color muy bonito.

CLIENTE      También necesito una corbata _____ mí.

VENDEDORA    ¿Con rayas o de un solo color? ¿De qué material?

CLIENTE      Todas mis corbatas son de _____. Y tengo muchas de rayas.

             Creo que quiero una azul.

VENDEDORA    Aquí hay _____ que _____ muy

             elegante.

CLIENTE      Perfecto.

VENDEDORA    ¿Cómo va a pagar?

CLIENTE      Con la tarjeta de Visa.

VENDEDORA    Si la talla no le queda _____ a su novia, yo siempre estoy aquí

             _____ las tardes.

CLIENTE      Muchas gracias.

VENDEDORA    De nada y buen viaje.

# Lectura

## Estrategia de lectura: Activating Background Knowledge

In order to best understand a reading, you should first think about the topic. You should think about what you know and what you would like to learn more about. This will help you focus and will increase your comprehension. You will get an opportunity to do this before reading Tomás's diary of a trip to Mexico.

**ACTIVIDAD 23** **Antes de leer** Before reading Tomás's journal entries about Mexico, answer these questions.

1. ¿Conoces México? Si contestas que sí, ¿qué lugares conoces?

_____

_____

2. ¿Sabes cuáles son las civilizaciones indígenas de México?

_____

_____

3. Write in the first column of the chart what you already know about these Mexican people or places. If you don't know anything, write **No sé nada.** After completing the first column, read Tomás's journal about the tour he is taking and fill in the second column with what you learned. Write in Spanish.

| Antes de leer | Después de leer |
|---|---|
| 1. Diego Rivera | |
| 2. El Museo de Antropología | |
| 3. Tenochtitlán | |
| 4. Chichén Itzá | |

# El diario de Tomás

### martes, 25 de marzo

Acabamos de hacer un *tour* por la ciudad para ver el Paseo de la Reforma y el Zócalo y conocer la Catedral y el Palacio Nacional donde se ve la historia de México en los murales de Diego Rivera. ¡Todo eso antes del almuerzo! Ahora estamos en el Parque de Chapultepec, donde está el Museo de Antropología. ¡Qué maravilla! Es impresionante la cantidad de objetos olmecas, mayas, toltecas y aztecas que hay: joyas, instrumentos musicales, cerámica, ropa y, por supuesto, el calendario azteca. La guía de

**Chichén Itzá**

la excursión dice que ya en el siglo XIV los aztecas eran capaces de calcular el año solar.

El imperio azteca constaba de una confederación de tres ciudades —una de ellas era Tenochtitlán, la capital, que estaba donde actualmente está la Ciudad de México. Es increíble lo bien planeada que estaba la ciudad: tenía agua potable y sistemas sanitarios mucho mejores que los de Europa en el siglo XVIII. (Esto no es información nueva para mí; estoy aprendiendo sobre los aztecas en la facultad).

Estamos saliendo del museo (demasiado corta la visita; tengo que regresar un día de estos) y vamos a ir a la Plaza de las Tres Culturas: ruinas aztecas, una iglesia colonial y edificios del siglo XX. ¡Qué buen ejemplo de la fusión de culturas del México actual!

### miércoles, 26 de marzo

Son las once y media de la noche y acabamos de llegar a Mérida, Yucatán. Estoy muy cansado por pasar horas y horas en autobús pero, por suerte, me divierto mucho hablando con el Sr. Ruiz, porque es muy gracioso. ¡Qué hombre más divertido! De verdad yo no entiendo por qué la Dra. Llanos no soporta al Sr. Ruiz. Bueno, ahora a dormir, porque mañana salimos temprano para visitar Chichén Itzá.

### jueves, 27 de marzo

Bueno, ahora puedo decir que conozco bien las ruinas de Chichén Itzá, lugar de una gran población maya entre los años 300 y 900 d.C. No se sabe bien el lugar de origen de esta civilización: unas personas dicen que es el Petén, Guatemala; otros creen que es Palenque, México. Los mayas son famosos por su astronomía y matemáticas muy avanzadas y por usar el cero antes que los europeos. Sabemos que entre sus cultivos están el maíz, el cacao, la batata o el camote [1] y el chile. Los mayas también son los inventores de un sistema de escritura jeroglífica. Todo esto es tan fascinante que ahora quiero conocer otras ciudades mayas como Copán en Honduras y Tikal en Guatemala.

Bueno, la parte de Chichén Itzá que más me gusta es Kukulkán. Es un templo impresionante; al entrar uno tiene miedo. Allí en una pared [2] hay un jaguar rojo con ojos de jade. Me fascina este lugar.

Mañana vamos a Uxmal, otras ruinas...

[1] *sweet potato*  [2] *wall*

*Jim Fox/Photo Researchers*

**ACTIVIDAD 24 Explícalo.** After reading the diary entries, explain in other words what the words in bold mean. Don't use English. Use phrases like: **Es un sustantivo/verbo/adverbio/adjetivo que significa...**

1. Tomás dice que está aprendiendo sobre los aztecas en **la facultad.**

   _____

   _____

2. La ciudad de Tenochtitlán se encuentra en el lugar donde **actualmente** está la Ciudad de México.

   _____

   _____

3. Tomás dice que el Sr. Ruiz es **gracioso.**

   _____

   _____

4. La Dra. Llanos no **soporta** al Sr. Ruiz.

   _____

   _____

# Repaso

**Capítulo 5**

## Future, Present, and Immediate Past

You have learned to talk about obligations and plans, to state preferences, to say what you do every day, and to say what you are doing right now. You have also learned to state what has just happened.

### Future obligations and plans:

Esta noche tengo que acostarme temprano.
Esta noche debo estudiar.
Esta noche voy a estudiar.
¿Cuándo vienes?
Pienso estudiar economía.
No puedo ir.

### Preferences:

Me gustaría salir con mis amigos.
Me gusta comer en restaurantes e ir al cine.
Quiero ir contigo.
Prefiero la blusa roja.

### What you do every day:

Yo me levanto temprano.
Vuelvo a casa tarde.
Voy al trabajo.
Miro la televisión.
Como con mis amigos.
Me acuesto temprano.

### What you are doing right now:

Estoy leyendo.
Estoy estudiando.
Estoy haciendo la tarea.

### What you just did:

Acabo de hablar con mi jefe.

**ACTIVIDAD 1** **Un email** Complete the following email to a friend. Write the correct form of the indicated verbs in the blanks.

estar

estar

gustar

gustar

deber, comprar

ser

ser

levantarse, ducharse

vestirse, tomar

levantarse

encontrar

gustar

querer

gustar

acabar

necesitar

ser, salir

ir, hacer

gustar

tener

ir, venir

ir, divertirse

venir

Querida Mariana:

¿Cómo _____? Yo bien. En este momento

_____ escuchando unas canciones de Paulina

Rubio. Me _____ mucho, ¿y a ti? Un día

me _____ ver uno de sus conciertos. Tú

_____ _____ su nuevo álbum porque

_____ excelente.

   Aquí con el trabajo, todos los días _____

iguales. _____ temprano, _____,

_____ y _____ un café en una cafetería

cerca del trabajo. Este sábado no voy a _____

hasta las doce.

   Tengo que _____ un trabajo nuevo. De

verdad, no me _____ mi jefe (boss). Además

_____ vivir en Mazatlán para estar cerca de

mis padres. Me _____ encontrar un trabajo

de profesora en una escuela. _____ de leer

en el periódico que _____ profesores en una

escuela bilingüe.

   ¿Cómo _____ tu vida? ¿_____ con

Tomás? ¿Qué _____ a _____ tú durante

la Navidad? Me _____ ir a una isla del Caribe,

pero no _____ dinero.

   Mis padres _____ a _____ aquí para

la Navidad. Nosotros _____ a _____

mucho. ¿Por qué no _____ tú?

Un fuerte abrazo de tu amiga,

Raquel

# Ayer y hoy

Capítulo
6

## Vocabulario esencial I

### Los números del cien al millón

**ACTIVIDAD 1** **Los números** Write out the following numbers. Remember that in Spanish a period is used instead of a comma when writing large numbers.

a. 564 _____

b. 1.015 _____

c. 2.973 _____

d. 4.743.010 _____

**ACTIVIDAD 2** **Una serie de números** Write the number that fits logically in each series.

1. doscientos, trescientos, cuatrocientos, _____

2. ochocientos, _____, seiscientos

3. cuatro millones, tres millones, dos millones, _____

4. _____, doscientos, trescientos, cuatrocientos

5. trescientos, seiscientos, _____

6. cuatro mil, tres mil, dos mil, _____

7. doscientos, trescientos, _____

# Preposiciones de lugar

**ACTIVIDAD 3** **¿Dónde están?** In the first blank, write **C (cierto)** if the statement is true and **F (falso)** if the statement is false. Correct the false statements by writing the correct preposition (including the word **de** when needed) in the second space. All questions are based on the following configuration of letters.

```
                      LH
        AB                      I
        C       D       EFG     J
```

| | C/F | PREPOSICIÓN |
|---|---|---|
| 1. La ce está debajo de la a. | _____ | _____ |
| 2. La efe está encima de la e y la ge. | _____ | _____ |
| 3. La ele está cerca de la ce. | _____ | _____ |
| 4. La i está encima de la jota. | _____ | _____ |
| 5. La ge está a la izquierda de la efe. | _____ | _____ |
| 6. La jota está debajo de la i. | _____ | _____ |
| 7. La be está cerca de la a. | _____ | _____ |
| 8. La e está a la derecha de la efe. | _____ | _____ |
| 9. La ge está al lado de la efe. | _____ | _____ |
| 10. La ele está encima de la e. | _____ | _____ |
| 11. La a está lejos de la jota. | _____ | _____ |
| 12. La de está lejos de la ce y la e. | _____ | _____ |

**ACTIVIDAD 4** **¿Dónde está?** Using the maps on the inside cover of your textbook, fill in each blank with a logical preposition to describe the geography of Colombia and Venezuela. Use the prepositions **cerca de, en, entre,** and **lejos de.**

1. Colombia está _____ Brasil y Panamá.

2. Cartagena está _____ la costa.

3. Cali está _____ Medellín y Popayán.

4. Barranquilla está _____ Popayán, pero está _____ Cartagena.

5. Zipaquirá está _____ Bogotá.

6. Venezuela está _____ Colombia y Guyana y también _____ Brasil y el mar Caribe.

7. Maracaibo está _____ el lago Maracaibo y el mar Caribe.

8. La Guaira está _____ Caracas.

9. El salto Ángel está _____ el interior del país, _____ la costa.

10. Ciudad Bolívar está _____ el río Orinoco.

# Gramática para la comunicación I

## Talking about the Past: The Preterit

**ACTIVIDAD 5** **El pasado** Complete the following sentences by selecting a logical verb and writing the appropriate preterit form.

1. Ayer yo _____ con el Sr. Martínez. (hablar, costar)

2. Anoche nosotros no _____ cerveza. (beber, comer)

3. Esta mañana Pepe _____ al médico. (empezar, ir)

4. ¿Qué _____ Ramón ayer? (hacer, vivir)

5. Anoche Marcos y Luis _____ cinco kilómetros. (llevar, correr)

6. El verano pasado yo _____ a Buenos Aires. (despertarse, ir)

7. Yo _____ un buen restaurante, no _____ uno y al final _____ en una cafetería. (buscar, nadar) (encontrar, pagar) (correr, comer)

8. Guillermo, ¿_____ anoche con Mariana? (bailar, entender)

9. ¿_____ Ud. mi email? (vivir, recibir)

10. Tú _____ la composición, ¿no? (escuchar, escribir)

11. Ayer yo _____ 25 pesos por una camisa. (pagar, salir)

12. Ellos _____ unos sándwiches. (hacer, beber)

13. Después del accidente, el niño _____ . (llorar, conocer)

14. Anoche yo _____ a estudiar a las siete. (asistir, empezar)

15. ¿A qué hora _____ la película? (pensar, terminar)

**ACTIVIDAD 6** **¿Qué hicieron?** Answer the following questions about you and your friends in complete sentences.

1. ¿Adónde fueron Uds. el sábado pasado? _____

2. ¿A qué hora volvieron Uds. anoche? _____

3. ¿Recibió un amigo un email de tu madre? _____
_____

4. ¿Visitaste a tus padres el mes pasado? _____

5. ¿Pagaste tú la última vez que saliste con un/a chico/a? _____
_____

6. ¿Tomaste el autobús esta mañana para ir a la universidad? _____
_____

7. ¿Fuiste a una fiesta la semana pasada? _____
_____

8. ¿Quién compró Coca-Cola y pizza para la fiesta?
_____

9. ¿Aprendieron Uds. mucho ayer en clase?

   _____

10. ¿Escribieron Uds. la composición para la clase de español?

   _____

11. ¿Quién no asistió a la clase de español esta semana?

   _____

**ACTIVIDAD 7 ¿Infinitivo o no?** Complete the following sentences with the appropriate form of the indicated verbs (present, preterit, infinitive) and add the preposition **a** if necessary.

1. Ayer nosotros _____ y _____ . (cantar, bailar)
2. Ayer Margarita _____ la clase de biología. (asistir)
3. Los músicos van a _____ tocar a las ocho. (empezar)
4. Necesito _____; tengo hambre. (comer)
5. Todos los días yo _____ cuatro horas. (estudiar)
6. Debes _____ más. (estudiar)
7. Me gusta _____ en el invierno. (esquiar)
8. Ayer yo _____ la piscina, pero no _____ . (ir, nadar)

**ACTIVIDAD 8 Un día horrible** Complete this conversation between two friends in Maracaibo, Venezuela. First, read the entire conversation. Then fill in the missing words by selecting verbs from the list and writing them in the appropriate forms.

| comer | hacer | perder | ser |
| dejar | ir | recibir | ver |
| encontrar | llegar | sacar | volver |
| escribir | pagar | | |

—Ayer _____ (1) un día increíble.

—¿Qué _____ (2) Uds.?

—_____ (3) a ver una película. Después _____ (4) algo en un restaurante.

—¿Y?

—Qué desastre soy. Yo _____ (5) el dinero en el cine. Por eso María _____ (6) su reloj en el restaurante con un camarero. ¡Qué vergüenza! El camarero _____ (7) su nombre en un papel y guardó *(put away)* el reloj. ¡Un Rolex! Y nosotros _____ (8) al cine. Por fin, yo _____ (9) el dinero.

—¡Huy! Gracias a Dios.

—No termina la historia.

—(Nosotros) _____ (10) al restaurante y no _____ (11) al camarero.

—¿Qué _____ (12) Uds. entonces?

—Por fin, el camarero _____ (13) y María _____ (14) su reloj.

—Yo _____ (15) el dinero de mi cartera y _____ (16) los 150 bolívares.

**ACTIVIDAD  9**  **¿Cuándo fue la última vez que... ?**  Explain when was the last time that you did the following things. The first one has been done as an example.

1.  ir al médico                                              ayer

2.  visitar a tus padres                                anteayer

3.  hablar por teléfono con tus abuelos       hace dos/tres días

4.  comer en un restaurante                       la semana pasada

5.  levantarte tarde                                      hace dos/tres semanas

6.  ir al dentista                                           el mes pasado

7.  hacer un viaje                                         hace dos/tres meses

8.  volver a tu escuela secundaria             el año pasado

9.  descargar una canción                           hace dos años

10.  ir a un concierto

1.  *Hace tres meses que fui al médico.* _____

2.  _____

3.  _____

4.  _____

5.  _____

6.  _____

7.  _____

8.  _____

9.  _____

10.  _____

**ACTIVIDAD 10 Un email** Write an email to a friend telling him/her what you did last weekend and with whom, as well as what you are going to do next week.

Hola, _____

¿Qué tal? ¿Cómo está tu familia? Por aquí todo bien. El viernes pasado _____

_____

_____

_____

El sábado pasado _____

_____

_____

El domingo pasado nosotros _____

_____

_____

La semana que viene yo _____

_____

_____

_____

Un abrazo,


(tu nombre)

## Indicating Relationships: Prepositions

**ACTIVIDAD 11 Espacios en blanco** Fill in the following blanks with the appropriate preposition or prepositional pronoun. Use only one word per blank.

1. ¿Este dinero es para _____? ¡Gracias!

2. No puedo vivir _____ ti. Eres fantástico.

3. Después _____ comer en el restaurante, fuimos al cine.

4. Entre _____ y _____ vamos a hacer el trabajo.

5. Ignacio se enamoró _____ mi hermana a primera vista.

6. Javier no asiste _____ muchas clases; por eso va a sacar malas notas.

7. Ahora comienzo _____ entender tu pregunta.

8. ¿Quieres ir _____ al cine el viernes?

9. El príncipe William se casó _____ Kate Middleton.

10. Estoy aburrida. ¿Por qué no salimos _____ aquí?

11. No quiero salir más _____. Eres un desastre.

**ACTIVIDAD 12** **La telenovela** One of your friends is in Colombia and cannot see her favorite soap opera. Complete the following summary for her of what happened during this week's episodes. First, read the entire summary. Then complete the story with the appropriate prepositions or prepositional pronouns.

Maruja dejó a su esposo Felipe y se va a casar _____ (1) Javier, el mecánico de la señora

rica. Entre _____ (2) y _____ (3), ella está loca porque, como tú sabes, Javier

no es simpático. Entonces, Felipe dejó _____ (4) ir a Alcohólicos Anónimos y empezó

_____ (5) beber otra vez. Él cree que no puede vivir _____ (6) ella. Felipe

compró un regalo muy caro y en la tarjeta escribió: "Para _____ (7), con todo mi amor para

siempre, tu Felipe". Después, ella habló _____ (8) Javier por teléfono sobre el regalo y él no

dijo nada.

   Pero más tarde ella fue a la casa de Javier, abrió la puerta y encontró a Javier _____ (9)

otra mujer. Ella empezó a llorar y salió corriendo _____ (10) la casa de Felipe. Y así terminó

el programa del viernes. Como me vas a llamar el martes, puedo hablar _____ (11) de qué

ocurre el lunes.

# Un poco de todo

**ACTIVIDAD 13** **¿Qué ocurrió?** Last night you went out to a restaurant and a club with some friends, including Carmen, Ramón's ex-girlfriend. Since Ramón couldn't go, he wants to know all the details of the evening. Read all of Ramón's questions first; then complete your part of the conversation.

RAMÓN   ¿Carmen salió contigo anoche?

TÚ   _____

RAMÓN   ¿Quiénes más fueron contigo?

TÚ   _____

RAMÓN   ¿Adónde fueron y qué hicieron?

TÚ   _____

RAMÓN   ¿Habló mucho Carmen con Andrés?

TÚ   _____

Continúa →

RAMÓN     ¿Qué más hizo con él?

TÚ     _____

RAMÓN     Bueno, ¿y tú qué hiciste?

TÚ     _____

# Vocabulario esencial II

## La familia de Julieta

**ACTIVIDAD 14 La familia** Julieta is talking about her family. Complete the following sentences.

1. La hermana de mi madre es mi _____.

2. El padre de mi padre es mi _____.

3. El hijo de mis padres es mi _____.

4. La hija de mi tío es mi _____.

5. Mi _____ es la hija de mi abuelo y la esposa de mi padre.

6. La esposa del hermano de mi padre es mi _____.

7. Mi _____ es el hijo de mis abuelos y el padre de mi primo.

8. Si en el futuro mi hermano y su esposa tienen hijos, van a ser mis _____.

9. Mis primos Sandra y Juan son los _____ de mis abuelos paternos.

10. No es mi hermana pero es la nieta de mis abuelos; es mi _____.

11. Si Wilmer se casa y esa persona tiene hijos de un matrimonio anterior, esos niños van a ser los _____ de Wilmer.

**ACTIVIDAD 15 Mi familia** Parte A. List five of your relatives. For each of these relatives, indicate his/her name, relationship to you, age, occupation, marital status (single, married, or divorced), any children he/she may have, and whether he/she is a favorite relative. Follow the format shown in the examples.

▶ *Betty: abuela—74 años—jubilada (retired)—divorciada—4 hijos—mi abuela favorita*
*Clarence: abuelo—69 años—pintor—casado (con Helen)—2 hijos*

1. _____
   _____

2. _____
   _____

3. _____
   _____

4. _____
   _____

5. _____
   _____

**Parte B.** Use information from **Parte A** to write a short composition about a member of your family.

_____

_____

_____

_____

_____

_____

# Gramática para la comunicación II

## Using Indirect-Object Pronouns

**ACTIVIDAD 16** **Pronombres de complemento indirecto** Complete the following sentences with the appropriate indirect-object pronouns.

1. ¿ _____ escribiste un email a tu hermano?

2. Ayer _____ diste (a mí) el libro de cálculo.

3. A ti _____ gusta esquiar.

4. Ayer _____ mandé el regalo a ellos.

5. No recuerdo. ¿ _____ diste a Carlos y a mí el reloj?

6. ¿Qué _____ regalaste a tus padres para su aniversario?

7. ¿ _____ diste mi trabajo al profesor Galarraga?

8. Carlos _____ explicó su problema, ¿no? Ahora entiendes por qué está tan triste.

**ACTIVIDAD 17** **Preguntas y respuestas** Answer the following questions in the affirmative in complete sentences.

1. ¿Te dio dinero tu padre el fin de semana pasado? _____

_____

2. ¿Le ofrecieron el trabajo a Juan? _____

_____

3. ¿Le dieron a Ud. el informe Ignacio y Fernando? _____

_____

4. ¿Me vas a escribir? _____

5. ¿Les explicaron a Uds. la verdad? _____

6. ¿Me estás hablando? _____

**ACTIVIDAD 18** ¿Qué hiciste? Your roommate is sick and asked you to do a few things. He/She still has a few more requests. Answer his/her questions, using indirect-object pronouns.

COMPAÑERO/A   ¿Le mandaste a mi tía la carta que te di?

TÚ            Sí, _____

COMPAÑERO/A   ¿Me compraste el champú y la pasta de dientes? ¿Cuánto te costaron?

TÚ            Sí, _____

             _____

COMPAÑERO/A   ¿Le diste la composición al profesor de historia?

TÚ            Sí, _____

             _____

COMPAÑERO/A   ¿Le dejaste la nota al profesor de literatura?

TÚ            No, _____

             _____

COMPAÑERO/A   ¿Nos dio tarea la profesora de cálculo?

TÚ            No, _____

             _____

COMPAÑERO/A   ¿Me buscaste el libro en la biblioteca?

TÚ            Sí, _____

             _____

COMPAÑERO/A   ¿Les vas a decir a Adrián y a Leonor que no puedo ir a esquiar mañana?

TÚ            Sí, _____

             _____

COMPAÑERO/A   ¿Esta noche me puedes comprar papel para la computadora?

TÚ            No, _____

             _____

## Using Affirmative and Negative Words

**ACTIVIDAD 19** Negativos Rewrite the following sentences in the negative. Use **nada, nadie,** or **nunca.**

1. Siempre estudio. _____

2. Hago muchas cosas. _____

3. Él sale con su novia. _____

4. Voy al parque todos los días. _____

5. Compró mucho. _____

**ACTIVIDAD 20 La negación** Using complete sentences, answer the following questions in the negative. Use **nada, nadie,** or **nunca.**

1. ¿Esquías todos los inviernos? _____

2. ¿Bailaste con alguien anoche? _____

3. ¿Quién fue a la fiesta? _____

4. ¿Qué le regalaste a tu madre para su cumpleaños? _____

5. ¿Siempre visitas a tus abuelos? _____

6. ¿Tiene Ud. 20 pesos? _____

**ACTIVIDAD 21 Niño triste** Complete the following paragraph with affirmative or negative words. Use **algo, alguien, siempre, nada, nadie,** and **nunca.**

Es el primer día de clases y Beto está triste, requetetriste porque está en un país nuevo. No tiene amigos, y no juega con _____ (1) en el parque. No estudia _____ (2) porque no entiende _____ (3). _____ (4) habla en inglés con él y _____ (5) comprende sus problemas. No tiene _____ (6) que hacer y quiere volver a su país. La madre de Beto no está preocupada porque ella sabe que él va a aprender a decir _____ (7) en el idioma pronto y que _____ (8) va a empezar a jugar con su hijo. Los niños _____ (9) hacen amigos nuevos y se adaptan a diferentes situaciones en poco tiempo.

# Un poco de todo

**ACTIVIDAD 22 La novia y los padres de él** Manuel's girlfriend, Laura, spent an afternoon with his parents while he was at a convention. It was the first time they met her. Complete Laura's side of the conversation with Manuel where he finds out how things went.

MANUEL ¿Hicieron Uds. algo especial?

LAURA No, no hicimos _____

MANUEL ¿Adónde fueron?

LAURA _____

MANUEL ¿Conociste a alguien más de mi familia?

LAURA No, no _____

MANUEL ¿Mi madre te habló de mí?

LAURA Sí, _____

MANUEL ¿Hablaron de algo en particular?

LAURA     No, no _____,
          solo un poco de los políticos corruptos, de las películas de Gael García Bernal, de los nuevos
          escándalos de Hollywood. Como ves, nada en particular. Ah... y claro, para ellos tú eres muy
          especial.

MANUEL    ¿Y te gustaron mis padres?

LAURA     Sí, son muy _____

# Lectura

## Estrategia de lectura: Skimming and Scanning

Skimming is a skill used for getting the gist of written materials. For example, you skim the contents of
a newspaper, reading only the headlines and glancing at the photos to see which articles might interest
you. Once you find an article of interest, you may then skim or scan it. Skimming means merely reading
quickly to get the general message. Scanning means looking for specific details to answer questions that
you already have in mind.

**ACTIVIDAD 23** **Lectura rápida**  Skim the article on page 101 and select the main topic.

a.  la geografía y la gente de Venezuela y Colombia

b.  la gente de Venezuela y Colombia

c.  la geografía de Venezuela y Colombia

**ACTIVIDAD 24** **Lectura enfocada**  Scan the following article to find the answers to these
questions.

1.  ¿Dónde está el Orinoco y qué es? _____

    _____

2.  ¿Cómo se llaman las montañas más altas de América? _____

    _____

3.  ¿Qué país tiene grandes reservas de petróleo? _____

    _____

# Venezuela y Colombia

Cristóbal Colón fue el primer europeo en pisar[1] tierra suramericana en 1498 cuando **llegó** a lo que hoy es Venezuela. Los conquistadores encontraron una tierra muy rica y variada, pero esta misma tierra **les** causó muchos problemas por su diversidad natural. No fue fácil explorar las tierras vírgenes del río Orinoco en Venezuela ni cruzar[2] los Andes colombianos con los picos
5 más altos cubiertos[3] de nieves perpetuas aun en zonas cerca de la línea del Ecuador.

   Cuando los conquistadores españoles llegaron a lo que hoy día es la ciudad de Cartagena, Colombia, vieron un lugar perfecto para sus carabelas[4]: un lugar con una península que les dio protección natural a las carabelas españolas. Por eso, resultó ser un sitio perfecto para los comerciantes. Pronto **fue** un lugar importante de entrada de esclavos africanos al continente
10 americano.

   Los españoles encontraron un continente habitado por indígenas y aprendieron de ellos muchas cosas. Así, siguiendo el ejemplo de los indígenas, en los ríos Orinoco y Amazonas la canoa resultó ser para ellos un medio de transporte mucho mejor que las carabelas y los caballos[5] españoles. Pronto los españoles aprendieron a moverse por esas tierras, explorando
15 diferentes lugares y conociendo la vida y las costumbres de los habitantes. Los indígenas **les** contaron leyendas regionales. Como en muchas otras leyendas, aparecen seres humanos y dioses. Por ejemplo, una leyenda muy conocida es la historia de un cacique que mató al amante de su esposa. Y luego ella, sin saberlo, comió el corazón de su amante muerto. Pero al saber la verdad, **se enfadó,** tomó a su hija y se fue con ella a una laguna. Vivió el resto de su vida debajo
20 del agua con su nuevo esposo: una serpiente. El cacique empezó la tradición de ir a la laguna todos los años y ofrecerle ofrendas de joyas y figuras de oro y luego cubrirse el cuerpo de oro antes de entrar en el agua. Esta leyenda y muchas más pasaron oralmente de generación en generación y hoy día forman parte del folclore suramericano. Los conquistadores oyeron la leyenda del cacique cubierto de oro e hicieron muchas expediciones en busca de ese mineral
25 que nunca encontraron.

   En el siglo XXI la diversidad natural de Suramérica todavía nos ofrece mucha belleza y recursos[6] naturales. Los ríos son majestuosos y les dan la oportunidad a países como Venezuela de construir lugares como el Centro Hidroeléctrico Simón Bolívar en el río Caroní que **le** da electricidad a un área muy extensa. Los tepuyes de Venezuela forman parte del Parque Nacional
30 Canaima que es magnífico para hacer ecoturismo. El petróleo de Venezuela y el carbón de Colombia son exportaciones importantes. Además, Colombia exporta flores, bananas, perlas y también su famoso café.

   Los españoles llegaron a América con la idea de conquistar, explorar y llevar mucho oro a España. Su llegada empezó un nuevo capítulo en la historia suramericana. Ahora, en el siglo
35 XXI, estamos empezando a escribir otro capítulo, pero debemos ser conscientes y no destruir[7] la belleza y las riquezas naturales que forman parte de esa tierra tan maravillosa.

[1] to set foot upon [2] to cross [3] covered [4] ships, caravels [5] horses [6] resources [7] to destroy

**ACTIVIDAD 25 Los detalles** Answer the following questions based on the reading.

1. ¿Cuál es el sujeto del verbo **llegó** en el párrafo 1? _____

2. ¿A quiénes se refiere **les** en el párrafo 1? _____

3. ¿Cuál es el sujeto del verbo **fue** en el párrafo 2? _____

4. ¿Qué usaron los españoles para navegar los ríos? _____

   _____

5. ¿A quién se refiere **les** en el párrafo 3? _____

6. ¿Cuál es el sujeto del verbo **se enfadó** en el párrafo 3? _____

7. ¿Cuál es un sinónimo de **se enfadó**? _____

8. ¿A qué o a quién se refiere **le** en el párrafo 4? _____

9. ¿Dónde se puede hacer ecoturismo hoy día en Venezuela? _____

   _____

10. ¿Qué productos exportan Venezuela y Colombia hoy día? _____

    _____

# Los viajes

## Vocabulario esencial I

### El teléfono

**ACTIVIDAD 1** **Hablando por teléfono** Match the sentences in Column A with the logical responses from Column B.

| A | B |
|---|---|
| 1. _____ ¿Aló? | a. Tiene Ud. el número equivocado. |
| 2. _____ ¿De parte de quién? | b. ¿Para hablar con quién? |
| 3. _____ ¿Hablo con el 233–44–54? | c. Buenos días, ¿está Tomás? |
| 4. _____ Operadora internacional, buenos días. | d. ¿Por qué? ¿Tienes poca batería? |
| 5. _____ Tenemos que hablar rápido. | e. Quisiera el número del cine Rex, en la calle Luna. |
| 6. _____ Información, buenos días. | f. Quisiera hacer una llamada a Panamá. |
| 7. _____ No estamos en casa. Puede dejar un mensaje después del tono. | g. No me gusta hablar con máquinas. Te veo esta tarde. |
| 8. _____ Lo siento, pero Carlos no está. | h. ¿Le puede decir que llamó Héctor? |
| | i. Habla Félix. |

**ACTIVIDAD 2** **Número equivocado** Complete the following conversations that Camila has as she tries to reach her friend Imelda by telephone.

1. SEÑORA     ¿Aló?

    CAMILA     ¿_____ Imelda?

    SEÑORA     No, _____.

    CAMILA     ¿No es el 4–49–00–35?

    SEÑORA     Sí, pero _____.

2. OPERADORA Información.

 CAMILA _____ Imelda García Arias.

 OPERADORA El número es 8–34–88–75.

 CAMILA _____.

3. SEÑOR ¿_____?

 CAMILA ¿_____?

 SEÑOR Sí, ¿_____?

 CAMILA _____ Camila.

 SEÑOR Un momento. Ahora viene.

# En el hotel

**ACTIVIDAD 3** **¿Quién es o qué es?** Complete the following sentences with the logical words.

1. Una habitación para una persona es _____.

2. Una habitación para dos personas es _____.

3. La persona que limpia (cleans) el hotel es _____.

4. La persona que trabaja en recepción es _____.

5. Una habitación con desayuno y una comida es _____.

6. Una habitación con todas las comidas es _____.

7. El dinero extra que le das al botones es _____.

**ACTIVIDAD 4** **En el Hotel Meliá** Complete the following conversation between a guest and a receptionist at the Hotel Meliá. First, read the entire conversation. Then go back and complete it appropriately.

RECEPCIONISTA Buenos días. ¿_____ puedo servirle?

CLIENTE Necesito una _____.

RECEPCIONISTA ¿Con una o dos camas?

CLIENTE Dos, por favor.

RECEPCIONISTA ¿_____? Es más económico si no tiene.

CLIENTE Con baño.

RECEPCIONISTA ¿_____?

CLIENTE No, con media pensión.

RECEPCIONISTA Bien, una habitación doble con baño y media pensión.

CLIENTE ¿_____?

RECEPCIONISTA 125 euros. ¿_____?

CLIENTE Vamos a quedarnos tres noches.

RECEPCIONISTA Bien. Su habitación es la 24.

# Gramática para la comunicación I

## Talking about the Past (Part I)

**ACTIVIDAD 5** **Los verbos en el pasado** Complete the following sentences with the appropriate preterit form of the indicated verbs.

1. ¿Dónde _____ tú las cartas? (poner)

2. Ayer yo no _____ ver a mi amigo. (poder)

3. ¿A qué hora _____ anoche el concierto? (comenzar)

4. La semana pasada la policía _____ la verdad. (saber)

5. Nosotros _____ la cerveza. (traer)

6. ¿Por qué no _____ los padres de Ramón? (venir)

7. Ustedes _____ las preguntas dos veces. (traducir)

8. Yo no _____ tiempo para estudiar. (tener)

9. Martín _____ el email que Paco le _____ a Carmen. (leer, escribir)

10. Nosotros no le _____ dar a José el número de teléfono de Beatriz. (querer)

11. Yo _____ varias horas en la cama, pero no _____ dormir. (estar, poder)

12. La compañía _____ unas oficinas nuevas en la calle Lope de Rueda. (construir)

13. Ellos no nos _____ la verdad ayer. (decir)

14. ¿_____ tú que el padre de Raúl_____ esa película? (oír, producir)

15. Anoche Gonzalo _____ en su carro. (llegar)

## Talking about the Past (Part II)

**ACTIVIDAD 6** **La vida universitaria** In complete sentences, answer the following survey questions from a student newspaper.

1. ¿Cuántas horas dormiste anoche? _____

_____

2. ¿Cuándo fue la última vez que mentiste? _____

_____

3. ¿Estudiaste mucho o poco para tu último examen? _____

_____

4. ¿Qué nota sacaste en tu último examen? _____

_____

5. ¿A cuántas fiestas fuiste el mes pasado? _____

_____

6. ¿Qué sirvieron en esas fiestas? _____

_____

7. La última vez que saliste de la universidad por un fin de semana, ¿llevaste tus libros? _____

_____

8. ¿Cuánto tiempo hace que leíste una novela para divertirte? _____

_____

9. ¿Comiste bien o comiste mal (papas fritas, Coca-Cola, etc.) anoche? _____

_____

**ACTIVIDAD  7  Las obligaciones** In Column A of the accompanying chart, write three things you had to do and did do yesterday **(tuve que)**. In Column B, write three things you had to do but refused to do **(no quise)**. In Column C, write three things you have to do tomorrow **(tengo que)**. Use complete sentences.

| A | B | C |
|---|---|---|
|   |   |   |
|   |   |   |
|   |   |   |

## Expressing the Duration of an Action: *Hace* + Time Expression + *que* + Verb in the Present

**ACTIVIDAD  8  ¿Presente o pretérito?** Answer the following questions in complete sentences, using either the present or the preterit.

1. ¿Cuánto tiempo hace que estudias español? _____

_____

2. ¿Cuánto tiempo hace que comiste? _____

_____

3. ¿Cuánto tiempo hace que viven tus padres en su casa? _____

_____

4. ¿Cuánto tiempo hace que asistes a esta universidad? _____

_____

5. ¿Cuánto tiempo hace que hablaste con tu madre? _____

_____

# Un poco de todo

**ACTIVIDAD 9** **¿Cuánto tiempo hace que...?** Look at this portion of Mario Huidobro's résumé. Complete the questions with the appropriate forms of the verbs **trabajar, tocar, vender,** or **terminar**. Then answer the questions. Remember: Use **hace** + *time period* + *present* to refer to actions that started in the past and continue to the present; use **hace** + *time period* + *preterit* to refer to actions that happened in the past and do not continue to the present.

> Salamanca, de 2003 a 2007: estudiante universitario y recepcionista en el hotel Puente Romano
>
> Barcelona, de 2007 al presente: pianista profesional
>
> Barcelona, de 2007 al presente: vendedor de computadoras para Dell

1. ¿Cuánto tiempo hace que Mario _____ como recepcionista?

   _____

2. ¿Cuánto tiempo hace que Mario _____ el piano profesionalmente?

   _____

3. ¿Cuánto tiempo hace que Mario _____ sus estudios universitarios?

   _____

4. ¿Cuánto tiempo hace que Mario _____ computadoras para Dell?

   _____

# Vocabulario esencial II

## Medios de transporte

**ACTIVIDAD 10** **El transporte** Write the transportation-related word that you associate with each of the following words or groups of words. Include the appropriate definite article.

1. Amtrak _____

2. Trek, Schwinn _____

3. Volkswagen, Honda, Buick _____

4. U-Haul, Ryder, Penske _____

5. United, Aeroméxico, Jet Blue, Iberia, Lacsa _____

6. BART (San Francisco), El (Chicago), T (Boston) _____

7. Harley-Davidson, Kawasaki _____

8. LAX, O'Hare, J.F.K., Logan _____

9. Titanic _____

10. Greyhound _____

**ACTIVIDAD 11** **Transporte en Barcelona** Complete the following travel guide description about the modes of transportation in Barcelona.

Al aeropuerto de Barcelona llegan _____ (1) de vuelos (flights) nacionales

e internacionales. Como el aeropuerto está a 12 kilómetros de la ciudad, se puede tomar un

_____ (2), pero hay un servicio de autobuses a la ciudad que cuesta menos. Como

Barcelona está en la costa, también llegan _____ (3) de Italia y de otras partes

del Mediterráneo. Existen dos estaciones de _____ (4); a muchas personas les

gusta este medio de transporte rápido porque pueden dormir durante el viaje en una cama. Dentro

de la ciudad, el transporte público es muy bueno y cuesta poco: hay _____ (5),

_____ (6) y, por supuesto, _____ (7), que cuestan más. El

_____ (8) es el medio más rápido porque no importan los problemas de tráfico.

Muchas personas prefieren conducir su _____ (9), pero es difícil encontrar dónde

dejarlo, especialmente en la parte vieja de la ciudad. Como en todas las ciudades grandes, hay pocos

lugares para aparcar.

## El pasaje y el aeropuerto

**ACTIVIDAD 12** **De viaje** Complete the following sentences with the word being defined.

1. La hora en que llega el vuelo es la _____.
2. Si un avión llega tarde, llega con _____.
3. Si vas de Nueva York a Tegucigalpa y vuelves a Nueva York, es un viaje de

   _____.
4. La hora en que sale el vuelo es la _____.
5. La persona que viaja es un _____.
6. Si vas de Nueva York a Tegucigalpa pero el avión va primero a Miami, el vuelo hace

   _____.
7. Si el vuelo no va a Miami (como en la pregunta anterior), es un vuelo _____.
8. La silla de un avión es el _____.
9. Iberia, LAN y Avianca son _____.
10. El equipaje que puedes llevar contigo en el avión es el _____.
11. El asiento que está entre el asiento de ventanilla y el de pasillo es el _____.
12. La tarjeta que presentas para subir al avión es la tarjeta de _____.

**ACTIVIDAD** **13** **Información** Give or ask for flight information based on the accompanying arrival and departure boards from Barajas, the airport in Madrid. Use complete sentences.

| Llegadas internacionales | | | | |
|---|---|---|---|---|
| **Línea aérea** | **N° de vuelo** | **Procedencia** | **Hora de llegada** | **Comentarios** |
| American | 952 | Lima | 10:20 | a tiempo |
| Air Europa | 354 | Santo Domingo | 10:25 | a tiempo |
| LAN | 988 | Santiago/Lima/Caracas | 12:45 | 13:10 |
| Aeroméxico | 904 | México/Barcelona | 22:00 | 22:35 |

| Salidas internacionales | | | | | |
|---|---|---|---|---|---|
| **Línea aérea** | **N° de vuelo** | **Destino** | **Hora de salida** | **Comentarios** | **Puerta** |
| Avianca | 357 | Panamá | 13:20 | 14:20 | 7 |
| Aeroméxico | 511 | México | 14:40 | 15:00 | 9 |
| Iberia | 750 | San Juan | 16:25 | 16:55 | 2 |
| Avianca | 615 | Bogotá | 16:45 | a tiempo | 3 |

1. — Información.

—¿ _____?

—Llega a las 10:25.

—¿ _____?

—No, llega a tiempo.

2. —Información.

—Quisiera saber si hay retraso con el vuelo de Avianca a la Ciudad de Panamá.

— _____

—¿A qué hora sale y de qué puerta?

— _____

—Por favor, una pregunta más. ¿Cuál es el número del vuelo?

— _____

—Gracias.

— _____

**ACTIVIDAD** **14** **El horario** You work at a travel agency. Refer to the accompanying flight schedule to answer the questions from the agency's clients. Use complete sentences.

| HORARIO DE VUELOS | | | |
|---|---|---|---|
| **DESDE CARACAS** | **N° de Vuelo** | **Hora** | **Día** |
| Caracas/Maracaibo | 620 | 7:00 | miércoles/sábado |
| Caracas/Porlamar | 600 | 21:00 | viernes/domingo |
| Caracas/Ciudad de Panamá*/ San Juan, Pto. Rico | 610 | 16:55 | viernes |
| Caracas/Barcelona | 614 | 21:00 | viernes |
| **HACIA CARACAS** | **N° de Vuelo** | **Hora** | **Día** |
| Maracaibo/Caracas | 621 | 19:00 | miércoles/sábado |
| Porlamar/Caracas | 601 | 22:25 | viernes/domingo |
| Barcelona/Caracas | 611 | 18:20 | viernes |
| Barcelona/Caracas | 615 | 22:25 | viernes |

*Cambio de avión

1. —Quiero ir de Caracas a Barcelona el sábado. ¿Es posible?

   —_____

2. —¿Puedo ir de Maracaibo a Caracas el lunes que viene?

   —_____

3. —¿Qué días y a qué horas puedo viajar de Porlamar a Caracas?

   —_____

   _____

4. —¿Hay un vuelo directo de Caracas a San Juan?

   —_____

   —¿Dónde hace escala?

   —_____

   —¿Tengo que cambiar de avión o solo hace escala?

   —_____

   —Bueno, entonces voy a comprar un pasaje.

   —¿Tiene Ud. pasaporte y visa para entrar en los Estados Unidos? ¿Y cuánto tiempo hace que sacó su pasaporte y la visa?

   —_____

   _____

# Gramática para la comunicación II

## Indicating Time and Age in the Past: *Ser* and *tener*

**ACTIVIDAD 15** **¿Qué hora era?** State what time it was when the following actions took place.

▶ despertarse

1. vestirse

2. preparar la comida

3. esposo / llegar

4. servir el almuerzo

5. esposo / volver al trabajo

Illustrations: © Cengage Learning 2013

▶ *Eran las ocho y diez cuando la mujer se despertó.*

1. _____

2. _____

3. _____

4. _____

5. _____

**ACTIVIDAD 16** ¿Cuántos años tenías? Answer these questions about you and your family.

1. ¿Cuántos años tenías cuando terminaste la escuela primaria? _____

_____

2. ¿Cuántos años tenías cuando recibiste tu primera bicicleta? _____

_____

3. ¿Cuántos años tenías cuando empezaste la universidad? _____

_____

4. ¿Cuántos años tenías cuando Barack Obama subió a la presidencia en el año 2009?

_____

**ACTIVIDAD 17** Feliz cumpleaños Answer the following questions in complete sentences.

1. ¿Cuántos años tenía tu madre cuando tú naciste? _____

_____

2. ¿Y tu padre? _____

3. ¿Qué hora era cuando tú naciste? _____

## Avoiding Redundancies: Direct-Object Pronouns

**ACTIVIDAD 18** *Lo, la, los, las* Rewrite the following sentences, replacing the direct object with the appropriate direct-object pronoun.

1. No veo a Juan. _____

2. No tenemos los libros. _____

3. Elisa está comprando comida. _____

4. No conoció a tu padre. _____

5. Juan y Nuria no trajeron a sus primos. _____

6. Vamos a comprar papas fritas. _____

**ACTIVIDAD 19** De otra manera Rewrite the following sentences in a different manner without changing their meaning. Make all necessary changes.

1. Tengo que comprarlos. _____

2. Te estoy invitando a la fiesta. _____

3. Lo estamos escribiendo. _____

4. Van a vernos mañana. _____

**ACTIVIDAD 20** **Pronombres de complemento directo** Answer the following questions in complete sentences, using direct-object pronouns.

1. ¿Me quieres? _____

2. ¿Vas a traer los pasajes? _____

3. ¿Nos estás invitando? _____

4. ¿Llevas la maleta? _____

5. ¿Compraste la pasta de dientes? _____

**ACTIVIDAD 21** **La respuesta apropiada** Construct a logical conversation by selecting the correct options.

CLIENTE  Quiero ver estas blusas, pero en azul.

VENDEDORA  a. ❑ Aquí los tiene.

b. ❑ No las tenemos en azul.

c. ❑ No la tengo.

CLIENTE  a. ❑ Entonces, en otro color.

b. ❑ Pues, deseo verlo en rosado.

c. ❑ Bueno, si no hay en otro color, quiero azul.

VENDEDORA  a. ❑ Las tengo en color rosado.

b. ❑ Voy a ver si los tengo en amarillo.

c. ❑ Sí, hay mucha.

CLIENTE  a. ❑ Este es muy elegante. Lo llevo.

b. ❑ No me gusta este. Lo siento.

c. ❑ Esta es muy bonita. La voy a llevar.

VENDEDORA  a. ❑ ¿La va a pagar?

b. ❑ ¿Cómo va a pagarla?

c. ❑ ¿Cómo va a pagarlas?

CLIENTE  a. ❑ Las pago con la tarjeta de crédito.

b. ❑ La pago con la tarjeta de Visa.

c. ❑ No, no voy a pagarla.

**ACTIVIDAD 22** **Las definiciones** Write definitions for the following objects without naming the objects themselves. To do this, you will need to use direct-object pronouns, as shown in the example. Remember that the word *it* is never expressed as a subject in Spanish.

▶ libros *Los compramos para las clases. Los usamos cuando estudiamos. Tienen mucha información. Son de papel. Los leo todas las noches. Me gustan mucho.*

1. computadora _____

_____

_____

2. pantalones _____

_____

_____

# Un poco de todo

**ACTIVIDAD 23** **Una conversación** Read this conversation between two friends who haven't seen each other in a long time. After reading it, go back and fill in each missing word with a logical verb from the list in the appropriate present, preterit, or imperfect. Do not repeat any verbs.

| dar | estar | mentir | tener |
|-----|-------|--------|-------|
| decir | explicar | pedir | trabajar |
| escribir | ir | ser | ver |

MARTA      Hace ocho años que te _____ (1) por última vez. ¿Cómo estás?

ANTONIO   Bien. ¿Todavía _____ (2) en el banco?

MARTA      No, te _____ (3) un email hace dos años donde te _____ (4) todo.

ANTONIO   Ah sí, tú les _____ (5) un cambio *(change)* de oficina a tus jefes.

MARTA      Exacto. Entonces me _____ (6) que sí, pero nunca me _____ (7) una oficina nueva.

ANTONIO   Así que ellos te _____ (8).

MARTA      Sí, y yo _____ (9) a trabajar en una compañía de electrónica.

Increíble ¿no? _____ (10) 52 años cuando pasó todo eso.

ANTONIO   ¿ _____ (11) contenta ahora?

MARTA      Muy contenta. El trabajo _____ (12) maravilloso.

# Lectura

## Estrategia de lectura: Identifying Main Ideas

As you read in your textbook, main ideas can be found in titles, headings, or subheadings and also in topic sentences, which many times begin a paragraph or a section of a reading. Other important or supporting ideas can be found in the body of a paragraph or section.

In the following reading about lodging in Spain, each section is introduced by a title and a topic sentence.

**ACTIVIDAD 24** **Alojamiento en tu país**  Before reading, make a list of different types of lodging available in your country for tourists. You can make this list in English.

_____

_____

**ACTIVIDAD 25** **Un esquema**  Fill in the boxes with the titles of the sections, write the topic sentences, and list the supporting evidence provided.

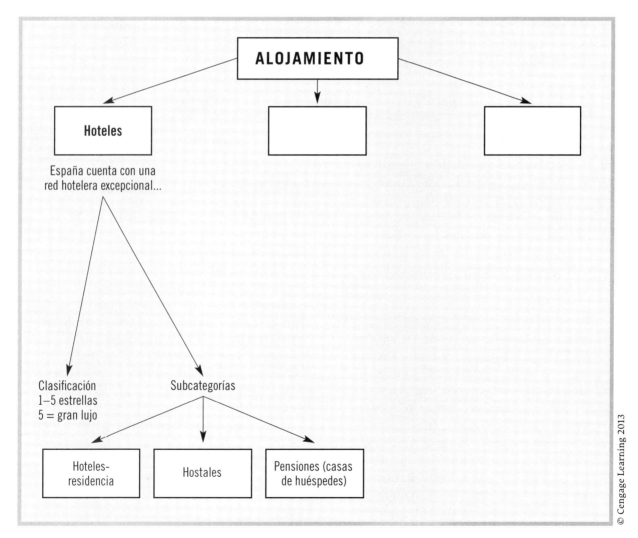

# ALOJAMIENTO

## HOTELES

España cuenta con una red hotelera excepcional por el número, la variedad y la calidad de unos establecimientos que se reparten por toda la geografía de nuestro país, y que son capaces de adaptarse a cualquier exigencia y posibilidad.

Los hoteles españoles están clasificados en cinco categorías, que se identifican con un número de estrellas que va de una a cinco, según los servicios y las características de cada uno. Existe también un reducido número de hoteles de cinco estrellas, de características auténticamente excepcionales, que ostentan además la categoría máxima de GRAN LUJO.

Los denominados **hoteles-residencia,** que se rigen por la misma clasificación que los demás hoteles, son aquellos que carecen de restaurante, aunque sirven desayunos, tienen servicio de habitaciones y poseen un bar o una cafetería. Los **hostales,** establecimientos de naturaleza similar a los hoteles, pero más modestos, constituyen otra modalidad de alojamiento. Están clasificados en tres categorías que van de una a tres estrellas.

Otra posible modalidad de alojamiento es la constituida por las **casas de huéspedes,** que en España se llaman **pensiones.** De gran tradición en nuestro país, resultan generalmente establecimientos acogedores y cómodos, cuyas instalaciones y servicios pueden variar entre la sobriedad y un lujo relativo. Regentados generalmente por la familia propietaria de la casa, su precio suele incluir solamente el alojamiento y las comidas, frecuentemente excelentes. Las pensiones resultan un tipo de alojamiento ideal para los visitantes que deseen conocer España en profundidad, apartándose de las rutas turísticas más frecuentadas.

**Patio del Parador Nacional de Zafra.**

Atlantide Phototravel/Corbis

## CAMPINGS

España cuenta con cerca de 800 campings, que reúnen una capacidad global de casi 400.000 plazas. Repartidos por todo el terreno nacional, son especialmente abundantes en las costas, y están clasificados en diversas categorías según sus características e instalaciones, como los hoteles. Sus tarifas varían en función de la cantidad y calidad de sus servicios. En el caso de que se opte por hacer acampada libre es recomendable informarse previamente acerca de la no existencia de prohibiciones municipales que afecten al lugar elegido. Si se desea acampar en un terreno privado, es preciso obtener previamente el permiso del propietario.

## PARADORES DE TURISMO

Los paradores de turismo constituyen la modalidad hotelera más original e interesante de la oferta turística española.

La red de paradores está constituida por 93 establecimientos, que ofrecen los servicios y comodidades de los más modernos hoteles, pero ocupan, en cambio, en la mayoría de los casos, antiguos edificios monumentales de valor histórico y artístico, como castillos, palacios, monasterios y conventos, que, abandonados en el pasado, han sido adquiridos y rehabilitados para este fin.

Enclavados casi siempre en lugares de gran belleza e interés, los paradores, que tienen generalmente categoría de hoteles de tres o cuatro estrellas, se reparten por todos los rincones de nuestro país. Para información y reservas: Paradores de Turismo, Velázquez 18, 28001 Madrid. Tels.: (91) 435 97 00 y (91) 435 97 44.

Alojamiento, reprinted by permission of Secretaría de Turismo / Turespaña, Ministerio de Industria, Comercio y Turismo.

**ACTIVIDAD 26** **El alojamiento en España** After reading the article, answer the following questions about lodging in Spain.

1. ¿Cuál es más impersonal, un hotel-residencia o una pensión? ¿Por qué? _____

_____

2. ¿Dónde hay más lugares para hacer camping? ¿En el centro de España o en la costa?

_____

3. ¿Cuántos paradores hay? ¿En qué tipo de edificios están? ¿Cómo son generalmente los lugares donde están?

_____

_____

4. ¿Dónde te gustaría pasar una noche: en un hostal, una pensión, un camping o en un parador? ¿Por qué?

_____

_____

_____

## The Details

Look at the following sentences and note how the use of an article **(el/un, la/una)** or lack of one can change the meaning.

| | |
|---|---|
| Voy a comprar **la chaqueta** que vimos ayer. | The speaker has a specific one in mind. |
| Voy a comprar **una chaqueta** para el invierno. | The speaker has none in mind; he/she will go to some stores and just look for one. |
| Mañana voy a comer en **el restaurante** Casa Pepe. | The speaker has a specific one in mind—Casa Pepe. |
| Mañana voy a comer en **el restaurante**. | Implying the specific one the speaker has in mind. |
| Mañana voy a comer en **un restaurante** chino. | The speaker will eat in a Chinese restaurant, but does not specify which. |
| Yo como en **restaurantes** con frecuencia. | Implying that the speaker goes to different restaurants. |

Look at how the use of **el/los** can change the meaning in these sentences.

| | |
|---|---|
| Trabajo **el** lunes. | I work on Monday. |
| Trabajo **los** lunes. | I work on Mondays. |

Note the use of these prepositions in Spanish:

Estudio **en** la Universidad de Georgetown.
Para mí, la clase **de** literatura moderna es muy difícil.
Normalmente estudio **por** la tarde.
Tengo que terminar un trabajo **para** el viernes.

Remember all the uses of **a:**

- the *personal* **a**

  Conozco **a** mi profesor de biología muy bien.

- before an indirect object (as with **gustar**)

  **A** Juan y **a** Verónica les gusta la clase de biología.
  Le doy el trabajo **al** profesor.

- **a** + *place*

  **asistir a** + *place/event*, **ir a** + *place/event*

  **Asisto a mi clase** de español todos los días.
  **Voy a la universidad** temprano todos los días.

- verbs that take **a** before infinitives

  aprender
  comenzar
  empezar ⎱ + **a** + *infinitive*
  enseñar
  ir

  Poco a poco **aprendo a escribir** español.
  **Empiezo a entender** las conversaciones del programa de laboratorio.
  El profesor nos **enseña a pronunciar** las palabras correctamente.

**ACTIVIDAD 1  Conversaciones** Complete the following conversations with the correct articles or prepositions. Only one word per blank.

1. —Mi padre está _____ _____ hospital.

   —¿Cuándo va _____ salir?

   —_____ miércoles, si Dios quiere.

2. —¡Carlitos! ¿Cuándo vas _____ aprender _____ comer bien?

   —Mamá, mamá, Ramón me está molestando.

3. —No quiero asistir _____ la reunión.

   —Yo tampoco. ¿Por qué no vamos_____ _____ restaurante _____ el centro?

   —Buena idea. Yo conozco _____ restaurante muy bueno.

4. —Por fin empiezo _____ entenderte.

   —¿Aprendiste _____ leer mis pensamientos?

   —No dije eso.

5. —¿Dónde estudias?

   —_____ la Universidad Autónoma en Madrid.

   —¿Cuándo empezaste?

   —Empecé _ _____ estudiar allí hace tres años.

   —¿Qué estudias?

   —Arte.

   —¿ _____ tus padres les gusta _____ idea?

   —Claro, ¡son artistas!

6. —Oye, voy _____ tener el carro _____ Felipe este fin de semana.

   —¿Adónde quieres ir?

   —Me gustaría ir _____ _____ capital. ¿Podemos ir?

   —¿Por qué no? Voy _____ ver _____ Pilar mañana _____ la noche.

   —¿Y?

   —Y su hermano comenzó _____ trabajar en la capital _____ mes pasado. Podemos dormir

   _____ el apartamento _____ él. Creo que está cerca _____ centro y que es muy grande.

   —Buena idea.

7. —¿Compraste _____ saco que vimos _____ otro día?

   —Sí, me costó _____ ojo de la cara.

   —Ahora necesitas corbata.

   —Sí, _____ corbata _____ seda roja.

8. —¿ _____ cuándo es la composición?

   —Es_____ _____ lunes.

# La comida y los deportes

## Vocabulario esencial I

### La comida

**ACTIVIDAD 1** **La palabra que no pertenece** Select the word that doesn't belong.

1. aceite, ensalada, servilleta, vinagre
2. arvejas, cordero, habichuelas, espárragos
3. cuchillo, bistec, chuleta, carne de res
4. cuchillo, tenedor, taza, cuchara
5. ternera, ajo, cordero, cerdo
6. tomate, maíz, papa, cuenta
7. lentejas, coliflor, frijoles, arvejas
8. fruta, helado, zanahorias, flan
9. plato, copa, vaso, taza
10. coliflor, huevo, cebolla, ajo

**ACTIVIDAD 2** **La mesa** Look at the following drawing and label the items. Remember to include the definite article in your answers.

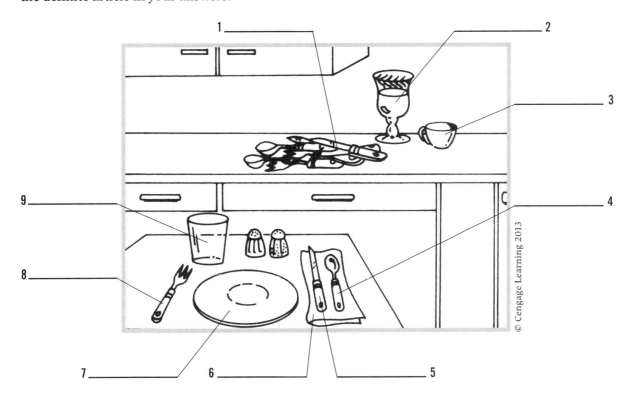

**ACTIVIDAD 3 Una cena especial** You are planning a dinner party at a restaurant for your parents' wedding anniversary. The restaurant manager suggests ordering two dishes for the first course, two dishes for the second, and something for dessert; that way your guests will have choices. You also need to plan a special vegetarian menu for your aunt and uncle. You can spend up to 500 **lempiras** (Honduran currency) per person. Look at the menu and complete the restaurant order form.

# Hotel Coral

### Restaurante Arrecifas

*Comidas regionales y del mundo para todos los gustos*

| Primer plato | lps |
|---|---|
| Sopa de verduras | 100,00 |
| Sopa de camarón | 120,00 |
| Espárragos con mayonesa | 125,00 |
| Tomate relleno | 100,00 |
| Ensalada rusa (papas, arvejas, zanahorias) | 110,50 |
| Pupusas (loroco, frijoles, queso) | 100,50 |

| Segundo plato | |
|---|---|
| Churrasco con casamiento | 300,00 |
| Bistec de ternera con puré de papas | 275,00 |
| Medio pollo al ajo con papas fritas | 250,00 |
| Tamales con carne de cerdo o con frijoles | 230,00 |
| Ravioles de queso | 225,00 |
| Kak'ik | 320,00 |

| Ensaladas | lps |
|---|---|
| Mixta | 100,00 |
| Zanahoria y huevo | 100,00 |
| Waldorf | 120,00 |

| Bebidas | |
|---|---|
| Agua con o sin gas | 50,00 |
| Media botella | 35,00 |
| Gaseosas | 50,00 |
| Té | 40,00 |
| Café | 40,00 |
| Vino tinto, blanco | 110,00 |
| Atol de elote | 100,00 |

| Postres | |
|---|---|
| Helado de vainilla, chocolate | 120,00 |
| Flan con dulce de leche | 130,00 |
| Arroz con leche | 100,00 |
| Pastel de tres leches | 140,00 |
| Frutas tropicales | 100,00 |

| Menú del día | |
|---|---|
| Ensalada mixta, medio pollo al ajo con papas, postre, café y pan | 475,00 |

Primer plato 1. _____

2. _____

Segundo plato 1. _____

2. _____

Postre _____

Champán ☐ Sí   ☐ No

Vino, agua, pan y café incluidos en el precio para grupos de veinticinco o más.

Señor Jiménez:

También necesitamos un menú especial para vegetarianos que va a incluir lo siguiente:

Primer plato _____

Segundo plato _____

Postre _____

**ACTIVIDAD  4  Rompecabezas**  Do the following newspaper puzzle. By finding the correct word for each definition, you will be able to complete a popular Spanish saying that means *he's blushing.*

1.  Es verde y es la base de la ensalada.            __ __ __ __ __ __
                                                        1          10

2.  Lloro cuando corto esta verdura; es blanca.     __ __ __ __ __ __
                                                      8       6

3.  Lo uso en la cocina y en mi carro.              __ __ __ __
                                                      4

4.  A Popeye le gusta comer esto mucho.             __ __ __ __ __ __ __ __
                                                         2

5.  Una banana es parte de este grupo.              __ __ __ __ __
                                                            3

6.  En una ensalada pongo aceite y esto.            __ __ __ __ __ __
                                                          11

7.  Son rojos, negros o marrones y se ponen en los burritos.  __ __ __ __ __ __ __
                                                                    7

8.  Para comer uso una cuchara, un cuchillo y esto.  __ __ __ __ __ __
                                                                  5

9.  Es la compañera de la sal; es negra.            __ __ __ __ __ __ __
                                                          9

El dicho secreto: __ __ __ __   __ __ __ __   __ __ __ __
                   1  2  3  4    5  6  7  6    8  6  9  6

                  __ __   __ __ __ __ __ __
                  10 11   3  6  9  4  3  1

# Grámatica para la comunicación I

## Expressing Likes, Dislikes, and Opinions: Using Verbs Like *Gustar*

**ACTIVIDAD  5  Verbos como *gustar***  Complete the following sentences with the correct form of the indicated verb. (Some function like **gustar** and need an indirect-object pronoun; others do not.)

1.  A mí _____ que estás loca. (parecer)

2.  A Bernardo y a Amalia _____ las películas viejas. (interesar)

3.  ¿A ti _____ mucho tiempo para terminar la tarea? (faltar)

4.  El Sr. Castañeda nunca _____ trabajar porque es millonario. (necesitar)

5.  Ahora, después de caminar tanto hoy, a Gustavo _____ los zapatos. (molestar)

6.  Ayer a Julio _____ el concierto. (fascinar)

7.  ¿Por qué no me _____ nunca cuando te pido ayuda? (ayudar)

8.  A Amparo siempre _____ dinero. (faltar)

9.  A mi padre y a mí _____ viajar y conocer otras culturas. (encantar)

**ACTIVIDAD** **6** **La universidad** You just received a questionnaire about university life. Answer the following questions, using complete sentences.

1. ¿Cuáles son tres cosas que te fascinan de esta universidad? _____

_____

2. ¿Cuáles son tres cosas que te molestan? _____

_____

3. ¿Te parecen excelentes, buenas, regulares o malas las clases? _____

_____

4. ¿Te parece excelente, buena, regular o mala la comida? _____

_____

5. ¿Te parece que hay suficientes computadoras en la universidad para hacer investigación *(research)*?

_____

6. ¿Te falta algo en la universidad? _____

_____

Algún comentario personal:

_____

_____

## Avoiding Redundancies: Combining Direct- and Indirect-Object Pronouns

**ACTIVIDAD** **7** **Combina** Rewrite the following sentences, using direct- and indirect-object pronouns.

1. Te voy a escribir una carta de amor. _____
2. Le regalé dos álbumes de rock. _____
3. Mi madre les pidió una sopa de verduras. _____
4. ¿Te mandé los papeles? _____
5. Estoy preparándote un café. _____

**ACTIVIDAD** **8** **De otra manera** Rewrite the following sentences that contain direct- and indirect-object pronouns without changing their meaning. Pay attention to accents.

▶ ¿Me lo vas a preparar? *¿Vas a preparármelo?*

1. Te lo voy a comprar. _____
2. Se la estoy escribiendo. _____
3. Me los tienes que lavar. _____
4. Nos lo está leyendo. _____
5. ¿Se lo puedes mandar? _____
6. Te las va a preparar. _____
7. ¿Me lo estás pidiendo? _____
8. Se los vamos a traer. _____

**ACTIVIDAD 9** **El esposo histérico** Your friend Víctor is preparing a romantic dinner for his wife's return from a long business trip and you are helping him. Víctor is very nervous and wants everything to be perfect. Complete the conversation between you and Víctor, using direct- and indirect-object pronouns when possible.

VÍCTOR   Gracias por tu ayuda. ¿Me compraste el vino blanco?

TÚ   Sí, _____.

VÍCTOR   ¿Pusiste las flores en la mesa?

TÚ   _____.

VÍCTOR   ¿Me limpiaste el baño?

TÚ   Sí, esta mañana _____.

VÍCTOR   ¿Qué crees? ¿Debo ponerme corbata?

TÚ   _____.

VÍCTOR   ¡Ay! Tengo los zapatos sucios *(dirty)*.

TÚ   ¡Tranquilo, hombre! Yo voy a _____.
¿Por qué no te sientas y miras la televisión? Tu esposa no llega hasta las tres. Te voy a preparar un té.

## Using *ya* and *todavía*

**ACTIVIDAD 10** **¿Ya o todavía?** Complete the following sentences, using **ya** or **todavía**.

1. Mi madre _____ sabe qué va a preparar para la cena: arroz con pollo.

2. _____ no tenemos carro, pero vamos a comprar uno mañana.

3. La gente _____ votó en las elecciones. ¡Hay un presidente nuevo!

4. _____ tengo que hablar con mis padres; esta mañana no contestaron el teléfono.

5. Lo estudié anoche, pero _____ tengo problemas. ¿Me lo puedes explicar?

6. Carolina me dijo lo que pasó. _____ sé la verdad.

7. Limpié la casa, preparé la comida y la sangría, compré el pastel. _____ no tengo que hacer nada más para la fiesta.

8. ¡Hombre, claro! _____ entiendo.

9. _____ no entiendo. ¿Puedes repetirlo?

**ACTIVIDAD 11** **Las actividades de esta semana** Look at the following list and state what things you have already done and what things you still have to do this week. Use **ya** or **todavía** in your responses.

▶   invitar a Juan a la fiesta     *Ya lo invité.*
*Todavía tengo que invitarlo.*

1. estudiar para el examen _____

2. comprar pasta de dientes _____

3. escribirle un email a mi abuelo _____

4. hablar por teléfono con mis padres _____

5. ir al laboratorio de español _____

6. aprender las formas del imperfecto _____

7. sacar dinero del banco _____

8. comprarle un regalo a mi novio/a _____

# Un poco de todo

**ACTIVIDAD 12 El primer mes** Parte A. Answer these questions about your first month at college. Use object pronouns when possible.

1. ¿Tus padres te mandaron dinero? _____

2. ¿Te mandó comida tu abuela? ¿Qué te mandó? _____

   _____

3. ¿Les escribiste emails a tus abuelos? _____

4. ¿Les mandaste fotos digitales a tus padres? _____

5. Para su cumpleaños, ¿les mandaste tarjetas virtuales a tus amigos de la escuela secundaria o les compraste tarjetas de Hallmark? _____

   _____

6. ¿Le dijiste tus problemas a tu compañero/a de cuarto? ¿Te escuchó? _____

   _____

7. ¿Los profesores te dieron ayuda extra? _____

8. ¿La universidad les ofreció a los estudiantes nuevos programas especiales de orientación? ¿Asististe a estos programas? _____

   _____

9. ¿Qué cosas te gustaron de tu nueva vida? _____

   _____

**Parte B.** Now that you have been at the university for a while, answer these questions.

1. ¿Tus padres todavía te mandan dinero? _____

   _____

2. ¿Todavía hablas con tus amigos de la escuela secundaria con mucha frecuencia? _____

   _____

3. ¿Ya eres experto/a o todavía hay más que tienes que aprender sobre cómo funciona la universidad?

   _____

4. ¿Te pareció fácil o difícil adaptarte a la vida universitaria? _____

   _____

# Vocabulario esencial II

## Los deportes

**ACTIVIDAD 13** **¡Qué partido!** Francisco is ready to play in an important soccer game, but it's a disaster. Read his teammates' complaints and complete each one with the appropriate sports-related word.

1. Julio y Felipe están enfermos. ¿Cómo podemos jugar si nos faltan dos _____?

2. Psstt... mira quién llegó. Es el _____ del partido del mes pasado. El mismo *(same one)* que nos dio dos tarjetas amarillas y una roja.

3. A ver cómo vamos a recordar las estrategias del juego sin nuestro _____. Acabo de hablar con él y dice que hoy llega tarde.

4. ¿Supiste lo que pasó? El otro _____ olvidó traer los uniformes.

5. ¡No puede ser! ¡Con todos estos problemas, y hoy hay más _____ en este estadio que nunca!

## Los artículos deportivos

**ACTIVIDAD 14** **El equipo de deportes** Match the sports-related items in Column A with the sports in Column B. Write all possible answers.

| A | B |
|---|---|
| 1. cascos _____ | a. béisbol |
| 2. uniformes _____ | b. basquetbol |
| 3. pelotas _____ | c. fútbol |
| 4. bates _____ | d. fútbol americano |
| 5. raquetas _____ | e. tenis |
| 6. guantes _____ | f. bolos |
| 7. palos _____ | g. golf |
| 8. estadio _____ | h. boxeo |
| 9. balón _____ | i. ciclismo |
| | j. squash |

**ACTIVIDAD 15** **Tus deportes favoritos** State what sports you do and what items you have or don't have to play those sports.

▶ *Me gusta jugar al basquetbol, pero no tengo balón y por eso siempre usamos el balón de mi amigo Chris.*

_____

_____

_____

_____

_____

# Grámatica para la comunicación II

## Describing in the Past: The Imperfect

**ACTIVIDAD 16** ¿Qué hacíamos? Complete the sentences with the appropriate imperfect form of the indicated verbs.

1. Todos los días, yo _____ a la escuela. (ir)

2. Mi familia siempre _____ a la una y media. (comer)

3. Todos los martes y jueves después de trabajar, ellos _____ al fútbol en un equipo. (jugar)

4. Cuando yo _____ pequeño, mi madre _____ en un hospital. (ser, trabajar)

5. Cuando mis abuelos _____ veinte años, no _____ teléfonos celulares. (tener, haber)

6. Pablo Picasso _____ todos los días. (pintar)

7. John F. Kennedy Jr., el hijo del presidente Kennedy, _____ muy guapo. (ser)

8. De pequeño, mi hermano nos _____ muchas cosas. (preguntar)

9. Todos los veranos, mi primo y yo _____ en torneos de tenis. Nosotros no _____ mucho, pero siempre _____. (participar, ganar, divertirse)

**ACTIVIDAD 17** Todos los días Complete the sentences with the appropriate imperfect form of the indicated verbs. As you have learned, the imperfect is used for habitual past actions, recurring past events, or to describe in the past. After completing the sentence, write **H/R** if the sentence describes habitual past actions or recurring past events and **D** for past description.

H/R or D

1. Nuestra casa _____ grande y _____ cinco dormitorios. (ser, tener) _____

2. Todos los viernes nosotros _____ al cine. (ir) _____

3. Todos los días, mis amigos y yo _____ al tenis y yo siempre _____. (jugar, perder) _____

4. De pequeño, Ernesto _____ mucho y ahora es médico. (estudiar) _____

5. Francisco Franco _____ bajo, un poco gordo y _____ bigote. (ser, tener) _____

6. En la escuela secundaria, nosotros _____ a las doce, y después de la escuela _____ a comer pizza. (almorzar, ir) _____

7. Mi madre siempre nos _____ a ver películas de Disney. (llevar) _____

8. Todos los días mi exesposo me _____ poesías horribles. (escribir) _____

9. Mi primera novia _____ muy inteligente, pero no le _____ nada la política y a mí me _____. (ser, gustar, encantar) _____

**ACTIVIDAD 18** **Mi vida en Tegucigalpa** Complete this description about Mario's life while he was living in Tegucigalpa. Use the imperfect.

Todos los días yo _____ (1. levantarse) temprano para ir a trabajar.

_____ (2. Caminar) al trabajo porque _____ (3. vivir) muy cerca.

_____ (4. Trabajar) en una escuela de inglés y _____ (5. enseñar)

cuatro clases al día, un total de veinticuatro horas por semana. Mis estudiantes

_____ (6. ser) profesionales que _____ (7. necesitar) el inglés para

su trabajo. Todos _____ (8. ser) muy inteligentes e _____ (9. ir) a clase

muy bien preparados. Me _____ (10. gustar) mis estudiantes y muchas veces ellos y yo

_____ (11. salir) después de las clases. _____ (12. Comer) en

restaurantes o _____ (13. ir) al cine. Tegucigalpa es fantástica y quiero volver algún día.

# Un poco de todo

**ACTIVIDAD 19** **Wimbledon** **Parte A.** Choose the appropriate verbs from the list to complete the following summary of a tennis match. Write the imperfect form of the verb if there is an **i** and the preterit form if there is a **p.** Note: This and the following activity preview use of the preterit and imperfect together. You will learn more about this in **Capítulo 9.**

|  |  |  |  |  |  |
|---|---|---|---|---|---|
| decir | esperar | estar | haber | poder | tener |
| empezar | estar | ganar | hacer | ser | |

Ayer _____ (1. i) mucha gente en el estadio de Wimbledon. _____ (2. i)

mucho calor y sol. Entre el público _____ (3. i) Nicolás Almagro, el príncipe William,

Penélope Cruz, Javier Bardem, Lionel Messi y otra gente famosa. Todo el mundo _____ (4. i)

ver el partido entre el español Rafael Nadal y el serbio Novak Djokovic. _____ (5. i)

las dos y media cuando _____ (6. p) el partido; todos _____ (7. i) en

silencio; nadie _____ (8. i) nada, esperando ansiosamente la primera pelota. Después

de hora y media de juego en el calor intenso, Nadal _____ (9. p) un accidente y no

_____ (10. p) continuar. Así que Novak Djokovic _____ (11. p) el

partido.

**Parte B.** Read the paragraphs again and answer these questions.

1. Is the imperfect or the preterit used to give past description? _____
2. Is the imperfect or the preterit used to narrate what occurred? _____

**ACTIVIDAD 20 El robo** Yesterday you witnessed a theft and you had to go to the police station to make a statement. Look at the drawings and complete the conversation with the police in complete sentences. Use the preterit and the imperfect as cued by the questions.

Illustrations: © Cengage Learning 2013

POLICÍA   ¿Qué hora era cuando vio Ud. el robo?

TÚ        _____

POLICÍA   ¿Dónde estaba Ud. y dónde estaba la víctima?

TÚ        _____

POLICÍA   ¿Qué hizo específicamente el ladrón *(thief)*?

TÚ        _____

          _____

POLICÍA   ¿Cómo era físicamente el ladrón?

TÚ        _____

          _____

POLICÍA   ¿Tenía bigote o barba? La víctima nos dijo que tenía barba.

TÚ        _____

POLICÍA   ¿Y la descripción del carro?

TÚ        _____

          _____

POLICÍA   ¿Quién manejaba? ¿Lo vio Ud. bien? ¿Sabe cómo era?

TÚ        _____

POLICÍA   Muchas gracias por ayudarnos.

Nombre _____  Sección _____  Fecha _____

**ACTIVIDAD 21** **Los niños de ayer y de hoy** Sonia, the Mexican-American blogger, and Julieta, the Venezuelan blogger, are comparing what they used to do when they were 13 years old with what 13-year-olds in the U.S. do now. Complete their conversation using the imperfect or the present.

SONIA   Cuando yo tenía trece años, _____

_____.

JULIETA   Yo iba al cine, salía con grupos de amigos y viajaba con mis padres.

SONIA   También _____

_____.

JULIETA   Pero hoy... ¡los adolescentes parecen adultos!

SONIA   Sí, es verdad, hoy los jóvenes en los Estados Unidos _____

_____.

JULIETA   ¡Es una lástima!

SONIA   Pero eso no es todo; también _____

_____.

JULIETA   Son como pequeños adultos; casi no tienen infancia *(childhood)*.

**ACTIVIDAD 22** **¡Cómo cambiamos!** Paulina went to the same high school as you. You saw her yesterday and couldn't believe your eyes; she seems like a different person. Look at the drawings of Paulina and write an email to your friend Hernando. Tell him what Paulina was like and what she used to do (imperfect), and what she is like and what she does now (present).

© Cengage Learning 2013

Hola, Hernando:

No lo vas a creer; acabo de ver a Paulina Mateos. ¿La recuerdas?

Recuerdas que era _____

_____

_____

_____

Pues ahora _____

_____

_____

Un abrazo,

_____

# Lectura

## Estrategia de lectura: Finding References

Understanding the relationship between words and sentences can help improve your understanding of a text. A text is usually full of pronouns and other words that are used to avoid redundancies. Common examples are possessive adjectives; demonstrative adjectives and pronouns; and subject, indirect-, and direct-object pronouns. Furthermore, as you have seen, subject pronouns are generally omitted when context allows it.

You will have a chance to practice identifying referents (the word or phrase to which a pronoun refers) while you read the next selection.

**ACTIVIDAD 23** **La geografía** Look at the map of Central America on the inside cover of your book and answer these questions.

1. ¿Con qué países limita Honduras? _____, _____ y _____

2. ¿Cuál de los tres países, Guatemala, Honduras o El Salvador, tiene más kilómetros de costa en el Caribe? _____

3. ¿Cuál de estos países no tiene costa en el Caribe: Guatemala o El Salvador? _____

4. ¿Qué país de Centroamérica limita con cuatro países? _____

**ACTIVIDAD 24** **Referencias** While you read the passage, write what the following words or phrases refer to.

1. línea 2: **esa región** _____

2. línea 8: **su** _____

3. línea 13: **Estas** _____

4. línea 22: **Allí** _____

5. línea 32: **ellos** _____

6. línea 38: **sus** _____

Now write what the subjects are of the following verbs.

7. línea 9: **fue** _____

8. línea 14: **construyeron** _____

9. línea 18: **se puede disfrutar** _____

10. línea 27: **es** _____

11. línea 34: **visitan** _____

# Un mosaico de tierras y de pueblos

Centroamérica es un mosaico de tierras y de pueblos[1]. Guatemala, Honduras, El Salvador y Belice forman la parte norte de Centroamérica. **En esa región** solo Belice es de habla inglesa. La zona tiene un paisaje diverso que incluye playas blancas, selvas tropicales[2], montañas de clima fresco, sabanas[3] fértiles y volcanes gigantescos. Su población incluye indígenas con costumbres
5   y lenguas precolombinas, descendientes de europeos, negros, mestizos y mulatos.

El Salvador, a pesar de ser el país más pequeño de la región, es el tercer exportador de café del mundo, después de Brasil y Colombia. El Salvador es además un país muy densamente poblado. La historia de ese país es "dolorosa y sangrienta", como dice **su** himno nacional, pero también **fue** el primer país en Centroamérica en levantarse contra la colonización española en
10   busca de su independencia.

Se puede decir que Honduras se divide en tres *grandes mundos*:

- **La civilización maya** Tanto para los arqueólogos como los turistas, las ruinas de Copán son un lugar de mucho interés. **Estas** contrastan con la arquitectura colonial de los pueblos y ciudades que **construyeron** los conquistadores y los edificios modernos del siglo XXI.

15   - **La naturaleza tropical** Honduras es un país relativamente pequeño de solo 112.090 kilómetros cuadrados de territorio, pero contiene 64 ecositemas diferentes.

- **Las recreaciones en el Caribe** Honduras tiene costa tanto en el Pacífico como en el Caribe, pero en las aguas del este del país **se puede disfrutar** de uno de los arrecifes de coral más grandes del mundo.

20   Gracias a esos tres *grandes mundos,* el turismo es la segunda industria de Honduras después de las maquiladoras (fábricas de otros países instaladas en Honduras).

Al norte de El Salvador y Honduras está Guatemala. **Allí** se encuentran ruinas de la civilización maya también. Tikal, con sus 576 kilómetros cuadrados, tiene la zona arqueólogica más grande de todo el continente americano. Pero hasta 1848, el mundo no sabía
25   nada de la existencia de este maravilloso lugar protegido, cubierto y escondido por las plantas de la selva tropical. La Universidad de Pennsylvania empezó las excavaciones iniciales hace unos 60 años; un proceso que continúa hoy bajo el control de Guatemala. Hoy día **es** una de las atracciones turísticas de mayor importancia de toda Centroamérica.

La sangre indígena predomina en esta zona. El 90% de la población de El Salvador y
30   Honduras es mestiza. Más de un 40% de los guatemaltecos son descendientes directos de los mayas y hablan una variedad de lenguas indígenas; ellos forman la población indígena de sangre pura más grande de Centroamérica. Entre **ellos,** una de las más famosas es Rigoberta Menchú (1959– ), defensora de derechos humanos y recipiente del Premio Nobel de la Paz.

Cuando **visitan** esta parte del hemisferio occidental, los turistas no solo ven las ruinas
35   que dan testimonio a la existencia de grandes civilizaciones sino también ven las caras de su gente, oyen hablar sus lenguas y pueden probar la misma comida que cocinaban en la época precolombina. Hoy día es común oír a los descendientes de los mayas hablando quiché, mam o chortí en **sus** conversaciones con familiares y amigos. Uno los ve hablando con su celular en las calles de las ciudades de la zona donde el pasado y el futuro se encuentran.

[1] *peoples*  [2] *tropical rainforests*  [3] *plains*

**ACTIVIDAD 25** **Preguntas** Place a check mark before the country or countries being described.

1. Tiene ruinas mayas de mucha importancia arqueológica.

    _____ Guatemala _____ Honduras _____ El Salvador

2. Este país tiene menos kilómetros cuadrados que los otros países de la zona.

    _____ Guatemala _____ Honduras _____ El Salvador

3. La lucha (struggle) contra la corona española para dar fin a la época colonial de Centroamérica comenzó en este país.

    _____ Guatemala _____ Honduras _____ El Salvador

4. Sus arrecifes de coral son impresionantes.

    _____ Guatemala _____ Honduras _____ El Salvador

5. Tiene el índice más alto de indígenas.

    _____ Guatemala _____ Honduras _____ El Salvador

6. Rigoberta Menchú es de este país.

    _____ Guatemala _____ Honduras _____ El Salvador

**ACTIVIDAD 26** **¿Qué aprendiste?** Write in Spanish five things that you learned from this reading.

_____

_____

_____

_____

_____

_____

_____

_____

# Cosas que ocurrieron

## Vocabulario esencial I

### La salud

**ACTIVIDAD  1**  **¿Buena salud?**  Unscramble the following letters to form health-related words. Write accents where necessary.

1. nacaamubil _____
2. gernsa _____
3. igper _____
4. nfniieócc _____
5. clseoísraof _____
6. irrdaea _____
7. ssáneau _____
8. dígraofaari _____
9. efbire _____
10. tceorsar _____
11. gaelair _____
12. aehidr _____

### Los medicamentos y otras palabras relacionadas

**ACTIVIDAD  2**  **Asociaciones**  Match the items from Column A with the medicine-related words in Column B.

| **A** | **B** |
|---|---|
| 1. _____ radiografía | a. receta médica |
| 2. _____ Contac | b. escalofríos |
| 3. _____ ACE | c. fractura |
| 4. _____ Robitussin | d. diarrea |
| 5. _____ 103ºF, 39ºC | e. dolor de cabeza |
| 6. _____ Pepto-Bismol | f. gotas |
| 7. _____ aspirina | g. jarabe |
| 8. _____ Band-Aid | h. fiebre |
| 9. _____ 2 pastillas al día por 1 semana | i. curita |
| 10. _____ Visine | j. cápsulas |
|  | k. vendaje |

**ACTIVIDAD 3** **Los remedios** Complete the following conversation that takes place in a pharmacy.

| | |
|---|---|
| CLIENTE | Tengo un dolor de cabeza terrible. |
| FARMACÉUTICA | ¿Por qué no _____? |
| CLIENTE | ¿Tiene Bayer? |
| FARMACÉUTICA | Claro que sí. ¿Algo más? |
| CLIENTE | Sí, mi hijo tiene un catarro muy fuerte y fiebre. |
| FARMACÉUTICA | Entonces, él tiene que _____. |
| CLIENTE | ¡Ay! No le gustan las cápsulas. ¿No tiene pastillas de Tylenol? |
| FARMACÉUTICA | _____. |
| CLIENTE | También tiene tos. |
| FARMACÉUTICA | Bien, pues debe comprarle _____. |
| CLIENTE | Y mi marido se cortó la mano. |
| FARMACÉUTICA | Entonces, _____. ¿Algo más? |
| CLIENTE | Creo que es todo. |
| FARMACÉUTICA | Ya entiendo por qué le duele la cabeza. |

# Gramática para la comunicación I

## Narrating and Describing in the Past (Part 1): The Preterit and the Imperfect

**ACTIVIDAD 4** **Me jugué la vida.** **Parte A.** Read the following description of how to use the preterit and imperfect when narrating in the past.

When narrating in the past, if you simply want to list a series of occurrences in the past, you need only the preterit.

> Three bears **left** their house.
> They **went** to the woods.
> A child **arrived** at the house, **knocked** on the door, and **opened** it.
> She **entered** the house.

If you want to go beyond the **who did what** (preterit) part of the story, you need to use the imperfect (shown in italics).

> There *were* three bears that *lived* in a cute little house in the woods. It *was* a beautiful day. The birds *were singing* and the sun *was shining*. So the three bears **decided** to go for a walk and **left** their house. While they *were enjoying* their walk, a child **arrived** at the house. She *was* young, blond, tired, and hungry. She **knocked** on the door, but no one **answered** because no one *was* home. The door *was* slightly ajar, so she **went** inside.

In **Part B** you will read a story in English and decide if the verbs should be in the preterit or the imperfect if the story were to be told in Spanish. First, read the following questions and answers; then refer back to them as needed.

1. Is this a completed action (similar to a photograph or a finger snap)? If yes, **preterit.**
   The child **knocked** on the door. (click/snap)
   She **opened** the door. (click/snap)

2. Does the verb indicate the start or end of a past action? If yes, **preterit.**
   The bears **started** their walk at 10:00 and **ended** it at 4:00.

3. Does the verb refer to a completed action that was limited by time? If yes, **preterit.**
   They **walked** for six hours.

4. Does the verb refer to a habitual action or recurring events in the past? If yes, *imperfect.*
   Every day Mama Bear *used to take* Baby Bear for a walk. Every Saturday Papa Bear *went* with them.

5. Does the verb refer to an action or state in progress in the past? If yes, *imperfect.*
   The bears *lived* in the woods and *were* very happy.

6. Does the verb refer to an action in progress that occurred while another action was happening? If yes, *imperfect.*
   While the bears *walked (were walking)* in the woods, the girl *explored (was exploring)* their house.

7. Does the verb refer to an action in progress that occurred when another action happened or interrupted it? If yes, *imperfect,* **preterit.**
   While the bears *walked (were walking)* in the woods, the girl **broke** a chair.

8. Is the verb being used to describe something in the past? If yes, *imperfect.*
   Baby Bear *was* little, but he *had* big paws and an engaging personality.

9. Is the verb being used to express time and age in the past? If yes, *imperfect.*
   It *was* 4:05 in the afternoon. Baby Bear *was* only one year old.

## Parte B. The following is a story about a car accident. As you read it, write *P* for preterit and *I* for imperfect for the indicated verbs.

I was _____ (1) a student in Buenos Aires and it was _____ (2) a Friday. I wanted _____ (3) to go to Mar del Plata to visit friends and didn't have _____ (4) a lot of money, so a friend and I decided _____ (5) to hitchhike. Classes ended _____ (6) and I went _____ (7) with my friend to the road to Mar del Plata. It was _____ (8) a beautiful day. We stuck out _____ (9) our thumbs and immediately a car stopped _____ (10) to give us a ride. The car was _____ (11) new and only had _____ (12) 5000 kilometers on the odometer. It was _____ (13) a four-door sedan. My friend sat _____ (14) in the front seat and I sat _____ (15) in the back. The driver was _____ (16) a very nice businessman.

I took off _____ (17) my shoes and soon fell asleep _____ (18) in the back seat. Some time later, we passed _____ (19) a car. We were going _____ (20) quite fast—about 130 kilometers per hour (80 mph), when our car hit _____ (21) a bump in the road and the axle broke _____ (22). The car began _____ (23) to zigzag. We collided _____ (24) head-on with another car. Both cars flew _____ (25) up in the air and our car started _____ (26) to burn. The driver and my friend were _____ (27) unconscious and still in the car. With the impact, my head pushed _____ (28) open the back door and I flew _____ (29) out of the car.

Two couples, who were _____ (30) about 70 years old, were returning _____ (31) from a vacation on the coast when they saw _____ (32) the accident. The men jumped _____ (33) out of their car and ran _____ (34) toward ours. First, they got out _____ (35) the driver. Then they went _____ (36) to get my friend. Her seat was tilted _____ (37) forward and was _____ (38) jammed. Her seatbelt was _____ (39) stuck. One of the men cut _____ (40) the seatbelt with a pocket knife and they finally got _____ (41) her out. While they were pulling _____ (42) her out of the car, one of the men's pants caught fire _____ (43). Then they saw _____ (44) me. I was _____ (45) unconscious on the pavement about 10 meters from the car, but they did not come _____ (46) closer since the car was burning _____ (47). The car never did explode ____ (48). When the fire died down _____ (49), the men came _____ (50) to check on me. I awoke _____ (51) 16 hours later, in a hospital.

Thank goodness no one died _____ (52) in the accident. I spent _____ (53) 17 days in the hospital and then went back _____ (54) to Buenos Aires and returned _____ (55) to my studies.

Today everyone is fine. I only have two little scars as reminders of the accident!

**ACTIVIDAD 5** **¿Imperfecto o pretérito?** Complete the following sentences with the correct preterit or imperfect form of the indicated verbs.

1. Ayer yo _____ a un gimnasio nuevo por primera vez. Allí la gente
   _____ gimnasia aeróbica, _____ y
   _____ pesas. (ir, hacer, nadar, levantar)

2. De pequeña todos los veranos yo _____ un mes en la playa con mi familia. A mí
   me _____. (pasar, encantar)

3. El año pasado durante cuatro meses Manuel y Carmen _____ con turistas en
   Punta del Este. Por eso, ellos _____ un apartamento. (trabajar, alquilar)

4. Todo el sábado pasado _____ náuseas y fiebre y por eso no fui a trabajar. (tener)

5. Javier _____ a 150 kilómetros por hora cuando lo _____ la
   policía. (manejar, ver)

6. Cuando Roberto me _____, yo _____ y por eso no
   _____ el teléfono. (llamar, ducharse, contestar)

7. El año pasado cuando nosotros _____ por Argentina, _____ a
   un concierto de Los Babasónicos. (viajar, ir)

**ACTIVIDAD 6** **¿Qué le pasaba?** Complete this excerpt of an email about a pair of newlyweds. For each blank, select the appropriate verb from the left margin and write the correct form in the imperfect or preterit.

entrar

estar

estar

levantarse

pasar

preparar

tener

Es increíble el cambio que veo en César después de que se casó. Tú sabes que él nunca _____ (1) en la cocina cuando estaba soltero. Y el viernes pasado yo _____ (2) por la casa de él para dejarle algo y mientras su esposa Isabel miraba la televisión, él _____ (3) la cena. Cuando él _____ (4) preparando la ensalada, yo _____ (5) segura que la ensalada _____ (6) demasiado vinagre; entonces _____ (7) del sofá para ayudarlo, pero resulta que César sabía exactamente cómo hacer una ensalada y al final, ¡qué ensalada más deliciosa!

creer

decir

empezar

poner

ser

Isabel me _____ (8) que el otro día mientras ella _____ (9) la ropa en la lavadora, César _____ (10) a ayudarla. Yo _____ (11) que él _____ (12) muy machista (sé que todavía es en ciertos sentidos), pero últimamente está cambiando. Él y su padre son muy similares.

**ACTIVIDAD 7** **El informe del detective** You are a private detective and you spent the morning tracking the husband of your client. Using complete sentences, write the report that you are going to give to your client. Say what her husband did during the morning.

**trabajar / la primera parte de la mañana**

**salir / 11:00**

**mientras tomar café / llegar**

**ellos entrar / tienda**

**mientras probarse vestido / comprar perfume**

**volver**

Illustrations:
© Cengage Learning 2013

_____

_____

_____

_____

_____

**ACTIVIDAD 8** **La verdad** Complete the following conversation between the husband from the previous activity and his wife.

ELLA   ¿Qué hiciste hoy?

ÉL   Nada; _____.

ELLA   ¿Toda la mañana _____?

ÉL   Sí, excepto cuando _____ para comprarte esto.

ELLA   Un regalo… A ver… ¡Un vestido y un perfume!

ÉL   Claro, hoy hace diez años que te _____.

ELLA   Es que… es que…

ÉL   ¿Quieres decirme algo?

ELLA   Es que yo creía que tú _____

_____.

ÉL   No, ella era _____.

Pero, ¿cómo supiste que fui con ella a la tienda?

**ACTIVIDAD 9** **¿Qué estaban haciendo?** The people in the drawing below heard an explosion and looked toward the street to see what happened. Write what they were doing when they heard the explosion.

▶ El mecánico *El mecánico estaba trabajando cuando oyó la explosión.*

1. La señora en la ventana _____ _____ la comida cuando

_____ la explosión.

2. Los dos señores en el banco _____ _____ cuando

_____ la explosión.

3. El niño _____ _____ al fútbol cuando

_____ la explosión.

4. El señor en el balcón _____ _____ en su cama cuando _____ la explosión.

5. La joven en el balcón _____ _____ en el baño cuando _____ la explosión.

# Narrating and Describing in the Past (Part II): Time Expressions

**ACTIVIDAD** **10** **Las vacaciones** Complete the following sentences about vacations using the preterit or the imperfect. Pay attention to time expressions.

1. De joven, durante los veranos, a menudo _____ en bicicleta con un grupo de amigos en el parque cerca de mi casa. (montar)

2. Estuve en Paraguay cuatro días en febrero. Todos los días _____ en la piscina del hotel por la mañana y por la tarde _____ al golf en el Paraná Country Club. (nadar, jugar)

3. Cuando Carlos _____ en Chile, de vez en cuando _____ a la playa de Viña del Mar con su familia. (vivir, ir)

4. Todos los años, mi familia _____ a la casa de mi abuela para la Navidad. Mi abuela _____ unas comidas espectaculares. (ir, preparar)

5. Después de terminar las negociaciones con la aerolínea LAN en Chile, yo _____ cinco días en Santiago. Cada día _____ viñedos *(vineyards)* diferentes de la zona. (pasar, visitar)

**ACTIVIDAD** **11** **El encuentro** Many people have a strict daily routine and when they do something different, interesting things can happen. Complete this paragraph to tell how Mr. and Mrs. Durán met. Fill in each blank with a logical word or words. Pay attention to the time expressions to help you decide whether to use the preterit or imperfect.

Con frecuencia el Sr. Durán _____ (1) y muchas veces _____ (2). Estas actividades eran parte de su rutina diaria. También _____ (3), _____ (4) y _____ (5). Pero el 3 de marzo fue diferente; no _____ (6). Fue a la playa de Viña del Mar y allí vio a la Srta. Guzmán. Pensaba que era una mujer muy _____ (7) y quería conocerla. Mientras ella _____ (8), él _____ (9). De repente, _____ (10). Así se conocieron y llevan diez años de casados.

# Un poco de todo

**ACTIVIDAD 12** **Los síntomas** Complete the following conversations between patients and their doctors.

1. PACIENTE A     Hace tres días _____

   _____

   _____.

   MÉDICO     Creo que Ud. le tiene alergia a algo, pero vamos a hacer unos análisis.

2. PACIENTE B     Toda la noche mi hijo tosió, _____

   _____.

   Ahora está bien, pero no quiere comer.

   DOCTORA     Creo que solo tenía gripe, pero debe obligarlo a comer algo.

3. PACIENTE C     Todas las mañanas _____

   _____.

   Ahora estoy mejor, pero no sé qué me pasa.

   MÉDICO     Vamos a ver. Creo que puede estar embarazada.

**ACTIVIDAD 13** **Un cuento** **Parte A.** In this workbook, normally you read a passage and then you answer questions to see if you understood the story. Now you're going to do the opposite. First, read through all the questions that follow. Then use your imagination to answer them.

1. ¿Adónde fueron Ricardo y su esposa de vacaciones? _____

   _____

2. ¿Cómo era el lugar y qué tiempo hacía? _____

   _____

3. ¿Qué hicieron durante las vacaciones? _____

   _____

4. ¿Cómo se murió la esposa de Ricardo? _____

   _____

5. ¿Qué estaba haciendo Ricardo cuando se fracturó la pierna? _____

   _____

6. La policía no dejó a Ricardo volver a su ciudad. ¿Por qué? _____

   _____

7. ¿Quién era la señora del vestido negro y los diamantes? _____

   _____

8. ¿Cómo era físicamente la señora? _____

   _____

Nombre _____ Sección _____ Fecha _____

9. ¿Qué importancia tiene ella? _____

_____

10. Al fin, la policía supo la verdad. ¿Cuál era? _____

_____

**Parte B.** Now create a story based on your answers from **Parte A.** Use the following words and phrases to enhance the telling of your story.

| | | |
|---|---|---|
| **primero** | **de repente** | **después** |
| **luego/más tarde** | **mientras** | **al final** |
| **media hora más tarde** | **después de una hora** | |

_____

_____

_____

_____

_____

_____

_____

_____

_____

_____

_____

_____

# Vocabulario esencial II

## El carro

**ACTIVIDAD 14** **Las partes del carro** Identify each numbered automobile part. Include the definite article in your answers.

1. _____
2. _____
3. _____
4. _____
5. _____
6. _____
7. _____

© Cengage Learning 2013

**ACTIVIDAD 15** **Problemas, problemas y más problemas** Complete this letter that Lorenzo Martín wrote to a car rental agency in Argentina following a terrible experience with a rental car.

---

Caracas, 15 de febrero de 2013

Estimados señores:

   Hace tres semanas, alquilé un carro de su compañía en Bariloche con transmisión automática y tuve muchísimos problemas. Primero, estaba bajando una montaña y de repente noté que no funcionaban muy bien los _____ (1). Por suerte no tuve un accidente. Paré en una gasolinera y me los arreglaron. Más tarde empezó a llover, pero no podía ver nada porque el _____ (2) del lado del conductor no funcionaba. Después, cuando llegué al hotel, no podía sacar las maletas del _____ (3) porque la llave que Uds. me dieron no era la llave que necesitaba; pero por fin un policía me lo abrió. Esa noche salí y no pude ver bien porque una de las _____ (4) no funcionaba. Al día siguiente hacía muchísimo calor y el _____ (5) no echaba aire frío, solo aire caliente. Y para colmo, me pusieron una _____ (6) por exceso de velocidad por ir a 140 kilómetros por hora, pero el velocímetro del carro marcaba solo 110.

   Hace muchos años que alquilo automóviles de su compañía sin problemas, pero después de esta experiencia, creo que voy a tener que ir a otra agencia de alquiler de carros.

Atentamente,

Lorenzo Martín

---

# Gramática para la comunicación II

## Narrating and Describing in the Past (Part III)

**ACTIVIDAD 16** **Las excusas** Read the following mini-conversations. Then complete them, using the preterit or imperfect of **ir** and **tener**. Remember that if you use **tuve/tuvo/**etc. **que** + *infinitive* or **fui, fuimos,** etc., it indicates that the action actually took place. The imperfect of **ir a** + *infinitive* means that the person intended to do the action, but did not. The imperfect of **tener que** + *infinitive* is ambiguous, therefore the listener does not know if the action took place or not.

1. —Había muchas personas en la fiesta.

   —Entonces, ¿te divertiste?

   —Sí y no. Y tú, ¿dónde estabas? Prometiste ir.

   —_____ a ir, pero _____ que ayudar a mi madre, que estaba enferma.

2. —_____ que ir al dentista ayer.

   —¿Fuiste o no?

   —No fui porque el dentista estaba enfermo.

3. —Nosotros _____ que ir al banco ayer.

   —¿Al final _____ o no?

   —Sí, y el director del banco nos ayudó con un problema que teníamos.

4. —¿Me compraste el champú?

   —_____ a comprártelo, pero no _____ a la tienda

   porque _____ un pequeño accidente con el carro.

   —¡No me digas! ¿Estás bien?

   —_____ que ir al hospital.

   —¡Por Dios! ¿Y qué te dijo el médico?

   —No mucho. Estoy bien, solo tengo que tomar aspirinas.

5. —Nosotros _____ a ir a ver una película, pero llegamos tarde al cine.

   —Entonces, ¿qué hicieron?

   —Volvimos a casa.

**ACTIVIDAD 17 ¿Pretérito o imperfecto?** Write the correct preterit or imperfect form of the indicated verbs. Remember that the preterit indicates the start of an action; therefore, use the preterit of **saber** to say *I/he/she/etc. found out something* and use the preterit of **conocer** to say *I/you/they/etc. met someone, became acquainted with someone or some place.*

1. El otro día mi novio _____ a mi padre. (conocer)

2. Ayer yo _____ la verdad, pero no le _____ nada a nadie. (saber, decir)

3. Ella no _____ su número de teléfono, por eso no lo _____. (saber, llamar)

4. Yo _____ en Asunción por tres años, por eso cuando _____ a esa ciudad

   el año pasado, no _____ mapa. Ya _____ la ciudad muy bien. (vivir, volver, usar, conocer)

5. Margarita _____ las vacaciones en Hollywood, pero tuvo mala suerte y no

   _____ a nadie famoso. (pasar, conocer)

6. Raúl _____ al profesor Guzmán en encro del año pasado. _____ con él

   varias veces sobre sus investigaciones. Así que cuando _____ a tomar su clase, ya lo

   _____ muy bien. (conocer, hablar, empezar, conocer)

**ACTIVIDAD 18** **La semana pasada** Write two sentences describing what you were going to do last week, but didn't. Then write two sentences describing what you had to do, but didn't. Finally, tell what you had to do last week and did. Use **iba a** + *infinitive* and **tenía/tuve que** + *infinitive*.

1. _____

2. _____

3. _____

4. _____

5. _____

## Describing: Past Participle as an Adjective

**ACTIVIDAD 19** **Descripciones** Complete the following sentences with the correct past participle form of the indicated verbs.

1. Llegamos tarde y el banco estaba _____. (cerrar)

2. El niño que perdió su perro está _____ allí. (sentar)

3. Nevó anoche en Portillo y las pistas de esquí están _____ de medio metro de nieve nueva: perfectas condiciones para esquiar. (cubrir)

4. Las tiendas están _____ los domingos, excepto en el centro comercial, donde están _____ de las doce a las cinco. (cerrar, abrir)

5. María, ¿por qué estás _____? (preocupar)

6. El contrato estaba _____, pero nadie quería firmarlo. (escribir)

7. Mi tío vende carros _____. (usar)

8. Después del accidente, el limpiaparabrisas estaba _____ y llevamos el carro a un garaje. Ahora el carro está _____ y _____. (romper, arreglar, lavar)

9. Los niños están _____ y _____. (bañar, vestir)

10. Los niños tienen las manos _____, la comida está _____ y la mesa está _____; ya podemos comer. (lavar, hacer, poner)

11. El libro *La gallina degollada y otros cuentos* de Horacio Quiroga está _____ al inglés. El título es *The Decapitated Chicken and Other Stories* y se puede comprar en Amazon.com. (traducir)

Nombre _____ Sección _____ Fecha _____

**ACTIVIDAD 20** **El mensaje** Finish this email message that Alicia sent to Paco, a professional pianist. Use the correct past participle form of the following verbs: **alquilar, morir, preparar, reservar,** and **vender.**

Ya está todo listo para tu viaje: La habitación está

_____ (1) en el Hotel El Cóndor. El carro está

_____ (2) en Hertz. Todas las entradas están

_____ (3). Todo está _____ (4)

para tu concierto del jueves. ¡Mucha suerte! Después de tanto

trabajo, estoy _____ (5) y creo que voy a dormir

por tres días.

Alicia

# Un poco de todo

**ACTIVIDAD 21** **Casi se mueren** Complete these stories about people in risky situations. Write the correct preterit or imperfect form of the indicated verbs that appear in the correct order.

1. Un amigo, que _____ celebrando el final de semestre, _____ mucho en una fiesta. De repente _____ un poco mareado, pero _____ la llave del carro de un amigo y _____ de la fiesta. Por suerte, una persona lo _____ y otros _____ para quitarle la llave. Al final, ellos lo _____ que llevar a casa.
   **(estar, beber, sentirse, tomar, salir, ver, salir, tener)**

2. Una amiga _____ manejando un carro alquilado e _____ a mucha velocidad cuando un niño _____ detrás de un balón de fútbol enfrente de su carro. Ella _____, pero en ese momento los frenos no _____. Mi amiga no _____ que el carro _____ problemas con los frenos. Por suerte no _____ al niño, pero _____ contra un árbol. Gracias a Dios, no le _____ nada a nadie.
   **(estar, ir, correr, frenar, funcionar, saber, tener, atropellar, chocar, pasar)**

**ACTIVIDAD 22 Un email** Rebeca, who is from Seattle but studying abroad, wrote the following email to a friend who is a Spanish-language professor in the United States. Complete her message by choosing a logical verb and writing the infinitive, present participle, or correct form in the present, preterit, or imperfect.

Querida Vicky:

Ya hace cinco meses que _____ a Uruguay y por fin hoy _____

unos minutos para _____ tu email. Las cosas aquí me van de

maravilla. Por cuatro meses _____ en una residencia estudiantil,

pero ahora _____ un apartamento con cuatro amigas suramericanas.

_____ muy simpáticas y estoy _____ mucho sobre el Cono Sur.

   **(alquilar, aprender, contestar, llegar, ser, tener, vivir)**

Durante el verano pasado, _____ clases de arte y arquitectura

de lunes a viernes por tres semanas. Durante este tiempo, nosotros

_____ a la universidad y _____ museos y lugares

históricos como la Plaza Independencia, el Parque Rodó y la Fortaleza del

Cerro. Cuando _____ por primera vez en el Museo Nacional de Artes

Visuales, me _____ grandísimo, y solamente _____ las

salas de los pintores nacionales, como Joaquín Torres García.

   **(entrar, ir, parecer, tener, ver, visitar)**

_____ enamorada de Uruguay. Me _____ la música porque

tiene mucha influencia del tango y de la milonga. El otro día _____

por la calle cuando _____ a un grupo de jóvenes tocando y bailando

"La cumparsita"; _____ unos veinte años y ellos me _____

que, con frecuencia, _____ en la calle para _____ dinero.

   **(bailar, caminar, decir, estar, fascinar, ganar, tener, ver)**

   Mis clases _____ hace dos meses; después _____ seis

semanas de vacaciones y las clases _____ otra vez la semana pasada.

Además de tomar clases, _____ enseñando inglés desde junio para

_____ técnicas nuevas de enseñanza. Y tú, ¿cómo estás? ¿Todo bien?

   **(empezar, estar, probar, tener, terminar)**

Un abrazo desde Montevideo de tu amiga,

Rebeca

**ACTIVIDAD 23** **¿Qué hiciste?** Using complete sentences, answer the following questions about the last concert you saw.

1. ¿A quién viste? _____

2. ¿Con quién fuiste? _____

3. ¿A qué hora empezó? _____

4. ¿Cuándo terminó? _____

5. ¿Dónde se sentaron Uds.? _____

6. ¿Pudiste ver y oír bien? _____

7. ¿Cuánto te costó la entrada? _____

8. ¿Qué canciones tocaron? _____

9. ¿Cuál de las canciones fue tu favorita? _____

**ACTIVIDAD 24** **¿Cómo era?** Answer these questions about the same concert using complete sentences.

1. ¿Había mucha gente? _____

2. ¿Cuántos músicos (musicians) había? _____

3. ¿Qué ropa llevaban los músicos? _____
   _____

4. ¿Cómo era el escenario (set)? _____
   _____

5. ¿Cómo reaccionaba el público mientras escuchaba las canciones? _____
   _____

6. ¿Usaron efectos especiales (láser, video, etc.)? Si contestas que sí: ¿qué hacían los músicos mientras Uds. veían los efectos especiales? _____
   _____
   _____

7. ¿Valió la pena ir al concierto o no? ¿Por qué sí o no? _____
   _____

**ACTIVIDAD 25** **Un concierto** In order to describe an event well, you need to use the preterit and the imperfect. Use the information from **Actividad 23** and **Actividad 24** to write an email to a friend telling him/her about the concert you saw. Describe what you did, what happened, and what the concert was like. Add more details if needed.

_____:

_____

_____

_____

_____

_____

_____

_____

_____

_____

_____

Un abrazo,

_____

# Lectura

## Estrategia de lectura: Finding References

In **Capítulo 8**, you practiced finding references while reading. In this chapter you will continue to practice this skill. Not only does indentifying references in reading help you to be a better reader, but it will also help you to be a better speaker and writer.

**ACTIVIDAD 26** **Predicción** Before reading the article about the Southern Cone, look at the following list of words and try to predict the topic of the article.

| indígenas | montañas | playas blancas |
| glaciares | mitología local | parque nacional |
| flora | fauna | patrimonio mundial |

1. ¿Cuál es el tema del artículo?
   a. la naturaleza del Cono Sur
   b. la destrucción de los ecosistemas del Cono Sur
   c. el abuso de las grandes compañías petroleras y su efecto en la ecología

**ACTIVIDAD 27** **Lectura detallada** Read the article and answer the following questions.

1. En el párrafo 1 (línea 3), ¿cuál es el sujeto del verbo **contrastan**? _____

2. En el párrafo 2 (línea 8), ¿cuál es el sujeto del verbo **existe**? _____

3. En el párrafo 3 (línea 11), ¿quién o qué es **Cai Cai**? _____

4. En el párrafo 3 (línea 13), ¿quién o qué convirtió a los dos guerreros en piedra?
_____

5. En el párrafo 4 (línea 18), ¿cuáles son dos cosas que contrasta la frase **más altas que**?
_____ _____ y _____

6. En el párrafo 5 (línea 25), ¿a qué se refiere **Esta**? _____

7. En el párrafo 5 (línea 27), ¿a quién se refiere **ella**? _____

8. En el párrafo 5 (línea 30), ¿cuál es un sinónimo de "se enojó"? _____

9. En el párrafo 5 (línea 30), ¿quién se enojó? ¿El dios, Tarobá o Naipí? _____

10. En el párrafo 5 (líneas 31–32), ¿quiénes son **los enamorados**? _____

# El Cono Sur y su belleza natural

El Cono Sur se caracteriza por su diversidad y su belleza natural. Esta belleza varía desde la selva paraguaya hasta el árido desierto de Atacama en el norte de Chile. También se encuentran las playas blancas de Chile y Uruguay que **contrastan** con los Andes y sus nieves eternas en Argentina y Chile. Entre las bellezas naturales también están el Parque Nacional Torres del
5 Paine y el Parque Nacional Iguazú.

El Parque Nacional Torres del Paine se encuentra en la zona de la Patagonia de Chile y es tan espectacular como el Parque Yellowstone o el Yosemite. Tiene una variedad de ecosistemas con flora y fauna que no **existe** en otras partes del mundo. Entre los lugares más interesantes para visitar están el lago y glaciar Grey y los Cuernos del Paine, dos montañas que son gigantescos
10 pilares de granito que se formaron hace 12 millones de años.

La mitología local dice que una serpiente llamada **Cai Cai** causó una inundación masiva para matar con el agua a la tribu guerrera[1] que vivía en Torres del Paine. Cuando el agua retrocedió, Cai Cai tomó a los dos guerreros más grandes y los convirtió en piedra; ahora son dos famosas montañas que se llaman los Cuernos del Paine que se pueden ver hoy día en ese parque
15 nacional chileno.

En el Parque Nacional Iguazú se encuentran las cataratas del Iguazú que están localizadas en el río del mismo nombre, en la frontera entre Argentina y Brasil cerca de Paraguay. Tienen una caída de ochenta metros y son veinte metros **más altas que** las cataratas del Niágara entre los Estados Unidos y Canadá. El salto o catarata más importante es la Garganta del Diablo[2]. En el
20 lado brasileño hay una vista panorámica de las cataratas, pero en el lado argentino se puede caminar muy cerca de cada salto. Las cataratas no solo son ricas en flora y fauna; también son una fuente de electricidad para Argentina, Brasil y Paraguay. En 1984 la UNESCO declaró las cataratas del Iguazú patrimonio mundial.

[1] *warrior* [2] *Devil's Throat*

Los indígenas de esta zona explican el origen de
25  estas cataratas con una leyenda. **Esta** dice que el
dios de los indígenas eligió a Naipí, la hija del jefe
de la tribu, como esposa, pero **ella** se enamoró de
Tarobá y un día Naipí y Tarobá se fueron en una
canoa por el río Iguazú ("agua grande" en la lengua
30  indígena). Cuando el dios escuchó esto, se enfureció
y decidió crear las cataratas para matar a **los
enamorados** con su torrente de agua. Así terminó
la vida de los jóvenes amantes.

Tanto el Parque Nacional Torres del Paine como el
35  Parque Nacional Iguazú reciben anualmente una

Las cataratas del Iguazú, Argentina

© Debbie Rusch

gran cantidad de turistas que llegan a los parques a practicar turismo de aventura. En estos dos
parques se puede hacer *trekking* y caminatas.

**ACTIVIDAD 28 Las leyendas** Read the following sentences about the two legends. Mark **C** for
**cierto** if the statement is true and **F** for **falso** if it is false.

**Leyenda sobre los Cuernos del Paine**

1. _____    Cai Cai es una persona.

2. _____    Las personas de la tribu son violentas.

3. _____    Cai Cai mató a muchas personas con un incendio (*fire*) grande.

4. _____    Ahora, los dos guerreros son montañas que se llaman los Cuernos del Paine.

**Leyenda sobre las cataratas del Iguazú**

5. _____    Un dios quería casarse con Naipí.

6. _____    Naipí se enamoró del dios.

7. _____    *Iguazú* significa "río corto" en la lengua indígena.

8. _____    El dios se enfureció y mató a Naipí y a Tarobá con agua.

9. _____    Hoy día, el torrente de agua se llama las cataratas del Iguazú.

# Repaso

## Saber and conocer

In Chapter 4, you studied when to use **saber** and **conocer.**

You use **saber** to say what someone *knows how to do* and to state factual information that someone *knows*.

> Ella **sabe** esquiar muy bien.

> Él **sabe** la dirección de mi casa y el número de teléfono.

You use **conocer** when saying that someone knows a person or is familiar with a place or a thing.

> Yo **conozco** a Jesús Covarrubias; es de Puerto Varas, Chile.

> **Conozco** Puerto Varas; es un pueblo muy bonito.

When **saber** and **conocer** are used in the preterit, they have a different meaning when translated into English. This is because the use of the preterit implies the beginning of an action. Study these examples and their explanations.

> Verónica me contó todo y así por fin **supe** la verdad.
> *Veronica told me everything and that's how I found out the truth. (The start of knowing something is to find it out.)*

> **Conocí** a Hernán en una fiesta en casa de mis amigos.
> *I met Hernán at a party at my friends' house. (The start of knowing someone is to meet him/her.)*

**ACTIVIDAD 1** **Conversaciones** Complete the following conversations with the correct present, preterit, or imperfect form of **saber** or **conocer.**

1.  —Por favor, señor, ¿ _____ Ud. dónde está la calle Lavalle?

    —Lo siento, no _____ muy bien esta ciudad. _____ que está cerca de

    aquí, pero no _____ exactamente dónde.

2.  —Juan ya _____ que Jorge iba a ir a Viña del Mar este fin de semana con Paulina, pero

    no nos dijo nada.

    —Es verdad. ¿Cuándo lo _____ tú?

    —Cuando me lo dijo Paulina. ¿Y tú?

    —Lo _____ cuando Ricardo me lo dijo.

    —¿Ricardo? Yo no _____ a ningún Ricardo. ¿De quién hablas?

    —Trabaja en la agencia de viajes de la calle Andrés Bello.

    —Ah sí... Ricky. Lo _____ en un viaje que hice a la Patagonia.

3. —Oye, Carmen, ¿_____ qué línea de metro debo tomar para ir a la calle Aconcagua?

—Lo siento, no _____ la calle Aconcagua.

—Está cerca del Parque O'Higgins.

—_____ que la línea 2 del metro pasa por allí y tiene una parada que se llama Parque

O'Higgins.

—Gracias.

4. —¿Dónde _____ tu padre a tu madre?

—La _____ en un accidente de coche.

—¡¿De veras?!

—Él dice que los frenos no funcionaron y por eso chocó con el carro de mi madre.

—Bueno, todos nosotros _____ que tu padre no maneja bien... siempre tiene por lo

menos un accidente al año.

# En casa

## Vocabulario esencial I

### Los números ordinales

**ACTIVIDAD 1** **La primera actividad** Completa cada oración con el número ordinal apropiado.

1. Ellos viven en el _____ piso. (2)

2. Ricardo llegó en _____ lugar. (3)

3. María fue la _____ persona en recibir su dinero. (5)

4. Ana terminó _____. (7)

5. Perú ganó el _____ premio *(prize)*. (4)

6. Carlos llegó _____. (3)

7. Tengo que estudiar _____; después puedo salir. (1)

8. Compraron un apartamento en el _____ piso y pueden ver toda la ciudad. (9)

9. Guillermo fue el _____ hijo de su familia que terminó la universidad. (1)

10. Esta es la _____ oración. (10)

**ACTIVIDAD 2** **¿En qué piso?** Imagina que eres portero/a. Estos son los buzones *(mailboxes)* del edificio de apartamentos donde trabajas. Usando oraciones completas, contesta las preguntas que te hacen las visitas que van al edificio.

| 101 Martín | 301 Pascual | 501 Robles |
|---|---|---|
| 201 Orozco | 401 Cano | 601 Fuentes |

1. ¿En qué piso vive la familia Robles? *Los Robles* _____

_____

2. ¿En qué piso vive Pepe Cano? *Pepe* _____

3. ¿Sabe Ud. en qué piso viven los Sres. Martín? *Sí, ellos* _____ _____

_____

4. La Srta. Pascual vive en el sexto piso, ¿no? *No, ella* _____

_____

## Las habitaciones de una casa

**ACTIVIDAD 3** **La casa** Asocia las siguientes acciones con las habitaciones de una casa.

1. preparar comida _____

2. mirar la televisión _____

3. dormir _____

4. vestirse _____

5. llegar a casa _____

6. comer _____

7. afeitarse _____

**ACTIVIDAD 4** **¡Muchos gastos!** Cuando una persona alquila un apartamento, tiene muchos gastos. Escribe a qué gasto se refiere cada una de las siguientes descripciones. Usa el artículo definido en tus respuestas.

1. El dinero que se paga cada mes por un apartamento. _____

2. El dinero extra que se paga antes de empezar a vivir en un apartamento. _____

3. Cuando usas computadoras o lámparas, tienes que pagar esto. _____

4. Cuando te bañas o te duchas, tienes que pagar esto. _____

5. Cuando preparas la comida, tienes que pagar esto. _____

6. Si hace mucho frío y quieres sentir calor, tienes que pagar esto. _____

# Gramática para la comunicación I

## Using Other Affirmative and Negative Words

**ACTIVIDAD 5** **Afirmativos y negativos** Completa las siguientes oraciones con **algún, alguno, alguna, algunos, algunas, ningún, ninguno** o **ninguna**.

1. No tengo _____ clase interesante.

2. —¿Cuántos estudiantes vinieron anoche?

   —No vino _____.

3. ¿Tienes _____ libro de economía?

4. —Necesitamos _____ álbumes de salsa para la fiesta.

   —¿Álbumes de salsa? Sí, creo que tengo _____.

5. —¿Tienes una tarjeta telefónica?

   —No, no tengo _____.

6. —¿Limpiaste todas las habitaciones?

   —No todas, pero limpié _____.

7. —¿Conoces _____ restaurante bueno cerca de aquí?

   —No hay _____ bueno, pero hay un restaurante muy barato.

**ACTIVIDAD 6** **El mensaje** Completa este mensaje que Camila le escribió a su nueva compañera de apartamento. Usa palabras afirmativas y negativas (**ningún, algún, ninguna,** etc.).

---

Pilar:

Busqué y no encontré _____ (1) toalla limpia. Si

tienes tiempo, favor de lavarlas. Voy a ir al supermercado esta tarde para comprar

_____ (2) cosas; si quieres algo en especial, voy

a estar en la oficina y no hay _____ (3)

problema, puedes llamarme allí. Otra cosa, iba a sacar fotos del apartamento

para mandárselas a mis padres, pero mi celular está roto y no encontré

_____ (4) cámara y sé que hay por lo menos dos en el

apartamento. Sé que tenemos _____ (5) fotos muy

bonitas pero creo que están en tu celular. ¿Me las puedes mandar?

    Camila

P. D. Esta noche van a venir _____ (6) amigos para

estudiar.

---

## Describing Wants and Needs: The Present Subjunctive

**ACTIVIDAD 7** **Busco apartamento** Miguel busca apartamento. Completa lo que dice con la forma correcta del subjuntivo de los verbos indicados.

1. Busco un apartamento que _____ cerca del trabajo. (estar)

2. No me gusta subir escaleras *(stairs)*; por eso necesito un apartamento que _____ ascensor *(elevator)*. (tener)

3. Necesito estudiar; por eso, busco un apartamento que _____ tranquilo. (ser)

4. Tengo muchas plantas. Quiero un apartamento que _____ balcón. (tener)

5. No tengo mucho dinero; por eso, busco un apartamento que _____ poco. (costar)

**ACTIVIDAD 8** **¿Subjuntivo o indicativo?** Completa las siguientes oraciones con la forma apropiada del indicativo o del subjuntivo de los verbos indicados.

1. Mi novio conoce a una secretaria que _____ noventa palabras por minuto. (escribir)

2. Quiero un novio que _____ inteligente. (ser)

3. Mi director necesita un recepcionista que _____ hablar italiano. (saber)

4. Hice la reserva y voy a quedarme en un hotel que _____ cuatro piscinas. (tener)

5. Necesitamos un carro que _____ nuevo. (ser)

6. Quiero una esposa que _____ bien. (bailar)

7. No veo a nadie que nos _____ ayudar. (poder)

8. Necesito unas clases que no _____ antes de las 10. (empezar)

9. Tengo una profesora que no _____ exámenes. (dar)

10. Tenemos unos profesores que _____ bien las lecciones. (explicar)

11. Busco un trabajo que _____ bien. (pagar)

12. Necesito un vendedor que _____ en Caracas. (vivir)

13. No conozco a nadie que _____ un Mercedes-Benz. (tener)

14. En la librería tienen unos libros de arte que _____ muy poco. (costar)

15. No hay ningún carro aquí que me _____. (gustar)

**ACTIVIDAD 9 El apartamento perfecto** El año que viene vas a buscar apartamento. Completa esta descripción del apartamento ideal con la forma correcta del subjuntivo de los verbos **costar, estar, ser** y **tener.**

Voy a buscar un apartamento que _____ (1) dos dormitorios, una sala grande y dos

baños. Quiero un apartamento que _____ (2) cerca de la universidad. También necesito

un apartamento que _____ (3) balcón porque me gusta mucho el sol. Prefiero un

apartamento que _____ (4) moderno y que _____ (5) en buenas

condiciones. Pero lo más importante es que busco un apartamento que _____ (6) poco,

porque soy estudiante y no tengo mucho dinero.

**ACTIVIDAD 10 Habitación libre** Buscas un/a compañero/a de apartamento. Escribe un anuncio *(advertisement)* para describir a la persona perfecta.

Busco un/a compañero/a que _____

_____

_____

_____

**ACTIVIDAD 11 Una clase fácil** Ya tienes varias clases difíciles para el próximo semestre, pero necesitas unos créditos más. Buscas la clase perfecta: interesante pero sin mucho trabajo. Tu compañero/a de habitación siempre encuentra clases "fáciles". Descríbele la clase que buscas.

Necesito una clase fácil con un profesor que _____

_____

_____

_____

_____

# Un poco de todo

**ACTIVIDAD 12** **Los anuncios personales** **Parte A.** Recibiste la siguiente nota de un amigo. Completa la nota con palabras afirmativas y negativas (**ningún, algún, ninguna,** etc.).

Tengo un problema. Nunca conozco a _____

chica que quiera salir conmigo. Quiero escribir un anuncio

personal. Escribí _____ líneas, pero no me

salieron bien. De verdad no tengo _____

idea sobre qué escribir. ¿Por qué no me escribes el anuncio tú?

Gracias,

   *Miguel Ángel*

**Parte B.** Como tú eres una persona cómica y escribes bien, vas a escribir un anuncio personal para tu amigo Miguel Ángel. Primero, describe cómo es él y qué le gusta hacer (indicativo). Luego, describe el tipo de mujer que busca (subjuntivo). Recuerda que estás escribiendo por él.

Yo _____

_____

_____

_____

_____

# Vocabulario esencial II

## En la casa

**ACTIVIDAD 13** **¿Dónde está...?** Escribe en qué habitación o habitaciones normalmente encuentras los siguientes muebles y electrodomésticos. Incluye el artículo definido (**el/la**).

1. sofá _____

2. inodoro _____

3. horno _____

4. cama _____

5. estante _____

6. mesa y seis sillas _____

7. lavabo _____

8. refrigerador _____

9. televisor _____

10. congelador _____

11. cómoda _____

12. espejo _____

**ACTIVIDAD** **14** **Necesitamos...** Gonzalo acaba de alquilar un apartamento semiamueblado y le escribió el siguiente email a su compañero de apartamento. Mira el dibujo y completa el mensaje con los muebles y electrodomésticos apropiados.

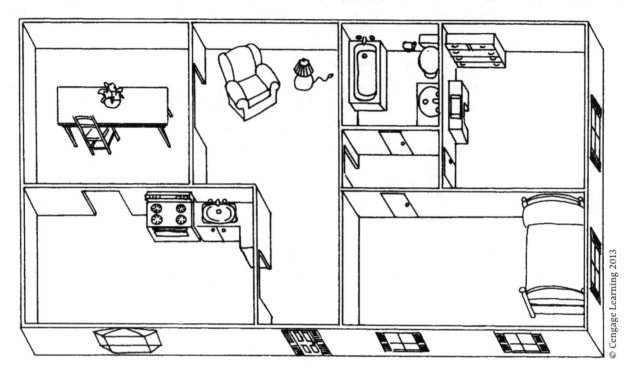

Paco:

En la sala solo hay _____ (1);

entonces necesitamos _____ (2).

En el comedor _____ (3).

Un dormitorio tiene _____ (4)

y el otro tiene _____ (5).

Por eso, necesitamos _____ (6).

Tenemos un problema enorme en la cocina: tenemos _____

_____ (7), pero _____

_____ (8).

Podemos hablar más esta noche.

    Gonzalo

# Gramática para la comunicación II

## Giving Advice and Stating Desires: Other Uses of the Subjunctive

**ACTIVIDAD 15** **Los consejos** Sara quiere vivir en California y sus amigas tienen muchos consejos para ella. Completa la conversación con el infinitivo o la forma apropiada del subjuntivo de los verbos indicados.

ANA  Te aconsejo que _____ (1) a Sacramento. (ir)

MARTA  Quiero que nos _____ (2) una vez al mes. (llamar)

ANA  Es importante que _____ (3) un carro nuevo antes del viaje. (comprar)

MARTA  Es mejor _____ (4) por avión. (viajar)

ANA  Necesitas buscar un trabajo que _____ (5) interesante. (ser)

MARTA  Te prohibimos que _____ (6) a fumar otra vez. (comenzar)

ANA  Te pido que me _____ (7). (escribir)

MARTA  No es bueno _____ (8) la primera oferta de trabajo. (aceptar)

ANA  Es importante que, antes de ir, _____ (9) información sobre apartamentos. (tener)

MARTA  Espero que _____ (10) fotos de tu apartamento nuevo. (sacar)

ANA  Te recomiendo no _____ (11) con cualquier *(any)* Fulano o Mengano. (salir)

MARTA  Es importantísimo que _____ (12). (divertirse)

SARA  Bien, bien... ¿y si decido ir a Colorado?

**ACTIVIDAD 16** **Los tíos preguntones** Magdalena pasó el día con sus tíos que son muy simpáticos, pero siempre le preguntan demasiado. Escribe lo que contestó Magdalena a sus preguntas, algunas discretas y otras indiscretas con el subjuntivo.

1. ¿Tus compañeros de apartamento quieren que cocines mucho?

   Sí, ellos _____.

2. ¿Les prohíbes a tus compañeros que hagan fiestas?

   No, no _____.

3. ¿Tus compañeros de apartamento y tú les prohíben a sus amigos que fumen en el apartamento?

   Sí, nosotros _____.

4. ¿Tu novio quiere que vivas con él?

   No, no _____.

5. ¿Tus padres quieren que vivas en una residencia en vez de un apartamento?

   No, no _____.

6. ¿Tus padres te aconsejan que cambies de especialización?

   No, no _____.

7. ¿Tu profesor de francés te prohíbe que otros te ayuden con tus composiciones?

   Sí, él _____.

8. ¿Tu profesor de francés les recomienda a Uds. que usen un diccionario?

   Sí, él _____.

9. ¿Quieres que tu tío y yo vayamos a visitarte el mes que viene?

   No, no _____.

10. ¿Quieres visitarnos durante tus próximas vacaciones?

    Sí, es buena idea que _____.

**ACTIVIDAD 17** **La queja** Lee esta carta que escribió Raimundo Cárdenas a una agencia de protección al consumidor en Nicaragua. Luego, completa la respuesta de la agencia.

Puerto Cabezas, 17 de abril de 2013

Estimados señores:

La semana pasada compré una tostadora. Funcionó por tres días y ahora no funciona. Busqué y no encontré ninguna garantía. Volví a la tienda para devolverla y recibir mi dinero, pero no me lo quisieron dar. Ahora tengo un problema: gasté 850 córdobas por una tostadora que no funciona. ¿Qué puedo hacer?

Gracias por su atención,

*Raimundo Cárdenas Zamora*

---

Managua, 20 de abril de 2013

Estimado Sr. Cárdenas:

Le aconsejamos que _____,

pero es importante que _____.

Si todavía tiene problemas, es mejor que _____

_____.

Atentamente,

*Susana Valencia Blanco*

Defensa del consumidor

**ACTIVIDAD 18** **Un problema serio** Tu hermano menor tiene problemas con las drogas. Tus padres no saben qué hacer y te pidieron consejos. Completa las siguientes oraciones para ayudarlos.

1. Es mejor que Uds. _____.

2. Les aconsejo que Uds. _____.

3. Es bueno que Uds. no _____.

4. Les pido que Uds. _____.

5. Es importante que Uds. _____.

Nombre _____ Sección _____ Fecha _____

# Un poco de todo

**ACTIVIDAD 19 Ayuda** Hablas con dos estudiantes de Bolivia que llegaron hace poco a tu ciudad. Dales algunos consejos para ayudarlos a buscar un apartamento.

*Tipo de apartamento*

1. Deben buscar un apartamento que _____

_____

*Precio de un alquiler típico*

2. Un alquiler normal _____

_____

*Depósito típico*

3. Es típico pagar _____

_____

*Buenas zonas de la ciudad para vivir*

4. Les aconsejo que _____

_____

**ACTIVIDAD 20 El estudiante confundido** Lee el siguiente email de un estudiante de inglés que pide consejos a estudiantes que ya tomaron el curso. Luego, completa el segundo email con consejos usando el infinitivo, el presente del indicativo o el presente del subjuntivo de los verbos indicados.

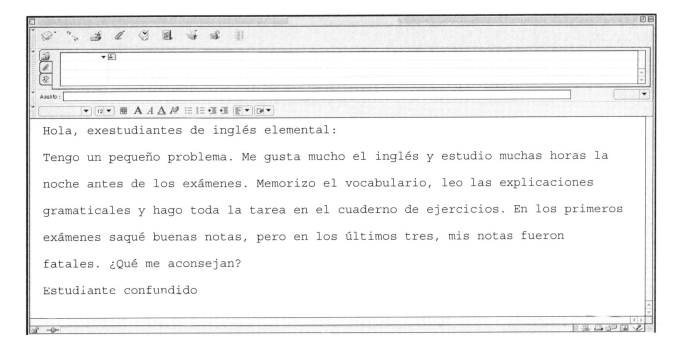

Hola, exestudiantes de inglés elemental:

Tengo un pequeño problema. Me gusta mucho el inglés y estudio muchas horas la noche antes de los exámenes. Memorizo el vocabulario, leo las explicaciones gramaticales y hago toda la tarea en el cuaderno de ejercicios. En los primeros exámenes saqué buenas notas, pero en los últimos tres, mis notas fueron fatales. ¿Qué me aconsejan?

Estudiante confundido

Hola, estudiante confundido:

Primero, es bueno estudiar inglés y es importante tener una actitud positiva. Tu problema es que esperas hasta el último momento para estudiar. Hay algunas cosas que _____ (1. ser) fáciles de hacer. Te aconsejamos que _____ (2. estudiar) un poco todos los días. Es mejor que _____ (3. empezar) a estudiar el vocabulario el primer día de cada capítulo y que después lo _____ (4. repasar) diez o quince minutos cada día. También debes _____ (5. hacer) las actividades de Internet. A nosotros nos gustan mucho porque el programa te corrige las actividades y te da la respuesta correcta en un segundo. Es importante _____ (6. comenzar) con las actividades de vocabulario y gramática y _____ (7. terminar) con las actividades de lectura (conversaciones y párrafos) que son más abiertas. También tienes que _____ (8. hacer) la tarea todos los días y no esperar hasta el último día. Una cosa más: Tenemos amigos que _____ (9. sacar) buenas notas y estudiamos con ellos; esto es una ayuda enorme. Es importante buscar gente que _____ (10. querer) trabajar con otros y que _____ (11. venir) preparada a colaborar.

Cuando estudias a última hora, recuerdas algunas cosas para el examen, pero después de dos días no sabes mucho. Por eso, es mejor _____ (12. estudiar) un poco todos los días; así vas a recibir una buena nota en la clase y vas a poder hablar inglés bien. Esperamos que _____ (13. sacar) una buena nota en la clase.

Un abrazo y buena suerte,
Exestudiantes de inglés elemental
P.D. Es muy importante que _____ (14. hablar) mucho en clase todos los días.

# Lectura

## Estrategia de lectura: Using the Dictionary

When you don't know what a word means, follow this procedure:

1. Skip it if it isn't important.

2. Discern meaning from context.

3. Check and see if the word is mentioned again in the reading.

4. Look it up in the dictionary.

Remember: The dictionary should be your last resort or you may become very frustrated trying to look up every single word you do not understand at first glance. See your textbook for information about how to use a dictionary.

**ACTIVIDAD 21 Cognados** Mientras lees el siguiente artículo sobre los mercados al aire libre, subraya *(underline)* los cognados.

---

### Los mercados en el mundo hispano

Si viajas a un país hispano, un lugar interesante para visitar es un mercado al aire libre. Hay muchas clases de mercados: mercados de artesanía, de antigüedades, de comida y también de cosas en general. Algunos de estos mercados son principalmente para turistas y otros son para la gente local. Vas a encontrar mercados que están abiertos todos los días y otros que
5   solo abren días específicos.

En general, se pueden conseguir buenos precios en los mercados y, a veces incluso, se puede regatear, pero tienes que tener cuidado con el regateo. En algunos lugares el regateo es común: el comerciante espera que el cliente no acepte el primer precio que se le dé y que haga una contraoferta o pida un precio más bajo. Por otro lado, hay mercados donde no se
10   regatea y si lo haces puedes insultar al comerciante. Para no meter la pata, es una buena idea ver qué hace la gente del lugar. Si ellos no regatean, pues entonces, es mejor no hacerlo.

Los mercados de artesanía y de comidas más conocidos de Hispanoamérica están en México, Guatemala y Perú. Allí prevalecieron las culturas azteca, maya e incaica, y hoy día sus descendientes venden al público productos de la región y la artesanía que aprendieron
15   a hacer de sus antepasados. En México, Guatemala y Perú están, por ejemplo, los mercados de San Cristóbal de las Casas en Chiapas, Chichicastenango y Huancayo, respectivamente, donde la gente local vende telas típicas, hamacas, cerámica, especias y comidas. Para saber si los precios de las artesanías que tienen son buenos o no, y para comparar precios, es buena idea ir a las tiendas artesanales del gobierno, donde tienen productos similares.

20   En la Ciudad de México y en Buenos Aires puedes encontrar mercados de antigüedades como la Lagunilla y la feria de San Telmo, respectivamente. Allí es posible regatear. El mejor día para ir a la Lagunilla es los domingos y ese es el único día que abre la feria de San Telmo.

Para comprar de todo, existen mercados como el Rastro en Madrid, que está abierto todos los domingos. Este mercado es enorme y está dividido en diferentes zonas donde se
25   venden cosas como antigüedades, ropa y artesanía moderna, y hay además una zona para comprar animales domésticos. En ese mercado normalmente no es apropiado regatear.

Si estás en un país hispano y quieres saber si hay mercados como los que se mencionan aquí, puedes averiguar en la oficina de turismo local o simplemente preguntarle a alguien del lugar.

---

**ACTIVIDAD 22** **Usa el diccionario** Adivina qué significan las siguientes palabras del texto que acabas de leer. Luego, consulta el diccionario de abajo para ver si tus predicciones son ciertas.

| | Guess | Dictionary Definition |
|---|---|---|
| 1. línea 2: **artesanía** | _____ | _____ |
| 2. línea 6: **conseguir** | _____ | _____ |
| 3. línea 10: **meter la pata** | _____ | _____ |
| 4. línea 13: **prevalecieron** | _____ | _____ |
| 5. línea 17: **telas** | _____ | _____ |

**ar·te·sa·ní·a** f. *(habilidad)* craftsmanship; *(producto)* crafts.
**con·se·guir §64** tr. *(obtener)* to obtain; *(llegar a hacer)* to attain; *(lograr)* to manage.
**pa·ta** f. ZOOL. *(pie)* paw, foot; *(pierna)* leg; COLL. *(pierna humana)* leg; *(base)* leg <*las patas de la mesa* the legs of the table>; ORNITH. female duck ◆ **a cuatro patas** on all fours • **a p.** COLL. on foot • **estirar la p.** COLL. to kick the bucket • **meter la p.** COLL. to put one's foot in it • **p. de gallo** crowfoot.
**pre·va·le·cer §17** intr. *(sobresalir)* to prevail; BOT. to take root.
**te·la** f. *(paño)* fabric; *(membrana)* membrane; *(nata)* film; *(de araña)* web; ANAT. film; BOT. skin; ARTS *(lienzo)* canvas; *(pintura)* painting ◆ **poner en t. de juicio** to call into question • **t. adhesiva** adhesive tape • **t. aislante** electrical tape • **t. metálica** wire netting.

**ACTIVIDAD 23** **Consejos para turistas** Después de leer el artículo, explica qué aconseja el autor sobre estos temas:

1. regatear _____
_____

2. cómo saber si los precios son buenos o malos _____
_____

3. cuándo ir a la Lagunilla y a San Telmo _____
_____

4. si se puede regatear en el Rastro de Madrid _____
_____

# El tiempo libre

Capítulo
## 11

## Vocabulario esencial I

### El tiempo libre y los pasatiempos

**ACTIVIDAD 1** **Asociaciones** Escribe la letra del pasatiempo de la Columna B que mejor corresponda con la(s) palabra(s) de la Columna A.

| A | B |
|---|---|
| 1. _____ plantas | a. hacer crucigramas |
| 2. _____ el póker | b. escribir poesía |
| 3. _____ mesa verde y bolas de colores | c. hacer jardinería |
| 4. _____ mecánico | d. jugar juegos de mesa |
| 5. _____ preparar comida | e. coleccionar tarjetas de béisbol |
| 6. _____ tres horizontal | f. jugar juegos electrónicos |
| 7. _____ sonetos, Shakespeare | g. conectarse a redes sociales |
| 8. _____ Pablo Picasso | h. cocinar |
| 9. _____ Wii, PlayStation, Xbox | i. jugar al billar |
| 10. _____ dinero | j. arreglar el carro |
| 11. _____ Monopolio, Scrabble | k. coleccionar monedas |
| 12. _____ fotos de amigos, mensajes, chat | l. jugar a las cartas |
| 13. _____ Yogi Berra, Alex Rodríguez | m. tocar un instrumento |
| 14. _____ canciones, sinfonías | n. pintar |

# Gramática para la comunicación I

## Expressing Doubt and Certainty: Contrasting the Subjunctive and the Indicative

**ACTIVIDAD 2** **Por las dudas** Completa las siguientes oraciones con la forma correcta del indicativo o del subjuntivo de los verbos indicados.

1. Dudo que Laura _____ mañana. (venir)

2. Es posible que él _____ crucigramas contigo. (hacer)

3. Es evidente que nosotros _____ un problema. (tener)

4. No es verdad que mi abuela _____ a redes sociales. (conectarse)

5. No creo que Paco _____ mucho a las cartas. (jugar)

6. No creo que Raúl _____ arreglar el carro. (saber)

7. Es cierto que yo _____ hacerlo. (poder)

8. El médico cree que tú _____ comer menos. (deber)

9. Estamos seguros de que el profesor _____ buenas notas. (dar)

10. Es probable que _____ la carta hoy. (llegar)

11. Es verdad que Uds. _____ mucho. (pescar)

12. Quizás mis hermanos _____ venir esta noche. (querer)

13. Es obvio que la clase _____ a ser difícil. (ir)

14. Es cierto que tú _____ poesías preciosas. (escribir)

15. No es probable que Jorge _____ aquí en Madrid, ¿verdad? (estar)

16. Tal vez yo _____ la lotería algún día. (ganar)

17. No cabe duda que tu padre _____ bien. (bailar)

18. Está claro que ella nos _____. (mentir)

19. Es dudoso que nosotros _____ juegos de mesa hoy. (jugar)

20. No es verdad que los crucigramas _____ aburridos. (ser)

**ACTIVIDAD 3** **Los pasatiempos** **Parte A.** Completa la siguiente encuesta *(survey)* sobre los pasatiempos. Luego, completa la encuesta otra vez, con las preferencias de uno de tus padres o de un/a amigo/a. Escribe tus iniciales y las de la otra persona en la columna apropiada, según las preferencias.

| Me/Le gusta: | mucho | poco | nada |
|---|---|---|---|
| 1. escuchar música | _____ | _____ | _____ |
| 2. pescar | _____ | _____ | _____ |
| 3. crucigramas | _____ | _____ | _____ |
| 4. juegos de mesa | _____ | _____ | _____ |
| 5. cocinar | _____ | _____ | _____ |
| 6. ajedrez | _____ | _____ | _____ |
| 7. pintar | _____ | _____ | _____ |

| Me/Le gusta: | mucho | poco | nada |
|---|---|---|---|
| 8. arreglar carros | _____ | _____ | _____ |
| 9. jugar a las cartas | _____ | _____ | _____ |
| 10. jugar al futbolito | _____ | _____ | _____ |

**Parte B.** Ahora, escríbele una nota a la persona de la **Parte A.** Uds. van a pasar el fin de semana juntos. Recomienda actividades que les gusta hacer.

▶ *Como a nosotros nos gusta el ajedrez, es posible que juguemos al ajedrez en mi casa. También, como siempre pintas, me puedes pintar…*

_____

_____

_____

_____

**ACTIVIDAD 4 Tal vez…** Lee las siguientes conversaciones y contesta las preguntas, usando oraciones completas. Usa **tal vez** o **quizás** en tus respuestas.

▶ —¿Puedo ver uno de esos?

—Claro que sí.

—Es muy bonito. ¿Cuánto cuesta?

—Solo 295 euros.

¿Dónde están?

*Tal vez estén en una tienda. / Quizás estén en una tienda.*

1. —Necesito una carta más.

—¿Solo una? Vas a perder.

—Yo siempre gano.

¿Qué están haciendo? _____

2. Bienvenidos al programa. Hoy vamos a preparar una ensalada. Primero lavo y corto la lechuga, después lavo bien los tomates y también los corto, pero no muy pequeños…

¿Dónde está esta persona? _____

3. —¿Cómo que no me queda dinero?

—No, señor, no hay nada.

—Pero, debo tener algo.

¿Dónde están? _____

4. —Javier, siéntate al lado de Gabriela. Y Verónica, tómale la mano a tu hermanito.

—¿Así, mamá?

—Así, perfecto. Ahora miren a la cámara y digan: "¡Patatas!".

—¡Patatas!

¿Qué están haciendo? _____

Creo que tengo problemas con mi esposa, pero tal vez sea mi imaginación. Hace dos meses empezó un trabajo nuevo como arquitecta. Al principio todo iba bien, pero comenzó a trabajar con un arquitecto joven y últimamente está trabajando muchas horas (anoche no regresó a casa hasta las diez y media). Dice que le gusta mucho el trabajo y sé que, para ella, es muy importante trabajar. Dice que, la semana que viene, ese arquitecto y ella tienen que ir a otra ciudad por dos días para asistir a una conferencia. Ella me dice que no pasa nada, pero yo tengo mis dudas. Anteayer, en vez de volver en autobús, él la trajo a casa.

Es posible que no sea nada, pero no estoy seguro. ¿Qué crees tú? ¿Qué debo hacer?

**Ernesto**

Es evidente que _____. Es posible que

_____

_____. También dudo que _____

_____. Pero es cierto que _____

_____. Te aconsejo que

_____ porque estoy seguro/a

de que _____. Te deseo

mucha suerte.

Un abrazo,

_____

## Saying How an Action Is Done: Adverbs Ending in -*mente*

**ACTIVIDAD 6** **¿Cómo?** Escribe oraciones, usando las siguientes palabras. Haz cambios y añade otras palabras si es necesario.

▶ yo / correr / rápido / clase    *Yo corro rápidamente a clase.*

1. general / ellas / estudiar / biblioteca _____

_____

2. mi / hermanos / hablar / constante / teléfono _____

_____

3. yo / saber / cantar / divino _____

4. ellos / jugar videojuegos / continuo _____

5. nosotros / poder / encontrar / trabajo / Caracas / fácil _____

_____

# Un poco de todo

**ACTIVIDAD 7** **Un anuncio** Lee este anuncio y contesta las preguntas.

**¿TE GUSTARÍA SER INSTRUCTORA DE YOGA?**

yoga libre

Profesoras entrenadas en la última metodología. Ambiente acogedor con el confort que buscas.

Formación para profesoras. Títulos pretigiosos. Estándares altos. Clases individuales o en grupo.

**Yoga libre** forma parte del Centro Deportivo Polígono Sur. Conoce el CDPS con dos piscinas, pesas, cintas corredoras, bicicletas estáticas, elípticas y clases de pilates y jazz.

Avenida Los Arcos 10
Tel: 7348-8234

© Cengage Learning 2013

1. Marca las actividades que se pueden hacer en Yoga Libre.

   ❐ levantar pesas

   ❐ nadar

   ❐ hacer ejercicio

   ❐ jugar al squash

2. ¿Crees que Yoga Libre busca personas que tengan experiencia? ¿Por qué sí o no?

_____

3. ¿Crees que es un gimnasio para hombres? ¿Mujeres? ¿Hombres y mujeres?

_____

¿Por qué crees eso? _____

# Vocabulario esencial II

## La vida saludable

**ACTIVIDAD 8** **Descripciones** Lee las descripciones y complétalas con la palabra correcta.

1. Me encanta correr, levantar pesas, pasear en bici, tomar clases de yoga... en fin, me gusta hacer ejercicio _____.

2. Martín trabaja muchas horas y no tiene nada de tiempo libre. Quizás esté un poco _____.

3. Claro que se debe comer pescado, verduras y frutas, pero una buena _____ es solo una parte de una vida saludable; también es importante hacer ejercicio y dormir bien.

4. Mis padres prefieren la comida _____ porque se cultiva sin pesticidas.

5. Algunos nutricionistas dicen que las verduras _____ tienen las mismas vitaminas que las que se compran frescas.

6. Si quieres _____ algo por la tarde entre comidas, es mejor que no sea comida procesada.

7. Hacer yoga es una buena forma de combatir el _____ y relajarse.

8. Por lo general, la comida rápida tiene muchas _____.

## La preparación de la comida

**ACTIVIDAD 9** **En la cocina** Escribe las letras de todas las cosas de la Columna B que asocias con cada frase de la Columna A.

| A | B |
|---|---|
| 1. comida que se fríe _____ | a. leche |
| 2. comida que se corta _____ | b. jamón |
| 3. comida que se añade _____ | c. cuchillo |
| 4. comida que se le da la vuelta _____ | d. olla |
| 5. comida que se hierve _____ | e. pimienta |
| 6. algo que se usa para sazonar _____ | f. pan |
| 7. cubierto que se usa para cortar _____ | g. papas |
| 8. cosa que se usa para freír _____ | h. huevos |
| 9. cosa donde se revuelve algo _____ | i. sartén |
| 10. cosa que se usa para hervir _____ | j. mantequilla |
| | k. recipiente |
| | l. sal |

# Gramática para la comunicación II

## Giving Instructions: The Passive *se*

**ACTIVIDAD 10** **Una receta** Completa la siguiente receta con la forma correcta de los verbos indicados. Usa el **se** pasivo.

UNA TORTILLA ESPAÑOLA

| | |
|---|---|
| Primero, _____ (1) cuatro patatas grandes | *cortar* |
| en trozos pequeños. Segundo, _____ (2) | *cortar* |
| una cebolla. Después _____ (3) aceite en | *poner* |
| una sartén a fuego alto. _____ (4) las patatas | *añadir* |
| y la cebolla al aceite caliente y _____ (5) a | *cocinar* |
| fuego alto. Mientras _____ (6) las patatas | *freír* |
| y la cebolla, _____ (7) cuatro huevos en un | *revolver* |
| recipiente. _____ (8) sal a los huevos. Después, | *agregar* |
| _____ (9) las patatas y la cebolla con los huevos | *revolver* |
| y _____ (10) todos los ingredientes en la sartén. | *poner* |
| Después de unos minutos, _____ | *darle* |
| (11) la vuelta y _____ (12) un poco más. Al final, | *cocinar* |
| _____ (13) una tortilla deliciosa con un grupo de amigos. | *comer* |

**ACTIVIDAD 11** **Una ensalada** Tu amiga es un desastre en la cocina. Para ayudarla, le escribiste un mensaje explicándole cómo se prepara una ensalada. Completa la receta con las palabras apropiadas. Usa el **se** pasivo, el infinitivo o el subjuntivo.

Primero se lava y _____ _____ (1) la lechuga. Después _____

_____ (2) y _____ _____ (3) los tomates. _____

_____ (4) la lechuga en el plato y _____ _____ (5) los tomates

encima de la lechuga. También puedes _____ (6) una cebolla si quieres y ponerla

encima de la lechuga. Como te gusta mucho el queso, te aconsejo que _____ (7)

un poco encima de todo. Ahora, _____ _____ (8) aceite y vinagre (pero poco

vinagre), después _____ _____ (9) sal (y también pimienta si quieres) y ya está.

Finalmente _____ _____ (10) todos los ingredientes y se come.

## Other Uses of *para* and *por*

**ACTIVIDAD 12** *¿Para o por?* Completa estas oraciones con **para** o **por**.

1. Le cambié mi radio _____ su chaqueta.

2. Anoche caminamos _____ la playa _____ varias horas.

3. _____ mí, el trabajo es muy aburrido.

4. Mañana Jaime sale _____ Punta del Este.

5. Mañana tengo que ir al médico; por eso Victoria va a trabajar _____ mí.

6. ¿Cuánto pagaste _____ los churros?

7. Eran las tres cuando me llamaste _____ teléfono.

8. Mis padres van en tren de Valencia a Madrid y van a pasar _____ Albacete.

9. Debes mandar los documentos _____ email.

10. _____ Álvaro, las tortillas de su abuela son deliciosas.

11. Trabajé más horas de lo normal _____ ganar un poco más de dinero.

12. Compré croissants y café _____ el desayuno.

## Expressing Emotions: More Uses of the Subjunctive

**ACTIVIDAD 13** *¡Qué emoción!* Completa estas oraciones con el infinitivo o la forma correcta del indicativo o del subjuntivo de los verbos indicados.

1. A Mercedes le sorprende que tú no _____ más. (leer)

2. Es una pena que _____ bombas atómicas. (haber)

3. Espero _____ dinero del banco esta tarde. (sacar)

4. A mi madre le gusta que yo la _____ con los crucigramas del periódico. (ayudar)

5. Mi padre espera que la universidad _____ a mi hermano. (aceptar)

6. Me alegro de que tú _____ aquí. (estar)

7. Sentimos no _____ venir mañana. (poder)

8. Temo que mi novia me _____. (mentir)

9. Es fantástico que a Guillermo le _____ arreglar carros. (gustar)

10. Miguel espera que su compañero le _____ un buen desayuno. (preparar)

11. Es una lástima no _____ tiempo hoy para jugar a las cartas. (tener)

12. Rogelio se sorprendió de _____ a Roberto en su clase. (ver)

13. Tenemos miedo de que el examen _____ difícil. (ser)

14. A mi hermana le molesta que yo _____ su guitarra. (tocar)

**ACTIVIDAD 14** **¿Qué sientes?**  Describe tus emociones y opiniones sobre tu universidad. Escribe sobre el presente o el futuro. No escribas sobre el pasado.

▶ Es bueno que la *universidad tenga una biblioteca grande.*

1. Me sorprendo de que _____.

2. Es fantástico que _____.

3. Me molesta que _____.

4. Es una pena que _____.

5. Me alegro de que _____.

6. Tengo miedo de que _____.

# Un poco de todo

**ACTIVIDAD 15** **Las mentes curiosas quieren saber**  Lee los siguientes titulares *(headlines)*. Algunos son de periódicos respetables y algunos de periódicos sensacionalistas. Escribe tus reacciones, usando estas frases: **Me sorprendo de que…, No creo que…, Es obvio que…, Me alegro de que…, (No) Es posible que…, Creo que…,** etc.

1. Viajes a Marte en el año 2025 _____

_____

2. Cumple 110 años y todavía hace artesanías _____

_____

3. Mujer de 72 años tiene bebé _____

_____

4. Nueva planta medicinal del Amazonas. ¿La cura del cáncer? _____

_____

5. Niño de 6 años va a competir en las semifinales de un campeonato de ajedrez contra adultos _____

_____

6. Costa Rica tiene más profesores que policías y no tiene militares _____

_____

7. Cada año España tiene más turistas que habitantes _____

_____

8. La fruta del futuro: La *nanzana,* una combinación de una naranja y una manzana _____

_____

# Lectura

## Estrategia de lectura: Reading an Interview Article

Prior to reading an interview article, you should go through the following steps to give you some background information:

- Read the headline and subheading.
- Scan the text for the interviewer's questions.

**ACTIVIDAD 16** **Lee y adivina** Lee el título, el subtítulo y las preguntas. Luego, contesta esta pregunta.

¿Cuál es la idea principal del artículo?

a. la comida de España

b. los modales en la mesa

c. la historia de la comida española

---

# LA BUENA EDUCACIÓN

### Entrevista con Carmen Pradillo, experta en etiqueta

#### POR LAURA RÓGORA

Nos sentamos en una mesa del restaurante La Corralada en la calle Villanueva en Madrid. Carmen es experta en protocolo y etiqueta. Hoy nos habla de los modales en la mesa.

En este momento tengo un estudiante de los Estados Unidos en mi casa por dos semanas y dentro de un mes mi hijo va a pasar un mes en su casa en los Estados Unidos. ¿Qué deben saber estos chicos para tener buenos modales a la hora de comer?

Bueno, primero vamos a hablar del uso del tenedor y del cuchillo para ciertas comidas. En España, es mucho más frecuente usarlos que en los Estados Unidos.

¿Me puedes dar un ejemplo?

Bueno, en casa o en restaurantes que no sirven comida rápida, es común usar tenedor y cuchillo para comer sándwiches, pizza y patatas fritas.

Y cuando mi hijo va a los Estados Unidos es mejor que use las manos, ¿verdad?

Exactamente. Pero hay más. Un norteamericano también tiene que aprender que al servir fruta de postre también se usan los cubiertos. Por ejemplo, la sandía o el melón se comen con tenedor y cuchillo.

Claro, ayer serví plátano de postre y el norteamericano lo agarró con las manos, pero vio que los demás no iban a comerlo de esta manera y nos empezó a imitar.

Muy inteligente el chico. Es exactamente lo que uno debe hacer en otro país: observar e imitar. A ver si ese chico es muy observador o no. Cuando come, ¿dónde pone la mano izquierda? ¿Encima de la mesa o debajo?

---

**La mano debajo de la mesa. Me pregunto por qué.**

Porque esto es lo que hacen en los Estados Unidos. Pero en España, no. Las dos manos deben estar encima de la mesa siempre. Bueno, esto también tiene que ver con cómo usamos el tenedor y el cuchillo al momento de cortar.

**¿Me puedes explicar esto?**

Sí, cómo no. En España, se pone el tenedor en la mano izquierda y el cuchillo en la mano derecha. Se pincha la carne con el tenedor, se corta con en cuchillo y se come sin cambiar el tenedor de mano.

**Pues claro.**

Pues claro no. En otros países no es así; en los Estados Unidos se cambia de mano el tenedor, luego se pone la mano izquierda debajo de la mesa y al final se come.

**¡Qué complicado! Tengo que decirle esto a mi hijo porque seguro que lo va a hacer mal en los Estados Unidos.**

Otra cosa que seguro que está aprendiendo tu estudiante norteamericano es qué hacer con el pan.

**No entiendo.**

Después de estar aquí unos días, muchos ven que los españoles siempre parten el pan en trozos pequeños al comer, trozos pequeños, solo lo que te puedes poner en la boca.

**¿Algo más?**

Es importante observar, observar y observar y después imitar.

**Es una pena que no tengamos mucho más tiempo para hablar. Tengo que decirles muchas cosas a mi hijo y a su amigo norteamericano.**

**ACTIVIDAD 17** **En tus palabras** Después de leer la entrevista, explica en tus propias palabras qué aprendiste sobre cómo se come en España.

1. ¿Dónde debes poner las manos? _____
   _____

2. ¿Cómo se coma fruta como el melón o el plátano? _____
   _____

3. ¿Cómo se parte el pan? _____

4  ¿Cuál es la cosa más importante que uno puede hacer cuando está en otro país? _____
   _____

# Repaso

## *Para* and *por*

In Chapters 5 and 11 you studied different uses of the words **para** and **por.** Study these examples and then complete the conversations that follow.

—¿**Para** qué estudias?

—Estudio **para** ser médico/abogado/etc.

—Pero trabajas también, ¿no?

—Sí, trabajo **para** J. Crew.

—En J. Crew, ¿la ropa es cara?

—Sí y no, depende. Es posible pagar $30 o $100 **por** un suéter.

—¿Cómo supiste del trabajo?

—**Por** un anuncio.

—¿Lo leíste en un periódico?

—No, un amigo me lo mandó **por** email.

—¿**Para** qué trabajas?

—Trabajo **para** tener dinero, **para** poder salir con mis amigos y **para** pagar mis estudios.

—¿Cuándo trabajas?

—Trabajo **por** la tarde los lunes, los martes y los jueves.

—En tu opinión, ¿es bueno estudiar y trabajar?

—**Para** otras personas, no sé, pero **para** mí, sí. En la universidad aprendo mucho, pero en el trabajo también aprendo.

—Pero si estudias, ¿hay días que no puedes ir a trabajar?

—Claro, pero tengo un amigo en el trabajo. Si él no puede trabajar, yo trabajo **por** él, y si yo no puedo, él trabaja **por** mí.

—¿Cuántos años más vas a estar en la universidad?

—Voy a estar aquí **por** dos años más.

—¿Y después de terminar?

—Pienso viajar **por** Suramérica.

—¿Cuándo te vas **para** tu pueblo **para** visitar a tus padres?

—Me voy **para** mi pueblo pronto.

—¿Cuándo es tu próxima visita?

—Voy **para** Navidad.

Nombre _____ Sección _____ Fecha _____

**ACTIVIDAD  1  Conversaciones** Completa las siguientes conversaciones con **para** o **por**.

Dos estudiantes de francés hablan:

—¿Entiendes la tarea que nos dio la profesora hoy en la clase de francés?

—_____ (1) mí, la tarea _____ (2) mañana es fácil, pero hay otras cosas que son problemáticas.

—Los verbos en francés son difíciles _____ (3) mí.

—_____ (4) los estudiantes de inglés, los verbos son fáciles.

Dos aficionados al fútbol hablan sobre un nuevo jugador:

—Ahora Jorge juega al fútbol _____ (5) los Huracanes.

—Juega solo _____ (6) tener dinero y _____ (7) ser famoso. No me gusta su actitud.

—A mí tampoco. Si Jorge está enfermo, Lorenzo juega _____ (8) él. ¿Sabías eso?

—Lorenzo es mejor jugador y él juega _____ (9) divertirse.

Dos personas hablan sobre el hermano de uno de ellos:

—¿Conoces a mi hermano Hernando?

—No, ¿cómo es?

—_____ (10) mis padres, es el hijo perfecto.

—¿Y eso?

—_____ (11) Hernando, la educación universitaria es muy importante. Él estudia _____ (12) ser maestro de niños pequeños. Tiene clases _____ (13) la mañana, trabaja _____ (14) la tarde _____ (15) una compañía internacional y estudia _____ (16) la noche. Los lunes, los miércoles y los sábados corre _____ (17) el parque _____ (18) hacer ejercicio. Los domingos Hernando sale de la ciudad y se va _____ (19) el pueblo _____ (20) visitar a nuestros padres. Normalmente los visita _____ (21) un par de horas. Después, al volver a casa pasa _____ (22) la casa de nuestra abuela _____ (23) ver si está bien.

—Ya veo. ¿El señor perfecto tiene novia?

—Claro. Ella vive en otra ciudad, entonces él siempre le manda regalos pequeños. Y también le manda mensajes románticos todos los días _____ (24) email.

—Tienes razón, su vida es perfecta.

—No, perdón. _____ (25) mí, esa no es una vida perfecta. No puede ir a caminar _____ (26) la calle todas las noches con su novia, no puede verla, solo puede hablar con ella _____ (27) teléfono o mandarle mensajes.

—Tu hermano piensa en su futuro y tú piensas en el presente.

—Sí, es verdad. Hablando del presente, ¿por qué no nos vamos _____ (28) una disco?

—Bueno, pero primero podemos pasar _____ (29) el banco; necesito sacar dinero.

—Bien.

# El campo y la ciudad

## Vocabulario esencial I

### La geografía

**ACTIVIDAD 1** **La variedad geográfica** Asocia las palabras de la Columna A con los términos geográficos de la Columna B.

© Debbie Rusch

**A**

1. _____ Misisipi, Amazonas, Ebro
2. _____ Caracas, Quito
3. _____ Etna, Osorno y Popocatépetl
4. _____ las Galápagos, Puerto Rico y Cuba
5. _____ los Pirineos, los Andes
6. _____ Jack y Jill
7. _____ Atlántico, Pacífico
8. _____ Malibú, Luquillo, Waikiki
9. _____ Michigan, Superior y Titicaca
10. _____ Sahara, Atacama

**B**

a. islas
b. desiertos
c. colina
d. playas
e. ríos
f. océanos
g. ciudades
h. lagos
i. montañas
j. volcanes

**ACTIVIDAD 2 La geografía** Completa este crucigrama.

### Horizontales

4. Es una carretera para vehículos de alta velocidad.

6. Es más pequeña que una montaña.

7. el Amazonas o el Orinoco

8. donde vive Tarzán

11. Un lugar entre dos montañas: Napa es un _____.

12. Titicaca es el _____ navegable más alto del mundo.

13. el Atlántico o el Pacífico

14. el Mediterráneo

### Verticales

1. Los romanos construyeron muchos, pero uno muy famoso y moderno conecta Manhattan y Brooklyn.

2. Iguazú o el salto Ángel

3. No es la ciudad.

5. Puerto Rico, Cuba o Mallorca

9. Hace erupción y produce lava.

10. Viajando por la _____ de Honduras, vimos el Caribe.

# Lugares de interés

**ACTIVIDAD 3** **Asociaciones** Asocia las frases de la primera columna con las palabras de la segunda.

1. Si visitas otra ciudad u otro país y necesitas saber cuáles son los sitios de interés, vas a este lugar. _____

2. Los musulmanes no van a una iglesia, sino a este lugar. _____

3. Es una estructura que se hace para conmemorar a una persona o una idea, por ejemplo, la Estatua de la Libertad. _____

4. Los mayas construyeron estas estructuras e hicieron sacrificios humanos encima de ellas. _____

5. Si quieres ver leones, tigres y otros animales exóticos, visitas este lugar. _____

6. En estos lugares hay exposiciones de objetos de importancia artística, histórica o científica. _____

7. Es más grande que una iglesia. _____

8. Los mexicanos celebran el Día de los Muertos en estos lugares. _____

9. Es un territorio bajo protección y administración federal y que se considera reserva natural. _____

10. Los judíos van a este lugar en Yom Kipur. _____

11. Si te gustan las rosas, debes visitar este lugar. _____

12. Si pierdes el pasaporte, tienes que ir a este lugar. _____

a. pirámides
b. sinagoga
c. zoológico
d. mezquita
e. cementerios
f. museos
g. parque nacional
h. catedral
i. centro de información turística
j. monumento
k. embajada
l. jardín botánico

**ACTIVIDAD 4** **A buscar** Usa Internet para buscar las respuestas a las siguientes preguntas.

1. ¿Dónde están las Pirámides del Sol y de la Luna? ¿Quiénes las construyeron y cuándo las construyeron?

_____

_____

2. ¿En qué cementerio y en qué ciudad está el cuerpo de Eva Perón? _____

_____

3. ¿Dónde está la embajada de los Estados Unidos en España? _____

_____

4. ¿Qué es Tibidabo? ¿Dónde está? Si no sabes, mira la página www.tibidabo.cat. No está en español. ¿Sabes en qué idioma está escrito? ¿En qué otros idiomas se puede ver esta página web?

_____

_____

5. Las ruinas mayas de Chichén Itzá están en la península de Yucatán. ¿Qué otras ruinas mayas hay en esa península? _____

_____

6. ¿Dónde está la basílica de Nuestra Señora de Guadalupe? ¿Cuándo construyeron la nueva basílica?

_____

_____

# Gramática para la comunicación I

## Making Comparisons (Part I)

**ACTIVIDAD 5** **Comparaciones** Escribe oraciones comparando estas personas o cosas. ¡Ojo! Algunas usan superlativos y otras usan comparativos.

▶ Paris Hilton / Rosie O'Donnell / Oprah / delgado
***Paris Hilton es la más delgada de las tres.***

1. Tom Cruise / Adam Sandler / bajo _____
_____

2. Cuba / Puerto Rico / isla Margarita / grande _____
_____

3. el tango / la salsa / sensual _____
_____

4. el Mini Cooper / costar / más / veinte mil dólares _____

5. George W. Bush / Bill Clinton / Barack Obama / joven _____
_____

6. el jazz / el merengue / el rock / bueno _____
_____

**ACTIVIDAD 6** **El ejercicio y la salud** Compara los siguientes gimnasios. Usa el comparativo o el superlativo.

|  | Cuerposano | Musculín | Barriguita |
|---|---|---|---|
| Número de clases aeróbicas | 14/semana | 7/semana | 21/semana |
| Precio | $1.700/año | $2.500/año | $1.875/año |
| Piscina | 50 metros | 25 metros | 40 metros |
| Número de miembros | 1.500 (hombres y mujeres) | 1.400 (para toda la familia) | 1.350 (solo mujeres) |
| Extras | Bar con jugos y sándwiches | Máquinas de Coca-Cola, boutique | Bar, cafetería y restaurante |

1. clases aeróbicas: Cuerposano / Musculín _____
_____

2. precio: Cuerposano / Musculín / Barriguita _____
_____

3. piscina: Cuerposano / Musculín / Barriguita _____
_____

4. número de miembros: Musculín / Barriguita _____

_____

5. En tu opinión, ¿cuál es el mejor gimnasio? ¿Por qué? _____

_____

**ACTIVIDAD 7** **Los hermanos Villa** Mira el dibujo de los hermanos Villa y lee las pistas *(clues)*. Después identifica el nombre de la persona en cada dibujo, su edad y qué hace.

© Cengage Learning 2013

**Pistas**

Felisa es la más alta de las hermanas.

El estudiante tiene un año más que el músico y un año menos que la secretaria.

La secretaria tiene el pelo más largo de todos.

David es más alto que el músico.

El menor de la familia tiene veinticinco años y se llama Felipe.

La persona que tiene dos años más que Felisa es doctora.

El estudiante no trabaja.

La mayor de todos los hermanos tiene treinta y cuatro años y es la más delgada.

La hermana más alta de las tres es arquitecta.

Maribel es mayor que Ana; Ana tiene solo veintisiete años.

| Nombre | Edad | Ocupación |
|---|---|---|
| 1. _____ | _____ | _____ |
| 2. _____ | _____ | _____ |
| 3. _____ | _____ | _____ |
| 4. _____ | _____ | _____ |
| 5. _____ | _____ | _____ |

**ACTIVIDAD 8** **¿Cómo es tu familia?** Escribe una pequeña descripción de tu familia usando comparativos y superlativos. Usa adjetivos como **interesante, inteligente, trabajador/a, mayor, menor,** etc.

_____

_____

_____

_____

_____

_____

## Making Requests and Giving Commands (Part I): Commands with *usted* and *ustedes*

**ACTIVIDAD 9** **Las órdenes** Completa estas oraciones con las órdenes correctas.

1. Sr. Mata, no _____ esto. Está caliente. (tocar)

2. Señores, _____ a la derecha para ver el Palacio Nacional. (mirar)

3. _____ Uds. del autobús ahora. Tienen una hora para caminar por el parque. (Bajar)

4. Sra. Martín, _____ la pirámide por la parte de la derecha de las escaleras. (subir)

5. Si Uds. no quieren enfermarse, _____ agua de botella solamente. (beber)

6. Srta. Pascual, ¿está Ud. mareada? _____ un momento. (sentarse)

**ACTIVIDAD 10** **Lo que deben hacer** Lee estas recomendaciones que se pueden escuchar en un aeropuerto y luego cámbialas a órdenes de **Ud.** y **Uds.** Usa pronombres de complemento directo e indirecto si es posible.

▶ Ud. tiene que sacar el pasaporte ahora.  *Sáquelo ahora.*

1. Deben hablar con el supervisor. _____

2. No debe beber Coca-Cola aquí. _____

3. Deben sentarse allí. _____

4. No pueden tocar la guitarra aquí. _____

5. Ud. tiene que explicarle su problema a mi supervisor. _____

6. Ud. debe darle su pasaporte al agente. _____

7. Señor, no puede poner los pies en la silla. _____

8. Aquí no pueden fumar. _____

9. Debe apagar el celular ahora. _____

10. Señora, el bolso de mano está roto; tiene que arreglarlo antes de abordar el avión. _____

_____

11. Señores, tienen que quitarse los zapatos, por favor. _____

12. Perdieron el vuelo a Miami y no hay más hoy. Deben volver mañana. _____

**ACTIVIDAD 11** ¡Ojo! Mira estos dibujos y escribe órdenes apropiadas. Usa pronombres de complemento directo cuando sea posible.

1.

2.

3.

4.

Illustrations: © Cengage Learning 2013

1. _____

2. _____

3. _____

4. _____

**ACTIVIDAD 12** **Sin supervisión** Los padres de Fabiana y Raúl se fueron de viaje a otra ciudad por el fin de semana. La madre les dejó un mensaje para recordarles lo que deben y no deben hacer. Completa el mensaje con las órdenes apropiadas de los verbos indicados.

Ya saben; vamos a quedarnos en el Hilton de Cartagena. Si necesitan algo,

_____ (1. llamarnos) al hotel. En el refrigerador hay una sopa de

verduras y unos filetes. _____ (2. Prepararlos) en una sartén

grande con un poco de aceite. Por la noche, _____ (3. salir)

pero _____ (4. regresar) a casa antes de las dos. No _____

(5. olvidar) que tienen tarea para el lunes; _____ (6. empezarla)

temprano. Si quieren, _____ (7. usar) la computadora de su padre.

_____ (8. Navegar) por Internet, pero no _____

(9. descargar) música ni _____ (10. visitar) salones de chat.

　　　Mamá

P. D. Por supuesto, no _____ (11. organizar) fiestas en la casa.

**ACTIVIDAD 13** **En la clase** **Parte A.** Escribe dos órdenes que un/a profesor/a normalmente les dice a los estudiantes de español elemental antes de un examen final.

1. _____

2. _____

**Parte B.** Ahora, tú tienes la oportunidad de decirle algunas cosas al/a la profesor/a de español elemental. Escribe dos órdenes que le dirías *(would say)* antes del examen final. Usa la forma de **Ud.**

1. _____

2. _____

# Un poco de todo

**ACTIVIDAD 14** **Instrucciones** Termina las siguientes instrucciones que les dio una profesora a sus estudiantes mientras viajan por España. Completa los espacios con una palabra relacionada con lugares de interés o con un comparativo. También debes usar los verbos indicados para escribir sus órdenes.

1. Vamos a visitar el _____ Real donde vivían los reyes de España. Una vez allí, no

   _____ (hablar) en voz alta.

2. Luego vamos al _____ del Prado para ver los cuadros de Velázquez, El Greco y Goya.

   Por favor, no _____ (tocarlos). El cuadro de *Las meninas* de Velázquez es el cuadro

   _____ famoso _____ todos en el museo.

3. Por la tarde vamos al _____ donde pueden ver osos panda, elefantes y otros

   animales. Pero recuerden, no _____ (darles) de comer. La comida para seres

   humanos es la _____ cosa que pueden comer los animales. No es bueno para ellos.

4. Mañana salimos temprano para Barcelona. Así que tienen que hacer las maletas. Por favor,

   _____ (hacerlas) esta noche y no mañana. Tenemos que salir temprano. El viaje va a

   ser de más _____ seis horas en autobús.

# Vocabulario esencial II

## Cómo llegar a un lugar

**ACTIVIDAD 15** **Por la ciudad** Asocia estas palabras con sus definiciones.

1. Tiene una luz roja, una amarilla y una verde; es _____.
2. El lugar por donde cruzas la calle es _____.
3. Necesitas uno para tomar el metro o el autobús; es _____.
4. El lugar donde dejas el carro es _____.
5. El lugar donde para el metro es _____.
6. Si no hay ascensor, tienes que subir por _____.
7. Es más pequeño que una calle y está entre edificios; es _____.
8. Una persona que camina por la ciudad es _____.

a. un boleto
b. el estacionamiento
c. un semáforo
d. las escaleras
e. un peatón
f. la estación
g. el cruce de peatones
h. un callejón

**ACTIVIDAD 16** **¿Qué está haciendo?** Di qué está haciendo el hombre en cada dibujo.
Usa **está + -ando / -iendo.**

▶ *Está entrando al edificio.*

1. _____

2. _____

3. _____

4. _____

5. _____

**ACTIVIDAD 17** **Las órdenes** Mira los dibujos de la **Actividad 16** y escribe una orden formal para
cada acción.

▶ *Entre Ud. al edificio.*

1. _____

2. _____

3. _____

4. _____

5. _____

**ACTIVIDAD 18** **Para llegar a mi casa** Escribe instrucciones para tu profesor/a de español para
ir desde tu clase hasta tu residencia, apartamento o casa para una comida especial para la clase. Dale
instrucciones muy completas e incluye órdenes. Por ejemplo: **Para llegar a mi casa, salga de la clase y
baje las escaleras. Al salir del edificio, doble a la derecha. Camine dos cuadras. Al llegar a la calle
Washington, doble a la derecha.** (etc.)

_____

_____

_____

_____

# Gramática para la comunicación II

## Making Comparisons (Part II): Comparisons of Equality

**ACTIVIDAD 19** **Comparaciones** Escribe comparaciones basadas en los dibujos.

1. Isabel    Paco

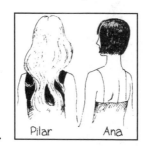
2. Pilar    Ana

3. Paula    María

4. Pedro    Martín

5. Pepe    Laura

6. Juana    Elisa

1. Isabel / Paco / alto _____

2. pelo / Pilar / Ana / largo _____

3. Paula / María / bonito _____

4. Pedro / Martín / dinero _____

5. Pepe / Laura / sueño _____

6. ojos / Elisa / Juana / pequeño _____

**ACTIVIDAD 20** **¿Idénticos?** Mario y David son dos hombres muy parecidos (*similar*). Escribe solo lo que tienen en común, usando **tan, tanto, tantos** o **tantas.** Escribe las respuestas en orden según esta información.

| | Mario | David |
|---|---|---|
| **altura** | 1'80 | 1'80 |
| **hermanos** | 1 | 0 |
| **hermanas** | 3 | 3 |
| **carros** | 2 | 2 |
| **novias** | 1 | 2 |
| **coeficiente intelectual (IQ)** | 146 | 146 |
| **trabajos** | 2 | 3 |
| **sueldo** | 700 euros/semana | 700 euros/semana |
| **relojes Rólex** | 3 | 2 |
| **teléfonos celulares** | 2 | 1 |
| **SMS recibidos por mes** | 1500 | 1500 |

1. _____
2. _____
3. _____
4. _____
5. _____
6. _____

**ACTIVIDAD 21** **Los anuncios** Trabajas para una compañía de publicidad. Tienes que escribir frases que llamen la atención *(catchy phrases)*. Usa **tan… como** en tus oraciones.

▶ el detergente Mimosil
   *El detergente Mimosil te deja la ropa tan blanca como la nieve.*

1. la película *Spiderman VI* _____
_____

2. el buscador Google _____
_____

3. la dieta Kitakilos _____
_____

4. el nuevo carro Mercedes Sport _____
_____

# Making Requests and Giving Commands (Part II): Commands with *tú*

**ACTIVIDAD 22** **Una vida de perros** Tienes un perro inteligente pero a veces es malo. Escribe órdenes para tu perro.

1. sentarse _____
2. traerme el periódico _____
3. bailar _____
4. no molestar a la gente _____
5. no subirse al sofá _____
6. acostarse _____
7. hacerse el muerto _____
8. no comer eso _____
9. quedarse allí _____
10. venir aquí _____

**ACTIVIDAD 23** **Consejos para tu hermano** Tu hermano menor va a comenzar sus estudios universitarios este año. Piensa tomar italiano elemental y, como estudias español, él te pidió consejos. Escríbele consejos usando órdenes e incluye otras palabras si es necesario.

1. llegar / clase / a tiempo _____
2. ir / oficina del profesor / si necesitar ayuda _____
_____

3. no / salir / noche / antes / examen _____

4. no / copiar / respuestas / cuaderno de ejercicios _____

_____

5. hacer / las actividades de Internet / frecuentemente _____

6. tener / actitud positiva _____

7. no / entregar / tarea / tarde _____

8. no / dormirse / en clase _____

9. ser / estudiante bueno _____

10. decirle / al profesor / si no entender _____

**ACTIVIDAD 24 Ayuda tecnológica** La abuela de Alejandra no sabe mucho de computadoras, pero quiere aprender a ver fotografías que recibe en email y saber cómo mandarles fotos a otros amigos. Termina esta conversación entre Alejandra y su abuela. Usa órdenes de **tú** y pronombres de complementos directos e indirectos si es posible.

ABUELA        Para abrir una foto de un email, hago clic aquí, ¿no?

ALEJANDRA     Sí, abuela, _____ (1) clic allí.

ABUELA        Lo hice. Ahhh, ¡qué bonita! ¿La descargo ahora?

ALEJANDRA     No, no _____ (2) ahora. Solo vas a descargarla si quieres tener la foto para siempre en tu computadora.

ABUELA        Huy, primero tengo que copiarla, ¿no?

ALEJANDRA     Sí, _____ (3) primero.

ABUELA        ¿Ahora abro un email nuevo?

ALEJANDRA     Sí, _____ (4) ahora.

ABUELA        ¿Escribo la dirección y el mensaje?

ALEJANDRA     Correcto, _____ (5) ahora.

ABUELA        ¿Y dónde copio la foto?

ALEJANDRA     _____ (6) allí mismo en el email después de lo que escribiste.

ABUELA        ¡Huy! Allí está. ¿Luego le mando el email a mi amigo?

ALEJANDRA     Exacto. _____ (7) ahora mismo.

ABUELA        Tengo una nieta superinteligente y muy buena profesora.

# Un poco de todo

**ACTIVIDAD 25 ¿Cuánto sabes?** Marca si estas oraciones son ciertas (**C**) o falsas (**F**). Corrige las oraciones falsas. Busca en Internet si no sabes la respuesta.

1. _____ El Aconcagua es la montaña más alta del mundo.

_____

2. _____ Hay más de veinticinco países de habla española en el mundo.

_____

3. _____ San Agustín, en la Florida, es una ciudad tan vieja como Plymouth, Massachusetts, en los Estados Unidos.

_____

4. _____ El salto Ángel, en Venezuela, es la catarata más alta del mundo.

_____

5. _____ La papa es tan importante en Centroamérica y en México como el maíz en los Andes en Suramérica.

_____

6. _____ Las montañas de los Andes son tan altas como las Rocosas en Norteamérica.

_____

7. _____ La Pirámide de la Luna es tan alta como la Pirámide del Sol.

_____

**ACTIVIDAD 26** **Imágenes satelitales** Un profesor chileno le explica a su clase de segundo grado cómo mirar imágenes satelitales de su ciudad, Santiago, en Google. Escribe órdenes formales o informales.

PROFESOR        ¿Todos están en la página web de mapas de Google?

ESTUDIANTES    Sí.

PROFESOR        Bien. Ahora _____ (1. mirar) el mapa,

_____ (2. buscar) la palabra "satélite".

PEPITO          ¿Dónde la busco?

PROFESOR        _____ (3. Buscarla) arriba a la derecha en el mapa.

PEPITO          Gracias, ahora la veo.

PROFESOR        Bueno, ahora _____ (4. hacer) Uds. clic en la palabra "satélite".

Una vez que hicieron esto, _____ (5. escribir) "Santiago, Chile" y

_____ (6. hacer) clic en el botón que dice "búsqueda".

ESTUDIANTES    ¡Qué bonito! ¡Increíble!

PEPITO          Yo no veo fotos.

PROFESOR        A ver, Pepito, ¿hiciste clic?

PEPITO          Ah, no, señor.

PROFESOR        Pues, _____ (7. hacerlo) ahora.

PEPITO          Ya veo.

PROFESOR        Bien. Es posible ver la foto de Santiago desde más cerca o más lejos. ¿Ven esta

línea vertical a la izquierda de la foto? _____ (8. Hacer)

clic, pero no _____ (9. levantar) el dedo, y luego

_____ (10. subir) o _____ (11. bajar) el

rectángulo. Si lo suben, van a ver la foto más de cerca.

| PEPITO | ¡No lo puedo creer! ¡Allá está mi casa! ¡También veo el estacionamiento de la escuela! Profesor, ¡allí está su carro! |
|---|---|
| ALICIA | Mi computadora no funciona. Lo subo y lo bajo y no pasa nada. |
| PROFESOR | Es que levantaste el dedo. _____ (12. Hacer) clic sin levantar el dedo. No _____ (13. levantarlo). Ahora _____ (14. subirlo) y _____ (15. bajarlo). |
| ALICIA | Ah, ya veo, ya veo. Mire señor, allí está el Palacio de la Moneda. Gracias. |

**ACTIVIDAD 27** **El entrenador personal** Carlos tiene que bajar de peso rápidamente antes de una operación y, por eso, va a un gimnasio todos los días con un entrenador personal. Termina estas instrucciones que le dio el entrenador a Carlos. Usa órdenes de **tú** para los verbos indicados y comparativos para completar los otros espacios en blanco.

1. _____ (Correr) 300 metros. Debes correr _____ rápido como _____

_____.

2. _____ (Sentarte) en esta silla. _____ (Levantar) la pierna derecha.

No _____ (bajarla). La pierna debe estar _____ recta (straight) como

_____. Después de un minuto _____ (hacer) lo mismo con la

izquierda.

3. Después de salir del gimnasio, no _____ (ir) a McDonald's y no _____ (comer)

comida con muchas calorías. Si haces ejercicio y si comes bien, después de tu operación vas a

recuperarte tan rápido _____ un abrir y cerrar de ojos.

# Lectura

## Estrategia de lectura: Understanding the Writer's Purpose

As you read, you need to focus your attention on the writer's purpose to best understand the text. Is the writer trying to inform, convince, entertain, or complain? To determine this, focus on how the writer describes or informs the reader.

**ACTIVIDAD 28** **El propósito** Lee el título y el artículo rápidamente para contestar esta pregunta. No pares para buscar el significado de palabras que no entiendes.

¿Cuál es la intención del autor?

a. convencer a posibles turistas de visitar estos lugares

b. informar sobre fenómenos inexplicables y costumbres interesantes del mundo hispano

c. entretener al lector con cosas curiosas

**ACTIVIDAD 29** **Oración principal e ideas de apoyo** Mientras lees el siguiente artículo, escribe las oraciones principales de los párrafos indicados y toma apuntes sobre las ideas de apoyo.

Párrafo 2: _____

    Ideas de apoyo:

    _____

    _____

    _____

Párrafo 3: _____

    Ideas de apoyo:

    _____

    _____

    _____

Párrafo 4: _____

    Ideas de apoyo:

    _____

    _____

    _____

    _____

Párrafo 5: _____

    Ideas de apoyo:

    _____

    _____

    _____

    _____

    _____

# Curiosidades y costumbres del mundo hispano

**Líneas de Nasca**

En algunos países hispanos se encuentran enigmas difíciles de comprender. Hay enigmas arqueológicos intrigantes que se están investigando, pero quizás nunca se encuentre una explicación para ellos. Por otro lado, hay fenómenos religiosos curiosos que tienen su origen en civilizaciones pasadas.

Uno de los fenómenos arqueológicos inexplicables son los dibujos de Nasca, Perú. Allí, en un desierto, hay imágenes gigantescas de animales y flores que solo pueden verse en su totalidad desde el aire. También hay unas líneas muy derechas. Algunos dicen que tal vez sean pistas de aterrizaje[1] que se hicieron en la época prehistórica para visitantes extraterrestres. Otros opinan que es el trabajo de una civilización avanzada para marcar fechas en el calendario.

Otro enigma que contradice toda lógica está en la Isla de Pascua, Chile. Está en medio del océano Pacífico a más de 3.500 kilómetros de Chile. Es una de las islas más remotas del mundo. Allí, al lado del mar, hay unas cabezas enormes de piedra volcánica que se llaman moáis. Hay mucha controversia sobre el origen de estos monolitos, pero se cree que se construyeron unos cuatrocientos años antes de Cristo. Algunas de estas piedras pesan más de veinte toneladas[2] cada una y, hoy en día, todavía es inexplicable cómo una pequeña población pudo moverlas tantos kilómetros, desde el volcán hasta la costa. Hay gente que afirma que es un fenómeno sobrenatural.

En el mundo hispano no solo hay fenómenos arqueológicos fascinantes; existen también algunas costumbres religiosas que muestran aspectos únicos de la cultura. Una de estas costumbres es cómo usan la hoja de coca los indígenas de Bolivia y Perú. Ellos le ofrecen la coca a la diosa Pachamama para que ella les dé buena suerte; también mascan[3] la hoja de coca para combatir el hambre y el cansancio que causa la altitud de las montañas andinas. La hoja de coca se usa además en esa zona para predecir el futuro y para diagnosticar enfermedades.

Un fenómeno religioso que coexiste con el catolicismo es la santería, común en varios países del Caribe. Es de origen africano y consiste en la identificación de dioses africanos con santos cristianos. Cuando los españoles trajeron a los esclavos a América, los forzaron a adoptar el cristianismo, pero ellos no abandonaron totalmente su propia religión y el resultado fue una mezcla de las dos religiones. La santería que se practica hoy en día varía de país en país. En Cuba, por ejemplo, los orishas (dioses) corresponden a los santos cristianos: Babalú es el nombre de San Lázaro y es el protector de los enfermos; Changó, el dios del rayo[4], es Santa Bárbara. Hay símbolos especiales asociados con cada orisha y rituales para honrarlos.

Estos fenómenos arqueológicos y estas costumbres religiosas nos muestran varios aspectos de la cultura hispana. Conocer las costumbres propias de otras culturas nos ayuda a comprenderlas mejor.

[1]pistas... *landing strips* [2]toneladas métricas (una tonelada métrica =2.204 libras) [3] *they chew* [4] *lightning*

Nombre _____ Sección _____ Fecha _____

**ACTIVIDAD 30** **Preguntas** Contesta estas preguntas, usando oraciones completas.

1. ¿Crees que las líneas de Nasca son para extraterrestres? _____
   _____

2. ¿Cuál es el fenómeno inexplicable de la Isla de Pascua? _____
   _____

3. ¿Para qué usan la coca los indígenas de Perú y Bolivia? _____
   _____

4. ¿Cuál es el origen de la santería? _____
   _____

5. ¿Conoces otros fenómenos inexplicables en otras partes del mundo? ¿Cuál o cuáles? _____
   _____

# LAB MANUAL

# Bienvenidos al mundo hispano

**Capítulo P**

## Tips for Using the Lab Audio Program

1. Listen to and do the pronunciation section when you begin to study each chapter.

2. Do the rest of the lab activities after studying the grammar explanation in the second half of each chapter.

3. Read the directions and the items in each activity in your Lab Manual before listening to the audio.

4. You are not expected to understand every word you hear on the audio. All you need to be able to do is to comprehend enough information to complete the activities in the Lab Manual.

5. Listen to the audio as many times as may be needed. At first you may feel that the speakers speak too quickly; however, with practice you will find that it becomes easier as you become more comfortable listening to Spanish.

## Mejora tu pronunciación

### The Spanish Alphabet

The Spanish alphabet has 27 letters, one more than in English, because it includes the letter **ñ.** The letters **k** and **w** are usually used with words of foreign origin.

**ACTIVIDAD** **1** **Escucha y repite** Listen and repeat the letters of the Spanish alphabet. You will hear alternate pronunciations for some letters.

| a | e | i | m | p | t | x |
|---|---|---|---|---|---|---|
| b | f | j | n | q | u | y |
| c | g | k | ñ | r | v | z |
| d | h | l | o | s | w | |

### Stressing Words

You have already seen Spanish stress patterns in the text. Remember that a word that ends in *n, s,* or a vowel is stressed on the next-to-last syllable; for example, **repitan, Honduras, amigo.** A word that ends in a consonant other than *n* or *s* is stressed on the last syllable; as in the words **español, favor, Madrid.** Any exception to these two rules is indicated by a written accent mark on the stressed vowel, as in **Andrés, Perú, ángel.**

Placing correct stress on words helps you to be better understood. For example, the word **amigo** has its natural stress on the next-to-last syllable. Listen again: **amigo,** not **amigo,** nor **amigo; amigo.** Try to keep stress in mind when learning new words.

**ACTIVIDAD 2** Escucha y subraya

**A.** Listen to the following names of Hispanic countries and cities and underline the stressed syllables. You will hear each name twice.

1. Pa-na-ma
2. Bo-go-ta
3. Cu-ba
4. Ve-ne-zue-la

5. Me-xi-co
6. Ma-drid
7. Te-gu-ci-gal-pa
8. A-sun-cion

**B.** Pause the recording and decide which of the words from part **A** need written accents. Write the missing accents over the appropriate vowels.

**ACTIVIDAD 3** Los acentos

**A.** Listen to the following words related to an office and underline the stressed syllables. You will hear each word twice.

1. o-fi-ci-na
2. di-rec-tor
3. pa-pel
4. dis-cu-sion

5. te-le-fo-no
6. bo-li-gra-fo
7. se-cre-ta-rio
8. ins-truc-cio-nes

**B.** Pause the recording and decide which of the words from part **A** need written accents. Write the missing accents over the appropriate vowels.

# Mejora tu comprensión

**ACTIVIDAD 4** **La fiesta** You will hear three introductions at a party. Indicate whether each one is formal or informal.

© Cengage Learning 2013

|  | Formal | Informal |
|---|---|---|
| 1. | ☐ | ☐ |
| 2. | ☐ | ☐ |
| 3. | ☐ | ☐ |

**ACTIVIDAD 5** **¿De dónde eres?** You will hear three conversations. Don't worry if you can't understand every word. Just concentrate on discovering where the people in the pictures are from. Write this information on the lines provided.

Illustrations:
© Cengage
Learning 2013

1. _____    2. _____    3. _____

**ACTIVIDAD 6** **¡Hola! ¡Adiós!** You will hear three conversations. Don't worry if you can't understand every word. Just concentrate on discovering whether the people are greeting each other or saying good-bye.

|  | Saludo *(Greeting)* | Despedida *(Saying good-bye)* |
|---|---|---|
| 1. | ❒ | ❒ |
| 2. | ❒ | ❒ |
| 3. | ❒ | ❒ |

**ACTIVIDAD 7** **La entrevista** A man is interviewing a woman for a job. You will only hear what the man is saying. As you listen, number the response that the woman should logically make to each of the interviewer's statements and questions. Before listening to the interview, pause the recording, and look at the woman's possible responses. You may have to listen to the interview more than once.

_____ Gracias.

_____ Soy de Caracas.

_____ Claudia Menéndez.

_____ ¡Muy bien!

**ACTIVIDAD 8** **Las capitales** You will hear a series of questions on the capitals of various countries. Select the correct answers. Before listening to each question, pause the recording, and read the three possible responses.

| | | | |
|---|---|---|---|
| 1. | Washington, DC | San Salvador | Lima |
| 2. | México | Guatemala | Madrid |
| 3. | Ottawa | Washington, DC | Buenos Aires |
| 4. | Lima | Bogotá | Tegucigalpa |
| 5. | Caracas | Santiago | Managua |

**ACTIVIDAD** **9** **Las órdenes** You will hear a teacher give several commands. Number the picture that corresponds to each command. If necessary, pause the recording after each item.

_____

_____

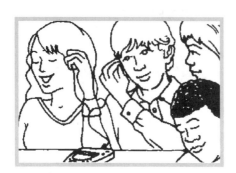

_____

_____

Illustrations: © Cengage Learning 2013

**ACTIVIDAD** **10** **Las siglas** Listen and write the following acronyms.

1. _____
2. _____
3. _____
4. _____
5. _____
6. _____

**ACTIVIDAD** **11** **¿Cómo se escribe?** You will hear two conversations. Concentrate on listening to the names that are spelled out within the conversations and write them down.

1. _____
2. _____

# ¿Quién es?

## Mejora tu pronunciación

### Vowels

In Spanish, there are only five basic vowel sounds: **a, e, i, o, u.** These correspond to the five vowels of the alphabet. In contrast, English has long and short vowels; for example, the long *i* in *pie* and the short *i* in *pit*. In addition, English has the short sound, schwa, which is used to pronounce many unstressed vowels. For example, the first and last *a* in the word *banana* are unstressed and are therefore pronounced [ ə ]. Listen: *banana.* In Spanish, there is no similar sound because vowels are usually pronounced the same way whether they are stressed or not. Listen: **banana.**

**ACTIVIDAD 1** **Escucha la diferencia**  Listen to the contrast in vowel sounds between English and Spanish.

| Inglés | Español |
|--------|---------|
| 1. map | mapa |
| 2. net | neto |
| 3. beam | viga |
| 4. tone | tono |
| 5. taboo | tabú |

**ACTIVIDAD 2** **Escucha y repite**  Listen and repeat the following names, paying special attention to the pronunciation of the vowel sounds.

1. **Ana Lara**

2. **Pepe Méndez**

3. **Mimí Pinti**

4. **Toto Soto**

5. **Lulú Mumú**

**ACTIVIDAD 3** **Repite las oraciones**  Listen and repeat the following sentences. Pay attention to the pronunciation of the vowel sounds.

1. ¿Cómo se llama Ud.?
2. Buenos días.
3. ¿Cómo se escribe?
4. ¿Quién es ella?
5. Juan Carlos es de Perú.
6. Las dos Coca-Colas.

# Mejora tu comprensión

**ACTIVIDAD 4** **Guatemala** You will hear a series of numbers. Draw a line to connect these numbers in the order in which you hear them. When you finish, you will have a map of Guatemala.

| | | | | | | | | | |
|---|---|---|---|---|---|---|---|---|---|
| 1 | 2 | 3 | 4 | 5 | 6 | 7 | 8 | 9 | 10 |
| 11 | 12 | 13 | 14 | 15 | 16 | 17 | 18 | 19 | 20 |
| 21 | 22 | 23 | 24 | 25 | 26 | 27 | 28 | 29 | 30 |
| 31 | 32 | 33 | 34 | 35 | 36 | 37 | 38 | 39 | 40 |
| 41 | 42 | 43 | 44 | 45 | 46 | 47 | 48 | 49 | 50 |
| 51 | 52 | 53 | 54 | 55 | 56 | 57 | 58 | 59 | 60 |
| 61 | 62 | 63 | 64 | 65 | 66 | 67 | 68 | 69 | 70 |
| 71 | 72 | 73 | 74 | 75 | 76 | 77 | 78 | 79 | 80 |
| 81 | 82 | 83 | 84 | 85 | 86 | 87 | 88 | 89 | 90 |
| 91 | 92 | 93 | 94 | 95 | 96 | 97 | 98 | 99 | 100 |

**ACTIVIDAD 5** **Los números de teléfono** You will hear a telephone conversation and two recorded messages. Don't worry if you can't understand every word. Just concentrate on writing down the telephone number that is given in each case.

1. _____  2. _____  3. _____

**ACTIVIDAD 6** **¿Él o ella?** Listen to the following three conversations and select the person who is being talked about in each case. Don't worry if you can't understand every word. Just concentrate on discovering to whom each discussion refers.

1. ☐   ☐        2. ☐   ☐        3. ☐   ☐

**ACTIVIDAD 7** **En el tren** Carlos is talking to a woman with a child on the train. Listen to the four questions that he asks. For each of the four questions, number the appropriate response 1 to 4. Note that there is one extra response below that will not be used. Before you begin the activity, pause the recording and read the possible responses.

_____ Dos años.

_____ Andrea.

_____ Son de México.

_____ De Tegucigalpa.

_____ Ella se llama Débora.

**ACTIVIDAD 8** **La conversación**

**A.** You will hear a series of sentences. Write each sentence or pairs of sentences you hear in the first column below. Be sure to use correct capitalization and punctuation. You will hear each sentence or pair of sentences twice.

| | |
|---|---|
| A. _____ | _____ |
| B. _____ | _____ |
| C. _____ | _____ |
| D. _____ | _____ |
| E. _____ | _____ |
| F. _____ | _____ |
| G. _____ | _____ |
| H. _____ | _____ |

**B.** Now stop the recording and put the sentences you have written in the correct order to form a logical conversation. Number each sentence in the blank in the right-hand column above.

**ACTIVIDAD 9** **En el hotel** You will hear a conversation between a hotel receptionist and a guest who is registering. Fill out the computer screen with the information about the guest. Don't worry if you can't understand every word. Just concentrate on listening for the information needed. You may have to listen to the conversation more than once. Remember to look at the computer screen before you begin the activity.

Huésped n.º 3586

NOMBRE:

OCUPACIÓN:

DIRECCIÓN: Calle 5 N.º 232

CIUDAD:                    PAÍS: Nicaragua

APARTADO POSTAL:

TELÉFONO:

**ACTIVIDAD 10** **Los participantes** Mr. Torres and his assistant are going over the participants they have chosen for a TV game show. Listen to their conversation and fill out the chart with information on the participants. Don't worry if you can't understand every word. Just concentrate on listening for the information needed to complete the chart. You may have to listen to the conversation more than once.

| Participantes | Nacionalidad | Ocupación | Edad |
|---|---|---|---|
| Francisco | *chileno* | | |
| Laura | | *abogada* | |
| Gonzalo | | | *30* |
| Andrea | *mexicana* | | |

**ACTIVIDAD 11** **Una hispana famosa** Listen to the following description of a famous Hispanic and complete the chart.

Nombre: _____

Nacionalidad: _____    Origen: _____ y cubano

Ocupación: _____ y _____

Edad: _____ años

# Capítulo 2

# ¿Te gusta?

## Mejora tu pronunciación

### The consonant *d*

The consonant **d** is pronounced two different ways in Spanish. When **d** appears at the beginning of a word or after *n* or *l,* it is pronounced by pressing the tongue against the back of the teeth; for example, **depósito.** When **d** appears after a vowel, after a consonant other than *n* or *l,* or at the end of a word, it is pronounced like the *th* in the English word *they*; for example, **médico.**

**ACTIVIDAD  1  Escucha y repite**  Listen and repeat the names of the following occupations, paying attention to the pronunciation of the letter **d.**

1. **d**irector
2. **d**eportista
3. ven**d**e**d**or
4. mé**d**ico
5. estu**d**iante
6. aboga**d**a

### Spanish *p, t,* and [*k*]

In Spanish, **p, t,** and **[k]** (**[k]** represents a sound) are unaspirated. This means that no puff of air occurs when they are pronounced. Listen to the difference: *Paul,* **Pablo.**

**ACTIVIDAD  2  Escucha y repite**  Listen and repeat the names of the following objects often found around the house. Pay attention to the pronunciation of **p, t,** and **[k].**

1. **p**erió**d**i**c**o
2. **t**eléfono
3. **c**ompu**t**adora
4. **t**elevisor
5. **c**ámara
6. es**c**ri**t**orio

**ACTIVIDAD  3  Las cosas de Marisel**  Listen and repeat the following conversation between Teresa and Marisel. Pay attention to the pronunciation of **p, t,** and **[k].**

TERESA    ¿Tienes café?
MARISEL   ¡Claro que sí!
TERESA    ¡Ah! Tienes computadora.
MARISEL   Sí, es una Macintosh. Me gusta la Macintosh.
TERESA    ¿De veras? A mí no me gusta la Mac.

# Mejora tu comprensión

**ACTIVIDAD** **4** **La perfumería** You will hear a conversation in a drugstore between a customer and a salesclerk. Select only the products that the customer buys and indicate whether she buys one or more than one of each item. Don't worry if you can't understand every word. Just concentrate on the customer's purchases. Before you listen to the conversation, read the list of products.

|   |   | Uno/a | Más de uno/a *(More than one)* |
|---|---|:---:|:---:|
| 1. | aspirina | ❑ | ❑ |
| 2. | crema de afeitar | ❑ | ❑ |
| 3. | champú | ❑ | ❑ |
| 4. | cepillo de dientes | ❑ | ❑ |
| 5. | desodorante | ❑ | ❑ |
| 6. | jabón | ❑ | ❑ |
| 7. | pasta de dientes | ❑ | ❑ |
| 8. | peine | ❑ | ❑ |
| 9. | perfume | ❑ | ❑ |

**ACTIVIDAD** **5** **El baño de las chicas** A little girl is visiting her older cousin, Teresa, at her dorm. She is now in the bathroom asking Teresa a lot of questions. As you hear the conversation, indicate in the drawing which of the items mentioned belong to whom.

© Cengage Learning 2013

**ACTIVIDAD** **6** **¿Hombre o mujer?** Listen to the following remarks and select the person or persons being described in each situation.

1. _____ _____     2. _____ _____

3 _____ _____     4. _____ _____

**ACTIVIDAD** **7** **El mensaje telefónico** Ms. Rodríguez calls home and leaves a message on the answering machine for her children, Esteban and Carina. Ms. Rodríguez reminds them to do four things. Select each item that she reminds them about. Before you listen to the message, pause the recording and read the list of reminders. Notice there are five items in the list and she only mentions four. Don't worry if you can't understand every word. Just concentrate on which reminders are for Esteban and which ones are for Carina.

|  | Esteban | Carina |
|---|---|---|
| 1. comprar hamburguesas | ❐ | ❐ |
| 2. llamar a Carlos | ❐ | ❐ |
| 3. estudiar matemáticas | ❐ | ❐ |
| 4. mirar una película | ❐ | ❐ |
| 5. no ir al dentista | ❐ | ❐ |

**ACTIVIDAD** **8** **El regalo de cumpleaños**

**A.** You will hear a phone conversation between Álvaro and his mother, who would like to know what she can buy him for his birthday. Select the things that Álvaro says he already has. Don't worry if you can't understand every word. Just concentrate on what Álvaro doesn't need. Before you listen to the conversation, read the list of items.

**Álvaro tiene…**

❐ escritorio     ❐ lámpara     ❐ reloj     ❐ silla     ❐ toallas

**B.** Now write what Álvaro's mother is going to give him for his birthday. You may need to listen to the conversation again.

El regalo es _____.

**ACTIVIDAD 9** Los planes de Diana

**A.** Pause the recording and write in Spanish two things you are going to do this weekend.

1. _____

2. _____

**B.** As you listen to a phone conversation between Diana, a new student who is in Puerto Rico for the semester, and her roommate Claudia, write what Diana is going to do this weekend. Don't worry if you can't understand every word. Just concentrate on Diana's plans. You may have to listen to the conversation more than once.

| DÍA | ACTIVIDADES |
|---|---|
| viernes | *3:00 p.m.: examen de literatura* |
| sábado | |
| domingo | |

**ACTIVIDAD 10** La conexión amorosa Mónica has gone to a dating service and has recorded a message describing her likes and dislikes. Listen to the recording and then choose a suitable man for her from the two shown. Don't worry if you can't understand every word. Just concentrate on Mónica's preferences. You may use the following space to take notes. Before you listen to the description, read the information on the two men.

A Mónica le gusta:

NOMBRE: Óscar Varone
OCUPACIÓN: profesor de historia
EDAD: 32
GUSTOS: música salsa, escribir

NOMBRE: Lucas González
OCUPACIÓN: médico
EDAD: 30
GUSTOS: música clásica, salsa, esquiar

Illustrations: © Cengage Learning 2013

El hombre perfecto para Mónica es _____.
(nombre)

**ACTIVIDAD 11** Un hispano famoso Listen to the following description of Junot Díaz and complete the chart.

| Junot Díaz | Nacionalidad: _____ |
|---|---|
| Ocupación: profesor y _____ | Premio *(award)*: _____ |
| Gustos: _____, _____ novelas y _____ | |

# ¿Qué haces hoy?

## Mejora tu pronunciación

### The consonants *r* and *rr*

The consonant **r** in Spanish has two different pronunciations: the flap, as in **caro,** similar to the double *t* sound in *butter* and *petty,* and the trill sound, as in **carro.** The **r** is pronounced with the trill only at the beginning of a word or after *l* or *n,* as in **reservado, sonrisa** *(smile).* The **rr** is always pronounced with the trill, as in **aburrido.**

**ACTIVIDAD  1  Escucha y repite**  Listen and repeat the following descriptive words. Pay attention to the pronunciation of the consonants **r** and **rr.**

1. enfermo
2. rubio
3. moreno
4. gordo

5. aburrido
6. enamorado
7. preocupado
8. borracho

**ACTIVIDAD  2  Escucha y marca la diferencia**  Circle the word you hear pronounced in each of the following word pairs. Before you begin, look over the pictures and word pairs.

1.   caro   carro
2.   coro   corro
3.   ahora   ahorra
4.   cero   cerro

**ACTIVIDAD 3** **Estudiante universitaria** Listen and repeat the following sentences about a college student. Pay attention to the pronunciation of the consonants **r** and **rr**.

1. Estudia turismo.

2. Trabaja en una agencia de viajes.

3. Su papá es un actor famoso de Costa Rica.

4. ¿Pero ella es costarricense?

# Mejora tu comprensión

**ACTIVIDAD 4** **¿Dónde?** You will hear four remarks. Match the letter of each remark with the place where it is most likely to be heard. Before you listen to the remarks, review the list of places. Notice that there are extra place names.

1. _____ farmacia

2. _____ biblioteca

3. _____ teatro

4. _____ supermercado

5. _____ agencia de viajes

6. _____ librería

**ACTIVIDAD 5** **Mi niña es...** A man has lost his daughter in a department store and is describing her to the store detective. Listen to his description and place a check mark below the drawing of the child he is looking for. Don't worry if you can't understand every word. Just concentrate on the father's description of the child. Before you listen to the conversation, look at the drawings.

Illustrations: © Cengage Learning 2013

1. ☐

2. ☐

3. ☐

**ACTIVIDAD** **6** **Su hijo está...** Use the words in the list to complete the chart about Pablo as you hear a conversation between his teacher and his mother. Fill in **en general** to describe the way Pablo usually is. Fill in **esta semana** to indicate how he has been behaving this week.

| aburrido | bueno | inteligente |
|----------|-------|-------------|
| antipático | cansado | simpático |

**Pablo Hernández**

En general, él es _____

_____.

Pero, esta semana él está _____

_____.

**ACTIVIDAD** **7** **La conversación telefónica** Patricia, a Puerto Rican student who is studying in Nicaragua, is talking with her father long-distance. You will hear her father's portion of the conversation only. After you hear each of the father's questions, complete Patricia's partial replies.

1. _____ _____ Claudia.

2. _____ economía.

3. _____ _____ la Universidad de Managua.

4. _____ de Colombia.

5. _____, pero ahora _____ en Quito de vacaciones.

6. _____ es comerciante.

7. _____ ama de casa.

8. _____ _____, gracias.

9. _____, _____ mucho.

10. _____ en la agencia de viajes del tío Alejandro.

11. _____ muy ocupado.

**ACTIVIDAD 8** **Intercambio estudiantil** Marcos contacts a student-exchange program in order to have a foreign student stay with him. Complete the following form as you hear his conversation with the program's secretary. Don't worry if you can't understand every word. Just concentrate on filling out the form. Before you listen to the conversation, read the form.

| C.C.D.I.E.: Consejo Costarricense de Intercambio Estudiantil | |
|---|---|
| Nombre del interesado: *Marcos Alarcón* | |
| Teléfono: | Celular: |
| Edad: | Ocupación: |
| Gustos: *leer ciencia ficción* | |
| Preferencia de nacionalidad: | |

**ACTIVIDAD 9** **Las descripciones**

**A.** Choose three adjectives from the list of personality characteristics that best describe each of the people shown. Pause the recording while you make your selection.

| artístico/a | optimista | serio/a |
|---|---|---|
| intelectual | paciente | simpático/a |
| inteligente | pesimista | tímido/a |

Illustrations: © Cengage Learning 2013

**Tu opinión**

1. _____

**Tu opinión**

2. _____

**B.** Now listen as these two people describe themselves, and enter these adjectives in the blanks provided. You may have to listen to the descriptions more than once.

**Su descripción**

1. _____

**Su descripción**

2. _____

**ACTIVIDAD 10** **El detective Alonso** Detective Alonso is speaking into his digital voice recorder while following a woman. Number the drawings in the upper left corner according to the order in which he says the events take place. Don't worry if you can't understand every word. Just concentrate on the sequence of events.

**ACTIVIDAD 11** **Un hispano famoso** Listen to the following description of Franklin Chang-Díaz and complete the following chart.

| Franklin Chang-Díaz |
|---|
| **Ocupaciones:** físico _____ |
| _____ _____ |
| **Personalidad:** _____ _____ |
| serio |

# Un día típico

**Capítulo 4**

## Mejora tu pronunciación

### The consonant *ñ*

The pronunciation of the consonant **ñ** is similar to the *ny* in the English word *canyon*.

**ACTIVIDAD 1** **Escucha y repite** Listen and repeat the following words, paying attention to the pronunciation of the consonants **n** and **ñ**.

1.  cana   caña   2.  una   uña

3.  mono   moño   4.  sonar   soñar

Illustrations: © Cengage Learning 2013

**ACTIVIDAD 2** **Escucha y repite** Listen and repeat the following sentences. Pay special attention to the pronunciation of the consonants **n** and **ñ**.

1.  Subo una montaña.
2.  Trabajo con **niños** que **no** tien**en** padres.
3.  Tú conoces al se**ñor** de Rodrigo, ¿**no**?
4.  ¿Cuándo es tu cumplea**ños**?

# Mejora tu comprensión

**ACTIVIDAD 3** **Los sonidos de la mañana** Listen to the following sounds and write what Paco is doing this morning.

1. _____

2. _____

3. _____

4. _____

**ACTIVIDAD 4** **El tiempo este fin de semana**

**A.** As you hear this weekend's weather forecast for Bolivia, draw the corresponding weather symbols on the map under the names of the places mentioned. Remember to read the place names on the map and look at the symbols before you listen to the forecast.

lluvia   nube   viento   nieve   sol

**B.** Now replay the activity and listen to the forecast again, this time adding the temperatures in Celsius under the names of the places mentioned.

**ACTIVIDAD 5 La identificación del ladrón** As you hear a woman describing a thief to a police artist, complete the artist's sketch. You may have to replay the activity and listen to the description more than once.

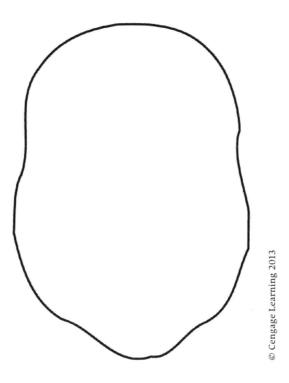

© Cengage Learning 2013

**ACTIVIDAD 6 Celebraciones hispanas**

**A.** A woman will describe some important holidays around the Hispanic world. As you listen to the description of each holiday, write the date on which it is celebrated.

**Fecha**

1. el Día de los Muertos                    el _____

2. el Día de los Santos Inocentes          el _____

3. el Día Internacional del Amigo          el _____

4. el Día de Reyes                          el _____

**B.** Now listen again and match the holiday with the activity people usually do on that day. Write the number of the holiday from the preceding list.

a. _____ Las personas reciben emails de otras personas.

b. _____ Las personas hacen bromas *(pranks)*.

c. _____ Las personas hacen un altar en casa.

d. _____ Los niños reciben juguetes *(toys)*.

**ACTIVIDAD 7** ¿Conoces a ese chico?

**A.** Miriam and Julio are discussing some guests at a party. As you listen to their conversation, draw lines to indicate which name goes with which person.

Miguel

Laura

Carmen

Ramón

Begoña

© Cengage Learning 2013

**B.** Now listen to the conversation again, and next to each name write who the person knows or what the person knows how to do using **conocer** or **saber.**

**ACTIVIDAD 8** **La entrevista** Lola Drones, a newspaper reporter, is interviewing a famous actor about his weekend habits. Cross out those activities listed in Lola's notebook that the actor does *not* do on weekends. Remember to read the list of possible activities before you listen to the interview.

se levanta tarde

corre por el parque

hace gimnasia en un gimnasio

ve televisión

estudia sus guiones (scripts)

sale con su familia

va al cine

© Cengage Learning 2013

**ACTIVIDAD 9** **Un hispano famoso** Listen to the following description of Mario Vargas Llosa and complete the chart.

| Mario Vargas Llosa | Nacionalidad: _____ |
|---|---|
| Vive en: _____, _____, París y Londres | Ocupación: _____ |
| Premio *(award)*: _____ | Cantidad de libros: _____ |
| Tema que le gusta: la _____ | Orientación política: _____ moderado |

# Los planes y las compras

**Capítulo 5**

## Mejora tu pronunciación

### The consonants *ll* and *y*

The consonants **ll** and **y** are usually pronounced like the *y* in the English word *yellow*. When the **y** appears at the end of a word, or alone, it is pronounced like the vowel **i** in Spanish.

**ACTIVIDAD 1** **Escucha y repite** Listen and repeat the following verse. Pay special attention to the pronunciation of the **ll** and the **y**.

Hay una toalla
en la playa amarilla.

Hoy no llueve.
Ella no tiene silla.

**ACTIVIDAD 2** **Escucha y repite** Listen and repeat the following sentences. Pay special attention to the pronunciation of the **ll** and the **y**.

1. **Y** por favor, otra cerveza.

2. ¿Tiene por casualidad un periódico de ho**y**?

3. Se come muy bien all**í**.

4. **Y** entonces, como es su cumpleaños, e**ll**a invita.

## Mejora tu comprensión

**ACTIVIDAD 3** **¿Qué acaban de hacer?** As you hear the following short conversations, select what the people in each situation have just finished doing. Remember to read the list of possible activities before you begin.

1. a. Acaban de ver una película.
   b. Acaban de hablar con un director.

2. a. Acaban de beber un café.
   b. Acaban de comer.

3. a. Acaban de ducharse.
   b. Acaban de jugar un partido de fútbol.

**ACTIVIDAD 4** **El cine** You will hear a recorded message and a conversation, both about movie schedules. As you listen, complete the information on the cards. Don't worry if you can't understand every word. Just concentrate on filling out the cards. Remember to look at the cards before beginning.

---

**GRAN REX**

*Abel*

Horario: _____, _____, _____, 10:00

Precio: $_____   $_____ matiné

---

**SPLENDID**

*La mujer cucaracha*

Horario: _____, 8:00, _____

Precio: $_____   $_____ matiné

---

**ACTIVIDAD 5** **Las citas del Dr. Malapata** As you hear Dr. Malapata's receptionist making appointments for two patients, complete the corresponding scheduling cards.

---

**DR. MALAPATA**

Paciente:
Fecha:                          Hora:
Fecha de hoy:

---

**DR. MALAPATA**

Paciente:
Fecha:                          Hora:
Fecha de hoy:

**ACTIVIDAD 6 Las sensaciones** Listen to the conversation between Alberto and Dora, and select the different sensations or feelings they have. Read the list of sensations and feelings before you listen to the conversation. Note that there are extra sentences.

|  | Alberto | Dora |
|---|---|---|
| 1. Tiene calor. | ❒ | ❒ |
| 2. Tiene frío. | ❒ | ❒ |
| 3. Tiene hambre. | ❒ | ❒ |
| 4. Tiene miedo. | ❒ | ❒ |
| 5. Tiene sed. | ❒ | ❒ |
| 6. Tiene sueño. | ❒ | ❒ |
| 7. Tiene vergüenza. | ❒ | ❒ |

**ACTIVIDAD 7 Ofertas increíbles** Listen to the following radio ad about a department store and select the articles of clothing that are mentioned. Remember to read the list of items before you listen to the ad.

_____ blusas de cuadros

_____ blusas de rayas

_____ camisas de manga corta

_____ camisas de manga larga

_____ chaquetas de cuero

_____ cinturones de plástico

_____ faldas de seda

_____ trajes de baño de algodón

_____ zapatos de diferentes colores

**ACTIVIDAD 8 La fiesta**

**A.** Look at the drawing of a party and write four sentences in Spanish describing what some of the guests are doing. Pause the recording while you write.

Pablo

_____

Fabiana

_____

Lucía

_____

Mariana

_____

© Cengage Learning 2013

1. _____

2. _____

3. _____

4. _____

**B.** Miriam and Julio are discussing four of the guests at the party. As you listen to their conversation, draw an arrow from each guest's name to the appropriate person in the drawing. Don't worry if you can't understand every word. Just concentrate on who's who.

**C.** Now listen to the conversation again and write the occupations of the four guests below their names.

**ACTIVIDAD 9** **Los fines de semana**

**A.** Write three sentences in Spanish describing things you usually do on weekends. Pause the recording while you write.

1. _____

2. _____

3. _____

**B.** Pedro is on the phone talking to his father about what he and his roommate Mario do on weekends. Listen to their conversation and select Pedro's activities versus Mario's. Remember to read the list of activities before you listen to the conversation.

|  | Pedro | Mario |
|---|:---:|:---:|
| 1. Se acuesta temprano. | ❏ | ❏ |
| 2. Se acuesta tarde. | ❏ | ❏ |
| 3. Sale con sus amigos. | ❏ | ❏ |
| 4. Se despierta temprano. | ❏ | ❏ |
| 5. Se despierta tarde. | ❏ | ❏ |
| 6. Duerme 10 horas. | ❏ | ❏ |
| 7. Duerme 14 horas. | ❏ | ❏ |
| 8. Juega al fútbol. | ❏ | ❏ |
| 9. Almuerza con sus amigos. | ❏ | ❏ |
| 10. Pide una pizza. | ❏ | ❏ |
| 11. Juega al tenis. | ❏ | ❏ |

**ACTIVIDAD 10** **Una hispana famosa** Listen to the following description of Carla Fernández and complete the chart.

| Carla Fernández | |
|---|---|
| **Nacionalidad:** _____ | **Ocupación:** _____ |
| **Taller Flora** | |
| • incentiva a _____ indígenas a no _____ sus habilidades artesanales | |
| • estas personas _____ técnicas para hacer y diseñar ropa | |
| • el dinero que reciben por su trabajo:   ❏ justo *(fair)*   ❏ injusto | |

# Ayer y hoy

## Mejora tu pronunciación

### The sound [g]

The sound represented by the letter *g* before *a, o,* and *u* is pronounced a little softer than the English *g* in the word *guy:* **gustar, regalo, tengo.** Because the combinations **ge** and **gi** are pronounced **[he]** and **[hi]**, a *u* is added after the *g* to retain the **[g]** sound: **guitarra, guerra.**

**ACTIVIDAD  1  Escucha y repite**  Listen and repeat the following phrases, paying special attention to the pronunciation of the letter **g.**

1. mi ami**g**a

2. te **g**ustó

3. es ele**g**ante

4. sabes al**g**o

5. no ten**g**o

6. no pa**g**ué

**ACTIVIDAD  2  ¡Qué guapo!**  Listen and repeat the following conversation between Claudio and Marisa. Pay special attention to the pronunciation of the letter **g.**

MARISA     Me **g**ustan mucho.

CLAUDIO    ¿Mis bi**g**otes?

MARISA     Sí, estás **g**uapo pero cansado, ¿no?

CLAUDIO    Es que ju**g**ué al tenis.

MARISA     ¿Con **G**ómez?

CLAUDIO    No, con López, el **g**uía de turismo.

### The sound [k]

The **[k]** sound in Spanish is unaspirated, as in the words **casa, claro, quitar,** and **kilo.** Hear the contrast between the **[k]** sound in English where a puff of air comes out as one pronounces the letter, and the **[k]** sound in Spanish where there is no puff of air: *case,* **caso;** *kilo,* **kilo;** *cape,* **capa.** The **[k]** sound in Spanish is spelled *c* before *a, o,* and *u; qu* before *e* and *i;* and *k* in a few words of foreign origin such as **kiwi, karate, kilómetro.** Remember that the *u* is not pronounced in *que* or *qui,* as in the words **qué** and **quitar.**

**ACTIVIDAD 3** **El saco** Listen and repeat the following conversation between a salesclerk and a customer. Pay attention to the [k] sound.

CLIENTE      ¿**Cu**ánto **cu**esta ese sa**co**?

VENDEDORA      ¿A**qu**el?

CLIENTE      Sí, el de **cu**ero negro.

VENDEDORA      ¿No **qui**ere el sa**co** azul?

CLIENTE      No. Bus**co** uno negro.

# Mejora tu comprensión

**ACTIVIDAD 4** **La tienda Beco** You are in Beco, a department store in Venezuela, and you hear about the sales of the day over the loudspeaker system. As you listen, write the correct price above each of the items shown. Remember that Spanish uses periods where English uses commas and vice versa: **3.500 bolívares fuertes** (Venezuelan currency).

**ACTIVIDAD  5  Los premios**

**A.** You will listen to a radio ad for a photo contest in Venezuela that mentions the prizes **(premios)** that will be awarded and how much each is worth. Before you listen to the ad, stop the recording and write down under **tu opinión** how much you think each item is worth in dollars.

|  | tu opinión | el anuncio |
|---|---|---|
| Volkswagen | $ _____ | _____ bolívares |
| viaje para dos por una semana a Colombia | $ _____ | _____ bolívares |
| cámara profesional | $ _____ | _____ bolívares |
| computadora portátil | $ _____ | _____ bolívares |
| entrada para el concierto de Chino y Nacho | $ _____ | _____ bolívares |

**B.** Now listen to the ad and write down how much each prize is worth in **bolívares** in the second column.

**ACTIVIDAD  6  La habitación de Jorge**  Jorge is angry because Juan Carlos, his roommate, is very messy. As you listen to Jorge describing the mess to Enrique, write the names of the following objects in the drawing of the room, according to where Juan Carlos leaves them.

**medias      teléfono      libros      periódico**

© Cengage Learning 2013

**ACTIVIDAD 7** **¿Presente o pasado?** As you listen to each of the following remarks, select whether the speaker is talking about the present or the past.

|   | Presente | Pasado |
|---|----------|--------|
| 1. | ❑ | ❑ |
| 2. | ❑ | ❑ |
| 3. | ❑ | ❑ |
| 4. | ❑ | ❑ |

**ACTIVIDAD 8** **El fin de semana pasado**

**A.** Write in Spanish three things you did last weekend. Pause the recording while you write.

1. _____

2. _____

3. _____

**B.** Now listen to Raúl and Alicia talking in the office about what they did last weekend. Write **R** next to the things that Raúl did, and **A** next to the things that Alicia did. Remember to look at the list of activities before you listen to the conversation.

1. _____ Fue a una fiesta.

2. _____ Trabajó.

3. _____ Comió en su casa.

4. _____ Se acostó temprano.

5. _____ Fue al cine.

6. _____ Tomó café.

7. _____ Habló con una amiga.

8. _____ Se acostó tarde.

9. _____ Jugó al tenis.

10. _____ Miró TV.

**ACTIVIDAD 9** **La familia de Álvaro** This is an incomplete tree of Álvaro's family. As you listen to the conversation between Álvaro and Clara, complete the tree with the initials of the names listed. Don't be concerned if you don't understand every word. Just concentrate on completing the family tree. You may have to listen to the conversation more than once.

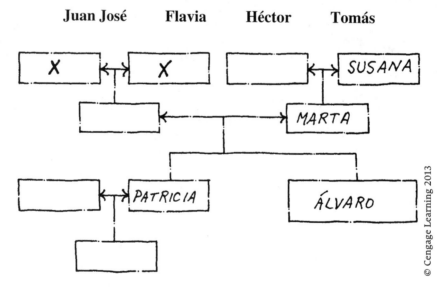

Juan José     Flavia     Héctor     Tomás

© Cengage Learning 2013

**ACTIVIDAD** **10** **Una cena familiar** Tonight there is a family dinner at Álvaro's, and his mother is planning the seating arrangements. Listen to Álvaro's mother, Marta, as she explains her plan to Álvaro. Write the name of each family member on the card in front of his/her place setting. You may have to refer to **Actividad 9** for the names of some of Álvaro's relatives.

**ACTIVIDAD** **11** **La boda de Nando y Olga**

**A.** Nando and Olga have gotten married, and now Hernán, Nando's father, gets a phone call. Read the questions; then listen to the phone call and jot **one-word** answers next to each question. You may have to listen to the conversation more than once.

1. ¿Quién llamó al padre de Nando por teléfono? _____

2. ¿A quién le hizo un vestido la Sra. Montedio? _____

3. ¿Qué le alquiló la mamá de Nando a su hijo? _____

4. ¿Quién les regaló una cámara de video a los novios? _____

5. ¿Quiénes les regalaron un viaje? _____

6. ¿A quiénes llamaron los novios desde la República Dominicana? _____

**B.** Now pause the recording and use your one-word answers to write down complete answers to the questions from part **A.**

1. _____

2. _____

3. _____

4. _____

5. _____

6. _____

**ACTIVIDAD 12** **Un hispano famoso** As you listen to a brief biography of Simón Bolívar, complete the following chart. Make sure you look at the chart before you listen.

| Simón Bolívar (_____–1830) | Nacionalidad: _____ |
|---|---|
| Ocupaciones:<br><br>1. _____<br><br>2. líder político<br><br>3. _____ de la Gran Colombia (1819–1830) | Se compara a Bolívar con: _____ |
| Contribuyó a liberar: _____, Colombia, _____, Perú, Bolivia y _____ | |
| País que lleva su nombre: _____ | Su estatua está en ciudades como:<br>_____, París y _____ |

# Los viajes

**Capítulo 7**

## Mejora tu pronunciación

### The consonants *b* and *v*

In Spanish, there is generally no difference between the pronunciation of the consonants **b** and **v**. When they occur at the beginning of a sentence, after a pause, or after *m* or *n*, they are pronounced like the *b* in the English word *bay;* for example, **bolso, vuelo, ambos, envío.** In all other cases, they are pronounced by not quite closing the lips, as in **cabeza** and **nuevo.**

**ACTIVIDAD 1 Escucha y repite** Listen and repeat the following travel-related words, paying special attention to the pronunciation of the initial **b** and **v**.

1. banco
2. vestido
3. vuelo
4. bolso
5. vuelta
6. botones

**ACTIVIDAD 2 Escucha y repite** Listen and repeat the following weather expressions. Remember that when a word starts with a **b** or a **v** and is preceded by another word, it is pronounced by not quite closing the lips.

1. Está nublado.
2. Hace buen tiempo.
3. ¿Cuánto viento hace?
4. Llueve mucho.
5. Está a dos grados bajo cero.

**ACTIVIDAD 3 En el aeropuerto** Listen and repeat the following sentences. Pay special attention to the pronunciation of **b** and **v**.

1. Buen viaje.
2. ¿Y su hijo viaja solo o con Ud.?
3. Las llevas en la mano.
4. ¿Dónde pongo las botellas de ron?
5. Vamos a hacer escala en Miami.
6. Pero no lo va a beber él.
7. Voy a cambiar mi pasaje.

# Mejora tu comprensión

**ACTIVIDAD 4** **¿Qué es?** As you hear each of the following short conversations in a department store, select the object that the people are discussing.

1. ☐ una blusa        ☐ un saco

2. ☐ unos pantalones     ☐ un sombrero

3. ☐ unas camas        ☐ unos carteles

**ACTIVIDAD 5** **Un mensaje para Teresa** Vicente calls his friend Teresa at work, but she is not there. Instead, he talks with Alejandro, Teresa's uncle. As you listen to their conversation, write the message that Vicente leaves.

---

**MENSAJE TELEFÓNICO**

Para: _Teresa_ _____

Llamó: _____

Teléfono: _____

Mensaje: _____

| Recibido por: | Fecha: | Hora: |
|---|---|---|
| tío Alejandro | el 6 de septiembre | |

---

**ACTIVIDAD 6** **La operadora** You will hear two telephone conversations. For each situation, select what happens.

1. ☐ tiene el número equivocado     ☐ no comprende a la persona

2. ☐ quiere el indicativo del país     ☐ quiere el prefijo de la ciudad

**ACTIVIDAD 7** **Las excusas** Two of Perla's friends call her to apologize for not having come to her party last night. They also explain why some others didn't show up. As you listen, match each person with his or her excuse for not going to the party. Before you listen, stop the recording and read the excuses. Notice that there are extra excuses.

**Invitados**

1. _____ Andrés

2. _____ Pilar

3. _____ Viviana

4. _____ Esteban

**Excusas**

a. Tuvo que estudiar.

b. No le gusta salir cuando llueve.

c. Conoció a una persona en la calle.

d. Se durmió en el sofá.

e. No pudo dejar a su hermano solo.

f. Se acostó temprano.

**ACTIVIDAD 8** **Aeropuerto Internacional, buenos días** You will hear three people calling the Barajas International Airport in Madrid to ask about arriving flights. As you listen to the conversations, fill in the missing information on the arrival board.

| LLEGADAS INTERNACIONALES | | | | |
| --- | --- | --- | --- | --- |
| Línea aérea | Número de vuelo | Procedencia | Hora de llegada | Comentarios |
| Iberia | | Lima | | a tiempo |
| LAN | 357 | | 12:15 | |
| Aeroméxico | | NY/México | | |

**ACTIVIDAD 9** **Las noticias** As you hear the news report, complete the following chart indicating who the people are and what happened in each case.

| | Quién es | Qué ocurrió |
| --- | --- | --- |
| 1. María Salinas | _____ | _____ |
| 2. Mario Estrada | _____ | _____ |
| 3. Pablo Bravo | _____ | _____ |
| 4. Sara Méndez Cordero | _____ | _____ |

**ACTIVIDAD 10** **¿Cuánto tiempo hace que...?** You will listen to a set of personal questions. Pause the recording after you listen to each question, and write a complete answer.

1. _____

2. _____

3. _____

4. _____

**ACTIVIDAD 11** **Mi primer trabajo** As you listen to Mariano tell about his first job, fill in each of the blanks in his story with one or more words. Pause the recording and read the paragraph before you listen to Mariano.

_____ cuando empecé mi primer trabajo.

_____ cuando llegué a la oficina el primer día. Allí con-

ocí a mis colegas. Todos eran muy simpáticos. Una persona estaba enferma, así que yo

_____ todo el santo día. _____

de la mañana cuando terminé. Ese fue un día difícil pero feliz.

**ACTIVIDAD 12 El horario de Nélida** After you hear what Nélida did this evening, figure out when each event happened. You may want to listen more than once.

¿Qué hora era cuando pasaron estas cosas?

1. Nélida llegó a casa. Eran _____

2. Alguien la llamó. _____

3. Entró en la bañera. _____

4. Comenzó *Los Simpson*. _____

5. Se durmió. _____

**ACTIVIDAD 13 Una hispana famosa** As you listen to a brief biography of **Isabel la Católica,** complete the following chart.

| Isabel la Católica ( _____ – _____ ) | Se casó con _____. |
|---|---|
| Fue reina de Castilla y de _____. | Él fue rey de Aragón. |
| En 1492... <br><br> • los reyes combatieron y ganaron contra los _____ que controlaban _____ (lugar). <br><br> • expulsaron a los _____. <br><br> • Isabel financió el primer viaje de _____. | |

# La comida y los deportes

## Mejora tu pronunciación

### Diphthongs

In Spanish, vowels are classified as weak **(i, u)** or strong **(a, e, o).** A diphthong is a combination of two weak vowels or a strong and a weak vowel in the same syllable. When a strong and a weak vowel are combined in the same syllable, the strong vowel takes a slightly greater stress; for example, **vuelvo.** When two weak vowels are combined, the second one takes a slightly greater stress, as in the word **ciudad.** Sometimes the weak vowel in a strong–weak combination takes a written accent, and the diphthong is therefore dissolved and two separate syllables are created. Listen to the contrast between the endings of these two words: **farmacia, policía.**

**ACTIVIDAD 1 Escucha y repite** Listen and repeat the following words.

1. las habich**ue**las
2. el m**aí**z
3. los cub**ie**rtos
4. la zanahor**ia**
5. la v**ai**nilla
6. c**ui**dar

**ACTIVIDAD 2 Escucha y repite** Listen and repeat the following sentences.

1. Alm**ue**rzo todos los d**ía**s en la universidad.
2. S**ie**mpre echo de menos la comida g**ua**temalteca.
3. Entre los ingred**ie**ntes principales está el m**aí**z.
4. Se come muy b**ie**n en este rest**au**rante.
5. Rec**ue**rden que estos son algunos platos que p**ue**den pedir.

**ACTIVIDAD  3  ¿Diptongo o no?** Listen and mark whether the following words have a diphthong or not.

|  | Sí | No |
|---|---|---|
| 1. | ☐ | ☐ |
| 2. | ☐ | ☐ |
| 3. | ☐ | ☐ |
| 4. | ☐ | ☐ |
| 5. | ☐ | ☐ |
| 6. | ☐ | ☐ |
| 7. | ☐ | ☐ |

# Mejora tu comprensión

**ACTIVIDAD  4  ¿Le molesta o le gusta?** As you listen to a series of statements, select the opinion of the speaker in each case.

1. a. Las clases le parecieron fáciles.
   b. Las clases le parecieron difíciles.

2. a. Le encanta ir a la casa de sus padres.
   b. Le molesta ir a la casa de sus padres.

3. a. Le fascina la luz.
   b. Le molesta la luz.

4. a. A él le pareció interesante la película.
   b. A él le pareció aburrida la película.

**ACTIVIDAD  5  Las compras** Doña Emilia is going to send her son Ramón grocery shopping and is now figuring out what they need. As you listen to their conversation, select the items they have, those they need to buy, and those they are going to borrow from a neighbor.

|  | Tienen | Necesitan comprar | Van a pedir prestado (borrow) |
|---|---|---|---|
| 1. aceite | ☐ | ☐ | ☐ |
| 2. lechuga | ☐ | ☐ | ☐ |
| 3. pan | ☐ | ☐ | ☐ |
| 4. vino blanco | ☐ | ☐ | ☐ |
| 5. pimienta | ☐ | ☐ | ☐ |
| 6. vinagre | ☐ | ☐ | ☐ |

**ACTIVIDAD** **6** **En el restaurante**  A family is ordering in a restaurant. Listen to them place their order and select what each person wants.

| MESA N.º 8 | | | CAMARERO: JUAN |
|---|---|---|---|
| Cliente N.º | | | Menú |
| 1 (mujer) | 2 (hombre) | 3 (niño) | |
| | | | **Primer plato** |
| | | | Sopa de verduras |
| | | | Espárragos con mayonesa |
| | | | Tomate relleno con pollo |
| | | | **Segundo plato** |
| | | | Ravioles |
| | | | Bistec de ternera |
| | | | Medio pollo al ajo |
| | | | Papas fritas |
| | | | Puré de papas |
| | | | **Ensalada** |
| | | | Mixta |
| | | | Zanahoria y huevo |
| | | | Espinacas, queso y tomate |

**ACTIVIDAD** **7** **Cómo poner la mesa**  You will hear a man on the radio describing how to set a place setting. As you listen to him, draw where each item should go on the place mat.

© Cengage Learning 2013

**ACTIVIDAD 8** **Los preparativos de la fiesta** Mrs. Uriburu calls home to find out if her husband has already done some things for tonight's dinner. While you listen to Mrs. Uriburu's part of the phone conversation, choose from the list the correct answers her husband gives her.

1. a. Sí, ya la limpié.
   b. Sí, ya lo limpié.

2. a. No, no lo compró.
   b. No, no lo compré.

3. a. No tuviste tiempo.
   b. No tuve tiempo.

4. a. Sí, te la preparé.
   b. Sí, se la preparé.

5. a. Sí, se lo di.
   b. Sí, se los di.

6. a. No, no me llamó.
   b. No, no la llamé.

**ACTIVIDAD 9** **La dieta Kitakilos**

**A.** Look at the drawings of María before and after Dr. Popoff's diet. Stop the recording and, under each drawing, write two adjectives that describe her. Also imagine and write two things she does now that she didn't use to do before.

**Antes**

Illustrations: © Cengage Learning 2013

**Después**

María era _____ y    Ahora es _____ y

_____.    _____.

Ahora puede _____

y_____.

**B.** Now listen to a radio ad on Dr. Popoff's diet and write two things María used to do before the diet and two things she does after the diet. It's not necessary to write all the activities she mentions.

| Antes | Después |
|---|---|
| _____ | _____ |
| _____ | _____ |

**240 •** Imágenes   Lab Manual

**ACTIVIDAD 10** **Los testimonios** There was a bank robbery yesterday and a detective is now questioning three witnesses. Listen to the descriptions the witnesses give and choose the correct drawing of the thief.

Illustrations: © Cengage Learning 2013

1. ☐                    2. ☐                    3. ☐

**ACTIVIDAD 11** **Un mensaje telefónico** The bank robber calls his boss at home and leaves her a very important message. Listen and write the message. When you finish, stop the recording and use the letters with numbers underneath them to decipher the secret message that the thief leaves his boss.

**Mensaje:**

___ ___ ___ ___ ___    ___ ___ ___ ___ .    ___ ___ ___ ___ ___ ___
      8          7   4   9       2     5    13

___ ___ ___    ___ ___ ___ ___ ___ ___ .    ___ ___ ___ ___ ___ ___
1        11      12      6      10

___ ___ ___ ___ .
3

**El mensaje secreto:**

__ __    __ __ __ __ __ __ __ __ __    __ __    __ __ __ __ __ .
1  2    3  4  5  2  6  7  8  13    4  9    6  10  7  11  12

**ACTIVIDAD 12** **Los regalos** María and Pedro are at a sporting goods store that has many items on sale. Listen to their conversation and write what they are going to buy their children.

Le van a comprar a...

1. Miguel _____

2. Felipe _____

3. Ángeles _____

4. Patricia _____

**ACTIVIDAD 13** **Diana en los Estados Unidos** Diana, an American who now lives in Spain, is talking to a friend about her life in the United States. Listen to their conversation and mark whether the following sentences about Diana are true or false.

|  | Cierto | Falso |
|---|:---:|:---:|
| 1. Vivía en una ciudad pequeña. | ☐ | ☐ |
| 2. Enseñaba inglés. | ☐ | ☐ |
| 3. Hablaba español casi todo el día. | ☐ | ☐ |
| 4. Se levantaba tarde. | ☐ | ☐ |
| 5. Ella vivía con sus padres. | ☐ | ☐ |
| 6. Estudiaba literatura española. | ☐ | ☐ |

**ACTIVIDAD 14** **Un hispano famoso** While you listen to a brief biography of Manlio Argueta, complete the following chart.

| Manlio Argueta (_____ – ) | Nacionalidad: _____ |
|---|---|

**Ocupación:** _____ y poeta

Su madre fue una gran influencia en su infancia:

• ella _____ poemas y a él le gustaban

• ella le traía _____ para leer

• para él, ella fue su primera (*first*) _____

Empezó a escribir poesía cuando tenía _____ años.

En 1972 tuvo que salir de El Salvador porque _____ al gobierno en sus publicaciones. Estuvo

exiliado durante _____ años.

Su novela más famosa es: *Un* _____ *en la* _____

# Cosas que ocurrieron

**Capítulo**
**9**

## Mejora tu pronunciación

### The consonants *c*, *s*, and *z*

In Hispanic America, the consonant **c** followed by an *e* or an *i,* and the consonants **s** and **z** are usually pronounced like the *s* in the English word *sin.* In Spain, on the other hand, the consonants **c** followed by an *e* or an *i,* and **z** are usually pronounced like the *th* in the English word *thin.*

**ACTIVIDAD  1  Escucha y repite**

**A.** Listen and repeat the following car-related words. Pay attention to the pronunciation of the consonant **c** followed by an *e* or an *i,* and the consonants **s** and **z**.

1.  estacionar

2.  el aceite

3.  revisar

4.  la luz

5.  acelerar

6.  la licencia

**B.** Now listen to the same words again as they are pronounced by a speaker from Latin America and then by a speaker from Spain. Do not repeat the words.

**ACTIVIDAD  2  El accidente**  Listen to a Spaniard as he describes an accident he had. Pay attention to the pronunciation of the consonant **c** followed by an *e* or an *i,* and the consonants **s** and **z**.

1.  Iba a Barcelona, pero tuve un accidente horrible en Zaragoza.

2.  Me torcí el tobillo.

3.  Luego me corté un dedo y tuve una infección muy grave.

4.  Gracias a Dios no me hicieron una operación.

5.  Pero ahora tengo un dolor de cabeza muy grande.

# Mejora tu comprensión

**ACTIVIDAD 3** No me siento bien

**A.** You will hear three conversations about people who have health problems. Listen and write in the chart the problem that each person has.

| | Problema |
|---|---|
| El hombre | |
| La niña | |
| Adriana | |

**B.** Now listen to the conversations again and write the solution to each person's problem in the chart below.

| | Solución |
|---|---|
| El hombre | |
| La niña | |
| Adriana | |

**ACTIVIDAD 4** **Tiene hipo** Clara is talking on the phone with a friend. She has the hiccups and can't finish some phrases. Listen to what Clara says and select a word to complete the idea that she is not able to finish each time her hiccups interrupt her. Number them from 1 to 4.

_____ hechos

_____ aburrido

_____ dormidos

_____ vestidos

_____ preocupada

_____ sentados

**ACTIVIDAD 5** **La fiesta inesperada** Esteban decided to have a "come as you are" party yesterday and immediately called his friends to invite them over. Today, Esteban is talking to his mother about the party. Listen to the conversation and mark what the people were doing when Esteban called them.

1. _____ Ricardo     a. Estaba mirando televisión.
2. _____ María        b. Estaba poniéndose los zapatos.
3. _____ Héctor       c. Estaba bañándose.
4. _____ Claudia      d. Estaba afeitándose.
5. _____ Silvio       e. Estaba comiendo.

## ACTIVIDAD 6 El accidente automovilístico

**A.** You will listen to a radio interview with a doctor who saw an accident between a truck and a school bus. Before listening, stop the recording and use your imagination to write what you think the people from the list were doing when the doctor arrived.

1. los niños _____

2. los paramédicos _____

3. la policía _____

4. los peatones *(pedestrians)* _____

**B.** Now listen to the interview and write what the people from the list were doing according to the doctor.

1. los niños _____

2. los paramédicos _____

3. la policía _____

4. los peatones _____

## ACTIVIDAD 7 Problemas con el carro
A man had a car accident and is on the phone talking to his car insurance agent about some of the problems his car has. Listen to the conversation and draw an **X** on the parts of the car that were damaged in the accident.

© Cengage Learning 2013

## ACTIVIDAD 8 Quiero alquilar un carro
Tomás is in Santiago, Chile, and wants to rent a car for a week to visit the country. Listen to the conversation and complete his notes.

Rent-a-carro: 698–6576

Por semana: $ _____

Día extra: $ _____

¿Seguro *(Insurance)* incluido? Sí / No                    ¿Cuánto? $ _____ por día

¿A qué hora debo devolver el carro? _____

¿Puedo devolverlo en otra ciudad? Sí / No

**ACTIVIDAD 9** **La novia de Juan** Juan is talking to Laura about his girlfriend. Read the questions and then, while you listen to the conversation, answer the questions with complete sentences.

1. ¿Conocía Juan a su novia antes de empezar la universidad? _____
_____

2. ¿Cuándo y dónde la conoció? _____
_____

3. ¿Qué era algo que no sabía sobre ella cuando empezaron a salir? _____

4. ¿Cómo y cuándo lo supo? _____
_____

5. ¿Qué piensa hacer Juan? _____
_____

**ACTIVIDAD 10** **Una hispana famosa** As you listen to a brief biography of **Eva Perón**, complete the following chart.

| Eva Perón (_____ – _____) | Nacionalidad: _____ |
|---|---|
| Se casó con Juan Domingo Perón que era... <br><br> • _____ <br><br> • futuro _____ del país | |
| Ella ayudó... <br><br> • a las mujeres a obtener el _____ <br><br> • a crear una fundación para construir escuelas y _____ | |
| Murió de cáncer cuando tenía _____ años. | |
| Nombre de obra de teatro musical y película: _____ | |

# En casa

**Capítulo 10**

## Mejora tu pronunciación

### The consonants *g* and *j*

As you saw in Chapter 6, the consonant **g**, when followed by the vowels *a, o,* or *u* or by the vowel combinations *ue* or *ui,* is pronounced a little softer than the *g* in the English word *guy;* for example, **gato, gordo, guerra**. **G** followed by *e* or *i* and **j** in all positions are both pronounced similarly to the *h* in the English word *hot,* as in the words **general** and **Jamaica**.

**ACTIVIDAD 1 Escucha y repite** Escucha y repite las siguientes palabras. Presta atención a la pronunciación de las consonantes **g** y **j**.

1. ojo
2. Juan Carlos
3. trabajar
4. escoger
5. congelador
6. **gi**gante

**ACTIVIDAD 2 Las asignaturas** Escucha y repite la siguiente conversación entre dos estudiantes. Presta atención a la pronunciación de las consonantes **g** y **j**.

ESTUDIANTE 1    ¿Qué asignatura vas a esco**ger**?

ESTUDIANTE 2    Creo que psicolo**gí**a.

ESTUDIANTE 1    Pero es me**j**or **ge**ografía.

ESTUDIANTE 2    ¡Ay! Pero no tra**j**e el papel para inscribirme.

ESTUDIANTE 1    ¿El papel ro**j**o?

ESTUDIANTE 2    No. El papel anaran**j**ado.

# Mejora tu comprensión

**ACTIVIDAD 3** **El crucigrama** Usa las pistas (clues) que escuchas para completar el crucigrama sobre aparatos electrodomésticos (electrical appliances). Mira la lista de palabras y el crucigrama antes de empezar.

aspiradora     horno      lavaplatos     secadora
cafetera       lavadora   refrigerador   tostadora

**ACTIVIDAD 4** **En busca de apartamento** Paulina ve el anuncio de un apartamento para alquilar y llama para averiguar más información. Escucha la conversación entre Paulina y el dueño del apartamento y completa sus apuntes.

Teléfono     986-4132

Apartamento:     1 dormitorio

Alquiler: $_____     Depósito: $ _____

Amueblado: Sí ☐  No ☐     Luz natural: Sí ☐  No ☐

Baño: bañera Sí ☐  No ☐     bidé: Sí ☐  No ☐

Dirección: San Martín_____     Piso _____  Apto. _____

© Cengage Learning 2013

**ACTIVIDAD 5** **¿Dónde ponemos los muebles?** Paulina y su esposo van a vivir en un nuevo apartamento y ahora planean en qué parte del dormitorio van a poner cada mueble u objeto. Mientras escuchas la conversación, indica dónde van a poner cada mueble u objeto. Pon el número de cada cosa en uno de los cuadrados *(squares)* del plano del dormitorio.

| 1 alfombra | 3 cómoda | 5 sillón |
|---|---|---|
| 2 cama | 4 mesa | 6 televisor |

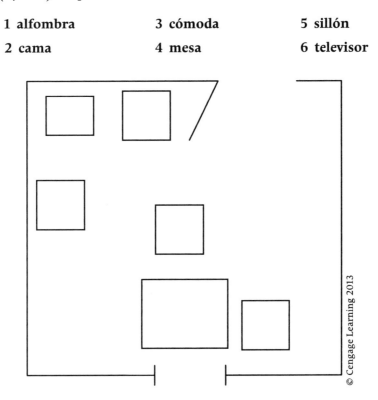

© Cengage Learning 2013

**ACTIVIDAD 6** **En el Rastro** Vicente y Teresa son compañeros de apartamento. Van al Rastro en Madrid para buscar unos estantes baratos. Escucha la conversación con el vendedor y, basándote en lo que escuchas, marca si las oraciones son ciertas o falsas.

|  | Cierto | Falso |
|---|---|---|
| 1. Hay poca gente en este mercado. | ❑ | ❑ |
| 2. Vicente ve unos estantes. | ❑ | ❑ |
| 3. Los estantes son baratos. | ❑ | ❑ |
| 4. Teresa regatea *(bargains).* | ❑ | ❑ |
| 5. El comerciante no baja el precio. | ❑ | ❑ |
| 6. Teresa compra dos estantes. | ❑ | ❑ |

**ACTIVIDAD 7 Busco un hombre que...**

**A.** Vas a escuchar un anuncio en la radio de una mujer que busca su compañero ideal. Antes de escuchar el anuncio, para la grabación *(recording)* y marca las características que buscas en un compañero o una compañera.

|  | tú | ella |
|---|---|---|
| **Busco/Busca un hombre/una mujer...** | | |
| que sea simpático/a | ____ | ____ |
| que sea inteligente | ____ | ____ |
| que tenga dinero | ____ | ____ |
| que tenga un trabajo estable | ____ | ____ |
| que salga por la noche | ____ | ____ |
| que sepa bailar | ____ | ____ |
| que sea guapo/a | ____ | ____ |

**B.** Ahora escucha el anuncio en la radio y marca en la lista de arriba las características que busca esta mujer en un hombre.

**ACTIVIDAD 8 Radio consulta**

**A.** Esperanza es la conductora del programa de radio *Problemas*. Escucha la conversación entre Esperanza y una persona que la llama para contarle un problema y marca cuál es su problema.

1. ☐ La señora está deprimida *(depressed)*.

2. ☐ La señora no sabe dónde está su animal.

3. ☐ La señora tiene un esposo que no se baña.

4. ☐ La señora tiene un hijo sucio *(dirty)*.

**B.** Antes de escuchar la respuesta de Esperanza, escoge y marca bajo "Tus consejos" qué consejos de la lista te gustaría darle a la persona.

|  | Tus consejos | Los consejos de Esperanza |
|---|---|---|
| 1. Debe poner a su esposo en la bañera. | ☐ | ☐ |
| 2. Debe hablar con un compañero de trabajo de su esposo para que él le hable a su esposo. | ☐ | ☐ |
| 3. Debe llevar a su esposo a un psicólogo. | ☐ | ☐ |
| 4. Ella debe hablar con una amiga. | ☐ | ☐ |
| 5. Tiene que decirle a su esposo que él es muy desconsiderado. | ☐ | ☐ |
| 6. Tiene que decirle a su esposo que la situación no puede continuar así. | ☐ | ☐ |

**C.** Ahora escucha a Esperanza y marca en la última columna los tres consejos que ella le da.

**ACTIVIDAD** **9** **El mensaje telefónico** La jefa de Patricio salió de la oficina y le dejó un mensaje telefónico para recordarle las cosas que tiene que hacer hoy. Escucha el mensaje y escribe una **P** delante de las cosas que ella le pide a Patricio que haga y una **J** delante de las cosas que va a hacer la jefa.

1. _____ comprar una cafetera

2. _____ escribirle un email al Sr. Montero

3. _____ llamar al Sr. Montero para conseguir *(get)* su dirección de email

4. _____ llamar a la agencia de viajes

5. _____ ir a la agencia de viajes

6. _____ ir al banco

7. _____ pagar el pasaje

# El tiempo libre

## Mejora tu pronunciación

### The consonant *h*

The consonant **h** is always silent in Spanish. For example, the word *hotel* in English is **hotel** in Spanish.

**ACTIVIDAD** **1** **Escucha y repite** Escucha y repite las siguientes palabras relacionadas con la salud.

1. **h**emorragia
2. **h**ospital
3. **h**acer un análisis
4. **h**erida
5. alco**h**ol
6. **h**epatitis

**ACTIVIDAD** **2** **La comida** Escucha y repite las siguientes oraciones relacionadas con la comida.

1. Tengo **h**ambre.
2. **H**ay que buscar recetas sanas por Internet.
3. Yo creo que voy a **h**ervir dos **h**uevos.
4. Y yo voy a **h**acer unas **h**amburguesas.

# Mejora tu comprensión

**ACTIVIDAD 3** ¿Certeza o duda? Vas a escuchar cuatro oraciones. Para cada una, indica si la persona expresa certeza o duda.

|   | Certeza | Duda |
|---|---------|------|
| 1. | ☐ | ☐ |
| 2. | ☐ | ☐ |
| 3. | ☐ | ☐ |
| 4. | ☐ | ☐ |

**ACTIVIDAD 4** Mañana es día de fiesta Silvia habla por teléfono con una amiga sobre sus planes para mañana. Mientras escuchas lo que dice, escribe cuatro oraciones sobre lo que quizás ocurra.

**Mañana quizás…**

1. _____

2. _____

3. _____

4. _____

**ACTIVIDAD 5** ¿Quién las hace? Escucha a cuatro personas e indica, en cada caso, si la persona expresa emoción por sus acciones o las acciones que hacen otras personas.

|   | Acciones de la persona que habla | Acciones de otra persona |
|---|----------------------------------|--------------------------|
| 1. | ☐ | ☐ |
| 2. | ☐ | ☐ |
| 3. | ☐ | ☐ |
| 4. | ☐ | ☐ |

**ACTIVIDAD 6** La receta de doña Petrona Vas a escuchar a doña Petrona mientras demuestra en su programa de televisión, *Recetas exitosas*, cómo preparar una ensalada de papas. Mientras escuchas la descripción de cada paso, numera los dibujos en el orden apropiado. ¡Ojo! Hay algunos dibujos extras.

_____    _____    _____    _____

_____    _____    _____    _____

**ACTIVIDAD 7** **Radio consulta** Escucha un programa de radio donde una mujer explica qué hacer para llevar una vida saludable. Marca las cosas que ella menciona.

1. ☐ hacer yoga
2. ☐ hacer ejercicio
3. ☐ relajarse
4. ☐ comer comida baja en calorías
5. ☐ no picar entre comidas
6. ☐ comer comida fresca

**ACTIVIDAD 8** **Un anuncio informativo**

**A.** Antes de escuchar un anuncio informativo para padres, lee la siguiente lista de pasatiempos. Marca, en la columna que dice **tú**, qué actividades hacías tú cuando eras niño o niña.

| | tú | el anuncio |
|---|---|---|
| 1. coleccionar algo | _____ | _____ |
| 2. jugar al ajedrez | _____ | _____ |
| 3. hacer crucigramas | _____ | _____ |
| 4. jugar juegos de mesa | _____ | _____ |
| 5. navegar por Internet | _____ | _____ |
| 6. jugar juegos electrónicos | _____ | _____ |
| 7. pescar | _____ | _____ |
| 8. hacer rompecabezas | _____ | _____ |

**B.** Ahora escucha el anuncio y marca en la lista de arriba las actividades que los padres les pueden enseñar a sus hijos según lo que dice el anuncio.

**ACTIVIDAD 9** **Cuando estudio mucho**

**A.** Antes de escuchar una conversación entre tres amigos, escribe en español tres cosas que te gusta hacer cuando tienes tiempo libre.

1. _____
2. _____
3. _____

**B.** Federico, Gustavo y Marisa están hablando de las cosas que les gusta hacer cuando tienen tiempo libre. Escucha la conversación y escribe oraciones para indicar qué actividad o actividades le gusta hacer a cada uno.

1. Λ Federico: _____ _____

_____

2. A Gustavo _____

_____

3. A Marisa _____

_____

**ACTIVIDAD 10** **El viaje a Machu Picchu** El Sr. López recibe una llamada. Antes de escuchar, lee las oraciones. Luego, escucha la conversación y marca si las oraciones son ciertas o falsas.

|  | Cierto | Falso |
|---|---|---|
| 1. El señor López ganó un viaje a Ecuador. | ☐ | ☐ |
| 2. La señora dice que una computadora escogió su número de teléfono. | ☐ | ☐ |
| 3. La señora dice que él ganó pasajes para dos personas. | ☐ | ☐ |
| 4. El señor López le da su número de tarjeta de crédito a la mujer. | ☐ | ☐ |
| 5. El señor López cree que la mujer le dice la verdad. | ☐ | ☐ |

# El campo y la ciudad

**Capítulo 12**

## Mejora tu pronunciación

### Linking

In normal conversation, you link words as you speak to provide a smooth transition from one word to the next. In Spanish, the last letter of a word can usually be linked to the first letter of the following word, for example, **mis amigas, tú o yo.** When the last letter of a word is the same as the first letter of the following word, they are pronounced as one letter, for example, **las sillas, te encargo.** Remember that the *h* is silent in Spanish, so the link occurs as follows: **la habilidad.**

**ACTIVIDAD 1** **Escucha y repite** Escucha y repite las siguientes frases prestando atención al unir las palabras.

1. las islas

2. la autopista

3. la colina elevada

4. la ciudad esta es maravillosa

5. la hospitalidad de este pueblo

6. me gusta nadar en el océano

**ACTIVIDAD 2** **En el restaurante argentino** Escucha y repite parte de la conversación entre unos novios en un restaurante argentino.

VICENTE   Espero que a la experta de tenis le gusten la comida y los tangos argentinos con bandoneón y todo.

NORA   Los tangos que cantaba Carlos Gardel me fascinan. El otro día, bajé de Internet Mi Buenos Aires querido cuando yo te vuelva a ver... Pero dime, Vicente, ¿cómo encontraste este restaurante?

VICENTE   Navegando por Internet. Bajé una lista de restaurantes argentinos y este tenía muy buenos comentarios.

# Mejora tu comprensión

**ACTIVIDAD 3** **La isla Pita Pita** Escucha la descripción de la isla Pita Pita y usa los símbolos que se presentan y los nombres de los lugares para completar el mapa incompleto. Los nombres de los lugares que se mencionan son **Blanca Nieves, Hércules, Mala-Mala, Panamericana** y **Pata**.

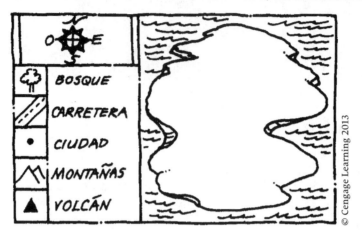

**ACTIVIDAD 4** **Visite Venezuela** ¿Sabes cuáles de los lugares de la lista forman parte de Venezuela y cuáles no? Escucha el anuncio comercial sobre Venezuela y marca solo los lugares que pertenecen a ese país.

_____ el salto Ángel

_____ la playa de La Guaira

_____ las cataratas del Iguazú

_____ las islas Los Roques

_____ las playas de Punta del Este

_____ el volcán de Fuego

_____ Mérida

_____ Ciudad Bolívar

_____ las islas Galápagos

**ACTIVIDAD 5** **Madrid y el D. F.**

**A.** Vas a escuchar dos anuncios comerciales: uno sobre Madrid y otro sobre la Ciudad de México. Para cada uno, marca qué lugares se pueden visitar. ¡Ojo! A veces se puede visitar el mismo tipo de lugar en las dos ciudades.

|  | Madrid (excursión a Segovia) | Ciudad de México (excursión a Teotihuacán) |
|---|---|---|
| castillo | _____ | _____ |
| catedral | _____ | _____ |
| palacio | _____ | _____ |
| parque | _____ | _____ |
| parque de atracciones | _____ | _____ |
| pirámide | _____ | _____ |
| ruinas | _____ | _____ |
| templo | _____ | _____ |
| zoológico | _____ | _____ |

**B.** Ahora escribe cuál de los dos lugares te gustaría visitar y por qué.

_____

_____

_____

**ACTIVIDAD 6** **Pichicho** Sebastián le está mostrando a su amigo Ramón las cosas que su perro Pichicho puede hacer. Escucha a Sebastián y numera los dibujos según las órdenes. ¡Ojo! Hay dibujos de ocho órdenes, pero Sebastián solo da seis.

Illustrations: © Cengage Learning 2013

**ACTIVIDAD 7** **En la oficina de turismo** Hay algunos turistas en una oficina de turismo. Escucha las conversaciones entre un empleado y diferentes turistas y completa el mapa con los nombres de los lugares adonde quieren ir los turistas: **el correo** (post office), **una iglesia** y **el Hotel Aurora**. Antes de empezar, busca en el mapa la oficina de turismo.

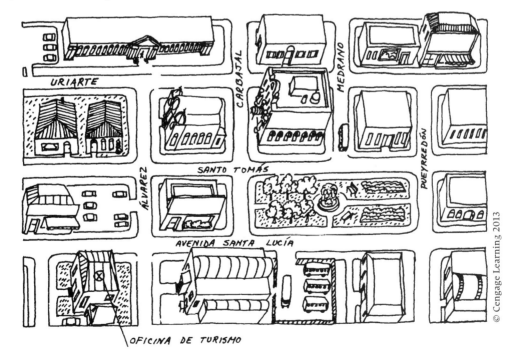

© Cengage Learning 2013

## ACTIVIDAD 8 La dieta

**A.** La Sra. Kilomás necesita bajar de peso *(to lose weight)* y está en el consultorio hablando con el médico. Antes de escuchar, escribe tres cosas que crees que el médico le va a decir que no coma.

1. _____

2. _____

3. _____

**B.** Ahora escucha la conversación y escribe en la columna correcta las cosas que la Sra. Kilomás puede y no puede comer o beber.

**Coma:**

_____

_____

**No coma:**

_____

_____

_____

_____

**Beba:**

_____

_____

**No Beba:**

_____

_____

## ACTIVIDAD 9 La llamada anónima
Unos hombres secuestraron *(kidnapped)* al Sr. Tomono, un diplomático, en Guayaquil, Ecuador, y quieren un millón de dólares. Llaman a la Sra. Tomono para decirle qué debe hacer con el dinero. Antes de escuchar, lee las oraciones que aparecen en el manual. Luego, escucha la conversación telefónica y marca si las oraciones son ciertas o falsas.

|  | Cierto | Falso |
|---|---|---|
| 1. La Sra. Tomono debe poner el dinero en una mochila marrón. | ❑ | ❑ |
| 2. Ella debe ir a la esquina de las calles Quito y Colón. | ❑ | ❑ |
| 3. Tiene que hablar por un teléfono público. | ❑ | ❑ |
| 4. Tiene que ir en taxi. | ❑ | ❑ |

**ACTIVIDAD 10  Las tres casas**

**A.** Llamas a una inmobiliaria *(real-estate agency)* para obtener información sobre tres casas y te contesta el contestador automático. Escucha la descripción de las casas y completa la tabla.

| | Tamaño (m²) | Dormitorios | Año | Precio (dólares) |
|---|---|---|---|---|
| Casa 1 | 175 | | | 380.000 |
| Casa 2 | | 2 | | |
| Casa 3 | | | 2010 | |

**B.** Ahora mira la tabla y escucha las siguientes oraciones. Marca **C** si son ciertas o **F** si son falsas.

      C         F

1. _____   _____

2. _____   _____

3. _____   _____

4. _____   _____

5. _____   _____

**ACTIVIDAD 11  La peluquería**

**A.** La Sra. López y la Sra. Díaz están en la peluquería hablando de sus hijos. Escucha la conversación y completa la información sobre sus hijos.

| Hijo | Edad | Ocupación | Sueldo *(salary)* | Deportes |
|---|---|---|---|---|
| Alejandro López | _____ | _____ | _____ | nadar  _____ |
| Marcos Díaz | _____ | abogado y  _____ | _____ | _____ |

**B.** Ahora escribe comparaciones sobre los dos chicos usando la información de la tabla y las palabras que aparecen en esta parte.

1. joven: _____

2. activo: _____

3. ganar dinero: _____